Taiwan Cinema as Soft Power

Taiwan Cinema as Soft Power

Authorship, Transnationality, Historiography

SONG HWEE LIM

OXFORD
UNIVERSITY PRESS

OXFORD
UNIVERSITY PRESS

Oxford University Press is a department of the University of Oxford. It furthers
the University's objective of excellence in research, scholarship, and education
by publishing worldwide. Oxford is a registered trade mark of Oxford University
Press in the UK and certain other countries.

Published in the United States of America by Oxford University Press
198 Madison Avenue, New York, NY 10016, United States of America.

Library of Congress Cataloging-in-Publication Data
Names: Lim, Song Hwee, 1965– author.
Title: Taiwan cinema as soft power : authorship, transnationality,
historiography / Song Hwee Lim.
Description: New York : Oxford University Press, [2022] |
Includes bibliographical references and index.
Identifiers: LCCN 2021030656 (print) | LCCN 2021030657 (ebook) |
ISBN 9780197503379 (hardback) | ISBN 9780197503386 (paperback) |
ISBN 9780197503409 (epub) | ISBN 9780197503416
Subjects: LCSH: Motion pictures—Taiwan—History—21st century. |
Motion pictures—Social aspects—Taiwan—History—21st century.
Classification: LCC PN1993.5.T28 L4946 2022 (print) |
LCC PN1993.5.T28 (ebook) | DDC 791.430951249—dc23
LC record available at https://lccn.loc.gov/2021030656
LC ebook record available at https://lccn.loc.gov/2021030657

DOI: 10.1093/oso/9780197503379.001.0001

1 3 5 7 9 8 6 4 2

Paperback printed by Marquis, Canada
Hardback printed by Bridgeport National Bindery, Inc., United States of America

Contents

Notes on Chinese Romanization, Translation, and Citation

As this is a book about Taiwan cinema, I have tried to render the names of Taiwanese directors, cast and crew, critics, and cultural figures in the Wade-Giles system to the best of my knowledge and ability. Names of those from Hong Kong and Southeast Asia also appear, where possible, in the way they would in their original locales. Names of those from the People's Republic of China and all Chinese characters and terms appear in pinyin as per convention, except for habitual spellings such as Kuomintang. For the sake of clarity, filmic characters whose first given name is the pinyin A (as in A Zhong) is spelled as Ah (as in Ah Zhong). All Chinese names and characters for terms used in the book are listed in the glossary. All translations from Chinese sources are mine unless otherwise stated. Some online database sources cited in endnotes and tables are not listed in the bibliography.

Illustrations

Tables

Acknowledgments

On a rackety train that would later emerge from a tunnel to reveal a mountain track, two teenage students have their eyes fixed on the textbooks in their hands whilst standing in a carriage. The girl is suddenly on the brink of tears because she did not know how to solve some problems in a mathematics test earlier in the day; the boy rebukes her lightly for not seeking his help when revising for the test. The single-carriage train arrives at the small station of Shifen. As they walk home along the railway track, the boy says, in Hoklo, "there's going to be a film screening," and the girl's face brightens up. The film cuts to their point of view to show a workman battling with the wind as he puts up the white screen above the railway track; gray clouds hover low over the mountains in the background. Thus begins Hou Hsiao-hsien's 1986 film, *Dust in the Wind*, and my lifelong love for Taiwan cinema.

This book is my long overdue homage to Taiwan New Cinema, which I first encountered during my undergraduate education at the National Taiwan University from 1985 to 1989. All my research monographs to date have been driven by deeply personal motivations. After living in Singapore for eight years as a condition of the scholarship for my undergraduate education, I simply had to get the issue of sexuality out of my system at the first opportunity when I embarked on postgraduate studies at Cambridge in 1997, the result of which led to the publication of *Celluloid Comrades: Representations of Male Homosexuality in Contemporary Chinese Cinemas* in 2006. Even though both my undergraduate and postgraduate studies were completed in the disciplines of Chinese literature and Oriental studies, my scholarly aspiration has always been to become a film specialist, a transformation facilitated in part by a career move from East Asian studies at Leeds to Film studies (later absorbed into English) at Exeter; *Tsai Ming-liang and a Cinema of Slowness* (2014) was an attempt to hone my skills as a film scholar through close analysis of a director's oeuvre with which I was—and remain—obsessed. This present book goes further back in time to the 1980s to mark the gravitation of my interest from literature to film, thanks in no small part to the Taiwan New Wave cinema that was at its heights during the time of my undergraduate studies. Today I still have vivid memories of skipping classes to catch free or cheap screenings on campus. I remember standing at the back of a full-house auditorium in the students' activities center throughout the screening of Edward Yang's *The Terrorizers* and failing to comprehend what the hell was going on. This book is, therefore, a crystallization of a devotion to

Taiwan New Cinema, albeit the focus is on its legacy in the twenty-first century instead. Whilst I use the notion of soft power as a discursive lens in the book, here I present myself as a concrete and incontrovertible evidence of this cinema's affective appeal for nearly 40 years. The wider lens cast upon my research object probably reflects my move into cultural studies at the Chinese University of Hong Kong (CUHK) in 2014.

The writing of the book has been long in gestation. I first tested out the conceptualization for this book in Exeter at a seminar in 2009 and then in an undergraduate course in 2012–13; I subsequently brought the course to CUHK where the chapter outline went through six revisions in as many years. I thank my students on the course over the years for their part in aiding me, however unconsciously, to figure out what works and what doesn't, and Regenia Gagnier at Exeter for her faith in my work. Relocating to Hong Kong has helped not least in terms of proximity to my research object and materials. The resources available both at CUHK and in funding bodies in Hong Kong are unimaginable for someone who had worked in England for over a decade. The research for this book was supported by a General Research Fund (2015–16) from the Research Grants Council of the Hong Kong Special Administrative Region, China (project no.: CUHK 14606815) and by a Direct Grant for Research (2014–15) from CUHK (project code: AL14904). The Department of Cultural and Religious Studies paid for a visit in October 2014 to Tsai Ming-liang's exhibition at the Museum of National Taipei University of Education; it also allowed me to take up a CUHK visiting fellowship to Clare Hall, Cambridge, in Term 2 of 2017–18 so I could work on the final chapters of the book. I hope I have not inadvertently left out any names among my army of research assistants and student helpers: Roberto Castillo, Chen Zhengheng, Bryan Choy, Ko Chun Kit, Ray Lai Kwok-wai, Silver Lee Wai-ming, Liu Haiping, Lu Xin, Richard Ng Wing-to, Katherine Peng Xin, Enoch Tam, Samson Tang, Zhang Zongyi, and Zhao Qing. I am grateful to colleagues in the UK who continue to involve me in their projects after my relocation to HK. Thanks to Stephanie Dennison for inviting me to act as a steering committee member on the Arts and Humanities Research Council (UK) international network "Soft Power, Cinema and the BRICS" between 2016 and 2018, which gave me the impetus to delve more deeply into the soft-power thesis. Daniela Berghahn, with whom I collaborated on a grant application on the exotic in cinema, had shown great enthusiasm for this book project, and I'm glad she and her family enjoyed watching *Blue Gate Crossing* after I recommended the film to her.

If it takes a village to raise a child, it similarly takes a community to build a scholar. The shaping of this book has benefited from feedback received at numerous presentations and in writing. Earlier parts and versions of the Introduction had been presented at CUHK, Leeds, Seoul, and Taiwan, and

I thank, respectively, Lai Chi Tim, Stephanie Dennison, Jaeho Kang, and Yu-lin Lee for their invitation and hospitality. Emilie Yueh-yu Yeh gave encouraging words on a paper based on Chapter 1; thanks to Luke Robinson for pointing me to the work of Philip Rosen and Jeffrey Skoller, and to Luke, Shi-yan Chao, and Guo-Juin Hong for a lovely time in snowy Toronto where this paper was presented as part of a panel at the Association for Asian Studies conference in 2017. Rey Chow read and commented on the portion on Hou Hsiao-hsien's *Flights of the Red Balloon* in Chapter 2; I thank her and Stephen Chu for inviting me to present this material at the University of Hong Kong and to Jeroen de Kloet for his comments. Sing Song-yong, my buddy in Tsai Ming-liang research, has been most generous in sharing his thoughts on a draft of Chapter 3 and any information about Tsai's works; I learned a lot on the subjects of expanded cinema and intermediality from conversations with him and with Elmo Gonzaga. Tsai and his assistant Claude Wang provided access to films in Tsai's "Walker" series. Chris Berry assured me that an earlier version of Chapter 4 was fine, though I later reframed parts of the chapter in relation to city branding and location tourism. Lisa Rofel gave me the splendid idea of "citizen-to-citizen soft power" in her feedback on materials that now appear as Chapter 5. Ko Chun Kit helped compile the tables in Chapters 3 to 5; Lin Yen-nan, whose PhD dissertation I supervised at Exeter, from which some data and figures were drawn for Table 5.1, responded promptly to every call for help for updates of information. I could not have completed the preparation of the manuscript in the final stages without the super-efficiency of Bryan Choy, who compiled the drafts for the glossary of Chinese terms, references, and filmography as well as configured the DVD screen grabs and pictures into the requisite technical specificities.

Professionally speaking, I feel I have finally found an institutional home at CUHK's Division of Cultural Studies as the discipline encompasses my research interests in cinema and beyond. I am blessed with a bunch of intellectually stimulating colleagues who open my eyes to an array of fascinating research topics I would not have otherwise encountered: Chan Ka-ming, Cheung Lik-kwan, Chung Peichi, Elmo Gonzaga, Oscar Ho, Katrien Jacobs, Li Tiecheng, Benny Lim, Janet Pang, Pang Laikwan, Tan Jia, Angela Wong, and Wu Kaming. I thank the two department heads, Lai Chi-Tim and Tam Wai-lun, for their support, and I am grateful to Elaine Chow, Loletta Jim, Leung Chun Kit, and Virginia Lo of the general office who continue to show me what true administrative help looks like. Cheung Chui-yu and Nocus Yung, project coordinators of the Center for Cultural Studies, made my role as director swimmingly smooth and easy. Chris Patterson and Roberto Castillo, both briefly postdoctoral fellows of the Center, and my research postgraduates Hu Wenxi, Ni Ziquan, Ong Yuin-ting, Samson Tang, Zhao Qing, and Zhu Mengmeng enriched my scholarly life through their own research from which I have learned a great deal. Wang Wan-jui, whose PhD

I supervised at Exeter, also worked at CUHK in 2014–2016 and could always be counted upon for conversations about Taiwan cinema—and dinners after work.

Hong Kong has been good to me in so many ways, most immediately in allowing me to reconnect with Chinese language in its various guises. I treasure my excitement at discovering Chinese-language publications that I had missed out on during the decade when I was living in England, the joy of writing film reviews and cultural critique in Chinese, and the challenge and fulfillment of teaching in Cantonese. I also made new friends and reconnected with some old ones. For their companion and friendship I thank Timmy Chen Chih-Ting, Rey Chow, Chow Yiu-fai, Du Ting, Lin Pei-yin, Gina Marchetti, Ng Oi Lam, Shu-mei Shih, James St. André, Enoch Tam, Tan Jia, Louisa Wei, Benz Wong, Harry Wu Yi-jui, and Zheng Bo. Whether in Hong Kong, Beijing, or Amsterdam, Jeroen de Kloet continues to be a source of wild inspiration (at times exasperation) and kind brotherhood. I feel more rooted in Hong Kong thanks to my god-sister Christine Fan. The final revision of this book was completed during my sabbatical leave in 2020–21, when I found myself back in Singapore rather than Taiwan owing to travel restrictions as a result of the coronavirus outbreak. My high school classmate Loong Li Ping brought me delicious food (and Yorkshire tea) during my quarantine period and subsequently introduced me to the local food and café scene. I enjoyed hanging out with Quah Sy Ren and Alex Chin and thank them for their immense hospitality. Chan Cheow Thia helped print chapter drafts and documents. Wong Koi Tet remained a dependable companion. My mom would always be happy and ready to make me a home-cooked meal. Meanwhile, I missed traveling and my winter clothes.

Sarah Wright pointed me in the direction of Oxford University Press where Norm Hirschy has been the most efficient editor I have ever encountered in my career; I am grateful also to India Gray, the copyeditor, and Suganya Elango, the project manager, for guiding me through the book's production. I am enormously grateful for his guidance each step of the way. Chris Berry and Margaret Hillenbrand, reviewers of the manuscript who waived their anonymity by subsequently writing to me directly, gave valuable feedback that benefited the revision of the book; all imperfections, of course, remain mine. Thanks to Jake Bevan for helping to compile, once again, the index. The Introduction incorporates materials from two previously published articles, namely "Taiwan New Cinema: Small Nation with Soft Power," in Carlos Rojas and Eileen Cheng-yin Chow, eds., *The Oxford Handbook of Chinese Cinemas* (New York: Oxford University Press, 2013), 152–169, and "Soft Power and Cinema: A Methodological Reflection and Some Chinese Inflections," in Stephanie Dennison and Rachel Dwyer, eds., *Cinema and Soft Power: Configuring the National and Transnational in Geo-Politics* (Edinburgh: Edinburgh University Press, 2021), 17–37. I thank Springer Nature for allowing the use, in Chapter 2, of material from "The Voice of the Sinophone," in Audrey Yue and Olivia Khoo, eds., *Sinophone Cinemas* (Basingstoke, Hampshire: Palgrave Macmillan), 62–76. Permission has been obtained for the reproduction of materials from previous publications in various chapters: in Chapter 2, Song Hwee Lim, "Domesticating Time: Gendered Temporalities in Hou Hsiao-hsien's *Café Lumière*," *Frontiers of Literary Studies in China* 10, no. 1 (2016): 36–57, © 2016, republished with permission of Springer, permission conveyed through Copyright Clearance Center, Inc.; in Chapter 3, Song Hwee Lim, "Walking in the City, Slowly: Spectacular Temporal Practices in Tsai Ming-liang's 'Slow Walk, Long March' Series," *Screen* 58, no. 2 (2017): 180–196, © 2017, DOI: 10.1093/screen/hjx015, republished with permission of Oxford University Press on behalf of *Screen*, permission conveyed through Copyright Clearance Center, Inc.; in Chapter 5, Song Hwee Lim, "Citizen-to-Citizen Connectivity and Soft Power: The Appropriation of Subcultures in 'Little Freshness' across the Taiwan Strait," *China Information* 33, no. 3 (2019): 294–310, © Sage Publications Ltd. 2019, reprinted by permission of Sage Publications, Ltd.

Introduction

Cinema as Soft Power, Soft Power as Method

The 2018 Golden Horse Awards, a Taiwanese competition for Chinese-language filmmaking across the world,[1] will be remembered less for the films and their cast and crew on whom it bestowed its accolades and more for the reaction from the People's Republic of China's (PRC) political regime and its agents (both official and unofficial) to the speech delivered at the Awards' ceremony by the director who won the Best Documentary category. Fu Yue, whose documentary *Our Youth in Taiwan* (*Women de qingchun, zai Taiwan*, 2018) traces the interaction between two leaders of the 2014 Sunflower Student movement, said in her acceptance speech that her greatest wish as a Taiwanese was that "our country can be treated as a truly independent entity."[2] Later in the ceremony when the Best Feature Film award was to be given out, customarily by the head of the jury panel (PRC film star Gong Li in that year) and the award's chairman (then Ang Lee), Gong refused to go on stage with Lee; Zhang Yimou, who won the Best Director award for his film *Shadow* (*Ying*, 2018), was the only PRC national to attend the post-ceremony reception, whereas his film's leads and other stars avoided the party and left Taiwan earlier than planned (Chen 2018). A meme entitled "China, Not One Less" (*Zhongguo, yidian dou buneng shao*), disseminated by the Communist Youth League of China, was quickly reposted on social media by PRC actors and actresses (Chen 2018) as well as by some Taiwanese and Hongkongers in the entertainment industry, many of whom were not at the ceremony. The next day, it was reported that China's Central Propaganda Department had issued an order to film companies in China that no PRC-produced or co-produced films would henceforth be allowed to participate in the Golden Horse Awards ("Chuan zhongxuanbu" 2018).

The following year, in 2019, an official boycott was announced in August by the PRC authorities, who scheduled China's film awards ceremony, the Golden Rooster Awards, to take place on the same day (November 23) as the Golden Horse Awards so that Hong Kong filmmakers with vested interests in China had to choose between the two, resulting in director Johnnie To resigning his position as head of the jury panel of the Taiwanese award (Frater 2019). Moreover, the 2019 Golden Rooster Awards was held in the city of Xiamen (Frater 2019), a location geographically closest to territories owned by Taiwan, whose official

Taiwan Cinema as Soft Power. Song Hwee Lim, Oxford University Press. © Oxford University Press 2022.
DOI: 10.1093/oso/9780197503379.003.0001

title is the Republic of China (ROC). Xiamen is a symbolic choice because it lays just around 30 kilometers from Kinmen (Quemoy/Jinmen), one of the two outlying islands (the other being Matsu/Mazu) whose first characters of their names together make up the Chinese name of the Taiwanese film award *Jinma* (which can be read, literally, as "golden horse"). The choice of Xiamen also serves to recall the August 23, 1958, artillery battle when Kinmen was shelled by Chinese communist forces, which carried on its bombardment for another 44 days ("Bombardment" 1988).

This fallout from the 2018 Golden Horse Awards is of academic interest not just to scholars of international relations and East Asian history who follow changes in geopolitical dynamics between China and Taiwan but also to those in cultural studies and film studies because it illustrates that the world of cinema is not immune to the play of power, whether hard or soft. Political scientist Joseph S. Nye Jr. famously coined the term "soft power," which identified key resources as culture, political values, and foreign policies (Nye 2004, 11), to contrast with a nation's hard powers, represented by the economy and the military; although, he qualified that these two forms of power "sometimes reinforce and sometimes interfere with each other" (Nye 2004, 25). The PRC regime and its agents coordinated condemnation of Fu's speech as advocating the independence of Taiwan suggests that, on the one hand, hard political tools can be readily deployed in cultural arenas in the forms of bans and boycotts, surveillance and censorship. On the other hand, hard and soft powers do not exist in mutually exclusive spaces; rather, they are drawn into an interplay of relations and dynamics, operating even remotely and without official orders as agents are fully aware of the stakes involved in making a clear stand—or not.

This book is an attempt to understand cinema as a form of soft-power tool. It proposes Taiwan as a paradigmatic example of cinema's effect in assisting a small nation gain prominence on the international stage despite its political stalemate with and sanction by a much bigger power. It aims to map the soft-power terrains of Taiwan's cinematic and other cultural outputs, focusing on those produced in the twenty-first century, by using the three keywords in the book's subtitle—authorship, transnationality, historiography—as prisms for examination. It argues that authorship is the secret weapon of Taiwan cinema's soft power thanks to the award-winning record of world-renowned auteurs (in particular, Hou Hsiao-hsien, Edward Yang, Ang Lee, and Tsai Ming-liang) at international film festivals.[3] As soft power invariably operates on the level of the transnational, this book tracks the impact that Taiwan cinema has made on foreign soils, filmmakers, audiences, institutions, agents, and cinemas. As such, it posits that historiographical writing of Taiwan cinema has to be re-envisioned in order to move beyond a national cinema framework and to depart from a lingua-centric model of cinema studies that privileges language as a unifying category for films.

Taken together, this book does not treat authorship, transnationality, and historiography as separate entities; rather, it brings them into a triangulated relationship to account for the reach of Taiwan cinema's soft power in the new millennium. In a nutshell, it suggests that authorship is central to Taiwan cinema's ability to transcend borders (both national and linguistic) to the extent that the historiographical writing of Taiwan cinema has to be reimagined. In presenting Taiwan cinema's significance as a case of a small nation with enormous soft power, this book hopes to recast the terms and stakes of both cinema studies and soft-power studies in academia.

Why Taiwan? Why Cinema? Why Soft Power?

This book's object of analysis is the legacy, in the twenty-first century, of Taiwan New Cinema (hereafter TNC), a movement, of sorts, beginning in the early 1980s, that has been attracting global attention as it travels the international film festival and art house cinema circuits across the world, making a lasting impact and impression upon filmmakers and cinephiles for nearly 40 years.[4] Taiwan offers an intriguing but important case for the study of soft power because its hard political and economic powers are highly circumscribed. An island isolated in the international community with no membership status in the United Nations or the International Olympic Committee,[5] Taiwan has, as of the end 2020, formal diplomatic ties with only 15 countries in the world,[6] having lost to the PRC three allies (Burkina Faso, the Dominican Republic, and El Salvador) in 2018 ("China accused" 2018; Kuo 2018) and two more (Solomon Islands and Kiribati) the following year (Lyons 2019). On the economic front, whereas Taiwan was, alongside Hong Kong, Singapore, and South Korea, one of the four "little dragons" whose staggering growth in the 1980s became the envy of developing countries, its gross domestic product (GDP) per capita figure now lags far behind Singapore, Hong Kong, and South Korea.[7] With limited and waning hard power in terms of political status (never mind military might) and economic prowess, Taiwan must increasingly rely on its soft power to make its voice heard on the international stage.

The study of soft power has, to date, paid the most attention to global giants to examine how soft power might supplement these giants' undisputed hard power. Nye's landmark book, *Soft Power: The Means to Success in World Politics*, takes the United States as the main focus whilst cursorily surveying selected countries around the world, and there is now a plethora of books on China's soft-power efforts and their effects (or lack thereof).[8] My choice of Taiwan will demonstrate, if somewhat counterintuitively, how a polity without hard political and economic power can exercise massive soft-power influence through the success of its cultural products (such as cinema) both globally and regionally.[9] More important, it is apt precisely because Taiwan's operation of soft power is not only often in the shadow of a much bigger and antagonistic power that is China, but Taiwan is also entangled in a triangulated relationship with China and the United States. As Chia-chi Wu argues, "Taiwan cinema's reception is constantly tempered by geopolitics and specific agendas of cross-cultural exchange" (Wu 2007, 76). She goes on to explain what this geopolitical dynamic has entailed for TNC since the 1980s:

> Inasmuch as Taiwan remains an "issue" that can be traded off at any time in Sino-American trade and military negotiations, and inasmuch as its attempts to reenter the United Nations or to act as an independent power have been thwarted, presentation of Taiwan cinema as an entity "separate from" and "equal to" that of China at international film festivals assists the assertion of Taiwan's difference. Such "self-assertion" rendered visible on a global scale was unprecedented in Taiwan's history of international relations. (Wu 2007, 79)

The role of cinema in the operation of soft power, defined as "the ability to get what you want through attraction rather than coercion or payments" (Nye 2004, x), cannot be underestimated. In a 2002 poll of 43 countries on dimensions of US attractiveness, technology and scientific advancement came first and American music, movies, and TV ranked second (Nye 2004, 35–36). Governments in many parts of the world are also aware of cinema's role in soft-power efforts. Apparently, "when the Taliban government fell in Afghanistan in 2001, the Indian foreign minister flew to Kabul to welcome the new interim government in a plane not packed with arms or food but crammed with tapes of Bollywood movies and music, which were quickly distributed across the city" (Nye 2004, 10).[10] Nye, however, notes that soft power can be a double-edged sword whose effectiveness is highly dependent on the context and also contradictory among different groups in the targeted nation. One example is China, where "the attraction and rejection of American culture among different groups may cancel each other out"; another is Iran, where "the same Hollywood images that repel the ruling mullahs may be attractive to the younger generation" (Nye 2004, 12–13).

On the whole, the study of soft power tends to pay overwhelming attention to the role of government agents in countries with hard power. However, to return to its original conception, Nye identifies soft-power resources as arising "in large part from the values an *organization* or country expresses in its culture, in the examples it sets by its internal practices and policies, and in the way it handles its relations with others" (Nye 2004, 8, emphasis mine). Nye, who served in the Clinton administration, goes on to qualify that soft power "does not belong to the government in the same degree that hard power does" (14). Therefore, to confine the understanding of soft-power use only to countries or governments is to make the mistake of equating soft power with cultural policy. The range of soft-power resources, albeit produced within the boundaries of nation-states but not necessarily (and often not) by governmental agents, that appeals to foreign audiences is too myriad and multiple to be possibly encompassed by official policies, strategies, or schemes formulated and executed by any single government. The government may reap rewards from some of these resources owing to their attractiveness, but the operation of such soft-power appeal does not hinge upon governmental initiatives alone. As Nye notes, soft power can be difficult to wield because "many of its crucial resources are outside the control of governments, and their effects depend heavily on acceptance by the receiving audience" (99).

Recent scholarship on the relationship between soft power and cinema has begun to scrutinize the roles of both nonstate agents and the audience. An edited volume, *Screening China's Soft Power* (Voci and Luo 2018a), contains at least two case studies. Luke Robinson's chapter investigates two Chinese-language film festivals in London organized by nonstate actors as a form of what he calls "quotidian soft power," in contradistinction to the "top-down, monological model of soft power that is assumed as its default mode of operation" (Robinson 2018, 111). Wanning Sun's chapter explores the popular reception of a Chinese reality show in Australia to advance a thesis of "soft power by accident" (rather than "by design") to illustrate how the show "almost shut down by the Chinese authorities, has caught the imagination of global viewers" and is now "widely touted as a rare window through which the world can get to know the real China" (Sun 2018, 197). This edited book can be said to be premised on displacing the role of state agents, as it begins with a section on "the limitations, or failure, of Chinese [official] soft power," evincing throughout the book, as the editors put it, the "incommensurability between the two ingredients in Nye's concept of soft power—state interest and cultural impact"—in this case, of China (Voci and Luo 2018b, 4).

Rather than being executed by the state and serving its interests alone, soft power may, in fact, generate cultural impact in ways that contravene state policies or challenge official ideologies. In the United States, "many soft-power resources are separate from the American government and are only partly responsive to its purposes. In the Vietnam [War] era, for example, American popular culture often worked at cross-purposes to official government policy" (Nye 2004, 15). As is often the case in banned or censored films from the PRC (or Iran, to cite another example), these films become all-the-more attractive to foreign audiences simply because the governments of the films' countries of origin have expressed disapproval toward them instead of using them as soft-power tools. As Yingjin Zhang writes wryly in the afterword of the aforementioned edited volume, rarely has one heard of "Taiwan's soft power deficit or failure" because Taiwan "has never banned a film for contradicting an officially sanctioned script since the late 1980s, even when many of its award-winning films present dismal images of Taiwan and challenging [sic] dominant bourgeois values" (Zhang 2018, 257). As I will show in this book, it is the relative *inaction* of Taiwanese government agents that has enabled, however unwittingly, the free-flowing of Taiwan cinema's soft power across the world over the past 40 years.

Taiwan and its cinema, therefore, serve as a prime example for the study of soft power because, according to Nye, the countries that are likely to gain soft power in the information age are those "whose dominant culture and ideas are closer to prevailing global norms (which now emphasize liberalism, pluralism, and autonomy); and whose credibility is enhanced by their domestic and international values and policies" (2004, 31–32). The election of Tsai Ing-wen in 2016 as Taiwan's first female president and the passing of the same-sex marriage bill in 2019 exemplify cultural and political values of liberalism and pluralism on the island. As political scientist Shelley Rigger puts it, Taiwan still matters to the world today because "democracy in Taiwan is an indicator and inspiration for democracy everywhere" (2011, 189). Taiwan cinema, embodying and representing such values of democracy, liberalism, and pluralism, tells moving stories that attract audiences worldwide via an exercise of soft power in subtle and sophisticated ways, which can be illustrated through the interrelationships between the three keywords of this book's subtitle: authorship, transnationality, and historiography.

Authorship, Transnationality, Historiography

For many film scholars and critics, Taiwan, having produced "some of the greatest works of art in the history of cinema, an achievement of breathtaking proportions" (Tweedie 2013, 145), can "reasonably claim one of the highest per-capita densities of international renowned film talent in the world" (Berry and Lu 2005b, 2). In relation to authorship, Hou Hsiao-hsien and Edward Yang emerged as key figures in the early years of the TNC movement as they, signaling a departure from their predecessors, turned to local realities and histories for their cinematic representations. A second generation, led by Ang Lee and Tsai Ming-liang, followed in the 1990s, heralding a transnational turn in Taiwan cinema through the production and distribution of their films. In English-language scholarship, Emilie Yueh-yu Yeh and Darrell William Davis (2005) have written a useful account of TNC's history and the quartet of auteurs mentioned earlier. My book shifts the context from the domestic to the foreign (or the national to the transnational) and updates the timeframe of analysis to the twenty-first century. It devotes three chapters (2 to 4) to the study of the cinematic and extra-cinematic soft power of Hou, Tsai, and Lee, with Yang excluded from discussion because his final film was made in the year 2000 before he passed away in 2007.

This book not only builds on the work of extant scholarship in pushing the study of Chinese-language cinemas beyond the national framework (Lu 1997; Wicks 2015), it also does so uniquely by reformulating Taiwan cinema *singularly* as a form of transnational cinema. That is to say, rather than mobilizing the concept of transnationality mainly to indicate cross-border cinematic connections, it envisions the transnational as inherent to the national body politic by adopting a "critical transnationalism" that interrogates how elements of transnationality negotiate with the national on all levels—"from cultural policy to financing sources, from the multiculturalism of difference to how they reconfigure the nation's image of itself" (Higbee and Lim 2010, 18). Moreover, it teases out several dimensions of this transnationality that also function as crucial "turns" in Taiwan cinema in the new millennium. These transnational turns include the production of a documentary that focuses on TNC's overseas reception (the historiographical turn in Chapter 1); the commissioning by foreign institutions of Hou to make non-Chinese-language films set outside Taiwan (the aural turn in Chapter 2); the expansion of Tsai's oeuvre from cinema to other medial forms that are staged in Europe as well as in virtual reality (the medial turn in Chapter 3); and Lee's trans-Pacific career in film industries located in the region, across the Taiwan Strait, and in the United States (the industrial turn in Chapter 4).

I have argued before (Lim 2011a, 41) that Taiwan cinema in the twenty-first century has rendered untenable conceptual models such as "Chinese-language film" (Lu and Yeh 2005) and Sinophone cinema (Shih S-m. 2007; Yue and Khoo 2014). In the context of this book, I would add that a national or lingua-centric historiography of cinema does not sufficiently recognize cross-cultural cinephilia as a form of soft power, which involves various agents (programmers, critics, audiences), institutions (festivals, museums), and mechanisms (distribution, exhibition), as much as the actual objects (films, auteurs), processes (reception, cultural translation), and discourses (critical, popular) of such transnational cinematic flows. The main body of this book opens, in Chapter 1, with an examination of a documentary—itself a form of historiographical writing—about the reception of TNC outside, rather than within, the island.[11] It closes, in Chapter 5, with another turn (this time affective) taken by Taiwan cinema in which local films and other cultural products eschew the global soft power of authorship and foreground instead structures of feeling that have a regional appeal across the Taiwan Strait, thus scaling down the historiographical frame. Finally, the book extends, in the Epilogue, its problematization of the notion of historiography by proposing that Taiwan cinema's resurrection may take place mainly among alien bodies on which this cinema's soft power has left indelible marks, generating an afterlife of Taiwan cinema that exists both within and beyond the island's shores. The rest of this Introduction will lay out the premise for Taiwan cinema's soft power and draw out some methodological implications for a study of this kind.

Cinema as Soft Power

How does one identify, never mind measure, the soft power of a cinema, national or otherwise? In 1995, the Danish film movement Dogme95 proposed that a cinema should be measured not only quantitatively by domestic production levels but also qualitatively in terms of international esteem indicators. With its now-famous 10-point manifesto, "The Vow of Chastity," and the histrionics of its founders (particularly Lars von Trier, the *enfant terrible* of European cinema), Dogme95 immediately captured the global imagination and spun out a transnational filmmaking movement that had led to over 30 films made in its name between 1998 and 2004.[12] Asked in an interview in the early days of the movement whether the Danes were proud to have provided the birthplace for the latest European avant-garde movement sweeping the globe, Dogme95's co-founder Thomas Vinterberg declared, "Well, it's the same thing as a guy with a small penis who wants a huge motorbike. I think part of the arrogance behind Dogme95 represents a very small country with very small penises. (*Laughs*) So it has to be very rigid and arrogant" (qtd. in Kelly 2000, 119–120). As an uncompromisingly rigid (the manifesto is replete with imperatives) and comparatively short-lived movement, Dogme95 certainly came and went quickly, but its impact was felt across the world, and it remains one of the most influential global film movements from the past 30 years or so.

Back in Taiwan, a "Taiwan Cinema Manifesto" was released in early 1987.[13] Drafted by Zhan Hongzhi, recognized as "a powerful opinion leader and a major backer of the New Cinema" (Yeh and Davis 2005, 76), the manifesto had 53 signatories comprising key TNC filmmakers as well as luminaries from other artistic fields. It called for a space, beyond "commercial film," for "another kind of cinema," one that can be "a consciously creative act," "an art form," and even "a national, cultural act with reflection and historicism" (Zhan 1988, 117, 111). This other kind of cinema was represented by TNC, and all but one of the core directors associated with the movement signed the manifesto.[14] However, unlike many manifestos that either preceded a cinematic movement (such as François Truffaut's "A Certain Tendency in French Cinema" and the French New Wave) or were launched in tandem with a new film (such as Fernando Solanas and Octavio Getino's 1969 "Towards a Third Cinema" and their 1968 film, *The Hour of the Furnaces*),[15] the "Taiwan Cinema Manifesto" was a last-ditch effort to save TNC from its impending death. By providing a diagnosis rather than a directive, it had the effect of describing TNC's end rather than beginning (Lu 2011, 122).

Whereas the Dogme95 movement perceived the survival of Danish cinema as threatened by external, Hollywood-style globalization (Hjort 2003, 31), TNC filmmakers and supporters sensed their animosity coming closer from home, alluding in the manifesto to a 1984 article entitled "Please Don't Kill Off Taiwan

Cinema" by critic Du Yun-chih. Since its inception, attributed in most discourses to the making of the omnibus film *In Our Time* (*Guangyin de gushi*, dir. Tao Te-chen, Edward Yang, Ko I-chen, and Chang Yi, 1982), the TNC movement had routinely been made a scapegoat as posing a threat to the survival of Taiwan cinema. Critics charged TNC's award-winning films as box-office poison, thus inventing and reinforcing a myth of bifurcation—and, more damningly, a causal relation—between TNC's high international prestige and Taiwan cinema's overall low domestic production and consumption levels.[16] In fact, while TNC had begun to win some awards in second-tier international film festivals in the 1986–87 period when the manifesto was drafted—Yang's 1986 *The Terrorizer* (*Kongbu fenzi*) was awarded a Silver Leopard at Locarno in 1987 and Hou's *A Time to Live, A Time to Die* (*Tongnian wangshi*, 1985) won Best Non-American/Non-European Film at Rotterdam in 1987—no Taiwan film or director had yet to bag a major award at any of the top three film festivals (Berlin, Cannes, and Venice). Fast-forward 25 years or so, and many top awards later, as Table I.1 indicates, in the heat of the phenomenal box-office miracle of Wei Te-sheng's *Cape No. 7* (*Haijiao qihao*, 2008), TNC was again accused, this time by an academic based in Taiwan's highest research institute, for "losing its storytelling ability, neglecting cinema's entertainment function, [and] walking into the cul-de-sac of art cinema" (Peng 2010, 124).

Rather than being celebrated by fellow citizens for its global soft power, TNC filmmakers were (and still are) held suspect, to extend Vinterberg's penile metaphor, for flaunting the prowess of their small penises or even, perhaps, for expanding beyond what is perceived to be their rightful size, rising above their station, so to speak. At stake, however, is not only the survival of a cinema (whether TNC as a movement or Taiwan "national" cinema as a whole) but also the historiography constructed as a result of such accusation and contention—manifestos, after all, are often a call to arms. In the case of Taiwan cinema, this remains a battle about different understandings of cinema and its function, which, as I will discuss later in the chapter, also has implications for the discipline of film studies.

The central tension, it seems to me, lies between the soft power of a film movement and the movement's position within what is regarded as its proper place in the nation's film industry and history; or, to put it differently, between cinema's external, outward-reaching potential and internal, inward-looking perspective. A major reason behind such tension, I would suggest, is the popular assumption of a national cinema model, which, despite acknowledgment of its limitations (Higson 2000) and the advancement of other frameworks—most notably, that of transnational cinema (Ezra and Rowden 2006)—still persists within film scholarship.[17] An edited book *The Cinema of Small Nations* (Hjort and Petrie 2007a) attempts to provide a different take on the national cinema model, though the

Table I.1 Major prizes won by Chinese cinemas at the top-three international film festivals (Berlin, Cannes, and Venice), 1988–2020

Year	Taiwan	China	Hong Kong
1988		*Red Sorghum* (Zhang Yimou), Golden Bear, Berlin	
1989	*A City of Sadness* (Hou Hsiao-hsien), Golden Lion, Venice	*Evening Bell* (Wu Ziniu), Silver Bear—Special Jury Prize, Berlin	
1990		*Black Snow* (Xie Fei), Silver Bear for Outstanding Single Achievement, Berlin	
1991		*Raise the Red Lantern* (Zhang Yimou), Silver Lion for Best Direction, Venice	
1992		*The Story of Qiu Ju* (Zhang Yimou), Golden Lion, Venice	Maggie Cheung for *Center Stage* (Stanley Kwan), Silver Bear for Best Actress, Berlin
1993	*The Wedding Banquet* (Ang Lee), Golden Bear, Berlin; *The Puppetmaster* (Hou Hsiao-hsien), Jury Prize, Cannes	*Women from the Lake of Scented Souls* (Xie Fei), Golden Bear, Berlin; *Farewell My Concubine* (Chen Kaige), Palme d'Or and FIPRESCI Prize, Cannes	
1994	*Vive L'amour* (Tsai Ming-liang), Golden Lion, Venice	Ge You, Best Actor for *To Live* (Zhang Yimou), Cannes; *To Live* (Zhang Yimou), Jury's Grand Prix Ex-aequo, Cannes	
1995		*Blush* (Li Shaohong), Silver Bear for Outstanding Single Achievement, Berlin	Josephine Siao for *Summer Snow* (Ann Hui), Silver Bear for Best Actress, Berlin
1996	*Sense and Sensibility* (Ang Lee), Golden Bear, Berlin*		Yim Ho, Silver Bear for Best Director for *The Sun Has Ears*, Berlin

1997	*The River* (Tsai Ming-liang), Silver Bear—Special Jury Prize, Berlin	Wong Kar-wai, Best Director for *Happy Together*, Cannes
1998		
1999	*Not One Less* (Zhang Yimou), Golden Lion, Venice	
2000	*The Road Home* (Zhang Yimou), Silver Bear: Jury Grand Prix, Berlin; *Devils at the Doorstep* (Jiang Wen), Grand Prix, Cannes	Edward Yang, Best Director for *Yi Yi*, Cannes; Tony Leung Chiu-wai, Best Actor for *In the Mood for Love* (Wong Kar-wai), Cannes
2001	*Beijing Bicycle* (Wang Xiaoshuai), Silver Bear—Jury Grand Prix, Berlin	Lin Cheng-sheng, Silver Bear for Best Director, Berlin, for *Betelnut Beauty*
2002		
2003	*Blind Shaft* (Li Yang), Silver Bear for Outstanding Artistic Contribution, Berlin	*Goodbye, Dragon Inn* (Tsai Ming-liang), FIPRESCI Award, Venice
2004		Maggie Cheung, Best Actress for *Clean* (Olivier Assayas), Cannes*
2005	*Peacock* (Gu Changwei), Silver Bear—Jury Grand Prix, Berlin; *Shanghai Dreams* (Wang Xiaoshuai), Jury Prize, Cannes	*The Wayward Cloud* (Tsai Ming-liang), Silver Bear for an outstanding single achievement, Berlin; *Brokeback Mountain* (Ang Lee), Golden Lion, Venice*
2006	*Still Life* (Jia Zhangke), Golden Lion, Venice	
2007	*Tuya's Marriage* (Wang Quan'an), Golden Bear for Best Film, Berlin	*Lust, Caution* (Ang Lee), Golden Lion, Venice
2008	Wang Xiaoshuai, Silver Bear for Best Script for *In Love We Trust* (Wang Xiaoshuai), Berlin	

Continued

Table I.1 *Continued*

Year	Taiwan	China	Hong Kong
2009		Lou Ye, Best Screenplay for *Spring Fever* (Lou Ye), Cannes	
2010		Wang Quan'an and Jin Na, Silver Bear for Best Script for *Apart Together* (Wang Quan'an), Berlin	John Woo, Golden Lion for Lifetime Achievement, Venice*
2011		*People Mountain People Sea* (Cai Shangjun), Silver Lion for Best Director, Venice+	Deanie Ip, Best Actress for *A Simple Life* (Ann Hui), Venice
2012		Lutz Reitemeier, Silver Bear for Outstanding Artistic Contribution for the photography in *White Deer Plain* (Wang Quan'an), Berlin+	
2013	*Stray Dogs* (Tsai Ming-liang), Grand Jury Prize, Venice	Jia Zhangke, Best Screenplay for *A Touch of Sin* (Jia Zhangke), Cannes	
2014		*Black Coal, Thin Ice* (Diao Yinan), Golden Bear for Best Film, Berlin; Liao Fan, Silver Bear for Best Actor in *Black Coal, Thin Ice* (Diao Yinan), Berlin; Zeng Jian, Silver Bear for Outstanding Artistic Contribution for the camera in *Blind Massage* (Lou Ye), Berlin	
2015	Hou Hsiao-hsien, Best Director for *The Assassin* (Hou Hsiao-hsien), Cannes		
2016	Mark Lee Ping-bing, Silver Bear for Outstanding Artistic Contribution for the cinematography in *Crosscurrent* (Yang Chao), Berlin+		

2017		Shi Nansun, Berlinale Camera, Berlin (Honorary Award)
2018	*An Elephant Sitting Still* (Hu Bo), GWFF Best First Feature Film Award (Special Mention) and FIPRESCI Award (Forum section), Berlin	
2019	Yong Mei, Silver Bear for Best Actress in *So Long, My Son* (Wang Xiaoshuai), Berlin; Wang Jingchun, Silver Bear for Best Actor in *So Long, My Son* (Wang Xiaoshuai), Berlin; *A Dog Barking at the Moon* (Xiang Zi), Jury Award (Teddy Awards), Berlin	Yonfan, Best Screenplay for *No. 7 Cherry Lane*, Venice
2020#	*Days* (Tsai Ming-liang), Jury Award (Teddy Awards), Berlin	Ann Hui, Golden Lion for Lifetime Achievement, Venice

Source: Information on awards won at Cannes and Berlin has been culled from relevant pages on their festival websites, respectively https://www.berlinale.de/en/archive/jahresarchive/2019/03_preistraeger_2019/03_preistraeger_2019.html. Information on awards won at Venice has been culled from various sources as its festival website does not contain a full list. Only awards for feature-length filmmaking and lifetime achievement at the main festivals are listed, but not ones for short films or for those won at side events (such as the Orizzonti/Horizon competition, the Venice Days, or a new category for virtual reality films at Venice).

* Awards won by director and actor for films made in non-Chinese-languages, except for John Woo, whose award recognizes both his Chinese- and English-language films.

+ 2011 award won by PRC director whose film was submitted as an entry for Hong Kong because it did not receive permission from the PRC authorities to participate in the festival (listed under China); 2012 award won by a German cameraman for a PRC film (listed under China); 2016 award won by a Taiwanese cameraman for a PRC film (listed under Taiwan).

Cannes Film Festival cancelled due to the coronavirus outbreak.

editors concede that "a definitive definition of small state cannot be provided." Nevertheless, they argue that the concept of small nationhood "gives priority to the question of levels of production, thereby blurring the distinction between the idea of a small nation that produces films and the idea of a country that produces a small number of films" (Hjort and Petrie 2007b, 4, 3). By asking their contributors to provide "information about the institutional parameters governing cinematic production in their context, to identify some of the persistent challenges faced by filmmakers in that context, and to discuss and assess the impact of any solutions that might have been explored over the years" (2), the editors clearly privilege issues of policy and production as instruments for measuring the state of a nation's cinema.

While Taiwan cinema may be classified as a cinema of a small nation, I would argue that the privileging of the quantitative (levels of production) as a measure of smallness misses the point—not because size doesn't matter but rather because, as the sexual connotation of this metaphor suggests, size alone cannot account for quality, whether measured by pleasure or prestige. Indeed, internal factors such as dismal domestic production levels or dysfunctional government policies are no necessary hindrance to the external dimension of a small cinema's global soft-power reach. If, according to Nye, the degree to which "a particular asset is a soft-power resource that produces attraction can be measured by asking people through polls or focus groups" (2004, 6), cinema as a soft-power resource can then be measured by awards conferred at international film festivals since these awards are, in effect, an index of attractiveness decided by panels of judges who act as voting focus groups. On this front, Taiwan cinema's winning streak at the top-three festivals is no mean feat for a small nation.

Taiwan Cinema's Soft Power

Authorship is key to this "small miracle" despite that, as James Udden notes in his chapter on Taiwan in the aforementioned edited book on the cinema of small nations, Taiwan cinema has never been respected by the Taiwanese government as "either an art form or even as a commercial industry" (2007, 158, 157). Averaging around one award every two years from 1989 to the time of this writing (2020), this small miracle can be largely attributed to the quartet of directors with an undisputed auteur status in world cinema. In fact, Hou, Yang, Lee, and Tsai are collectively responsible for almost all the top prizes that Taiwan cinema has won at Berlin, Cannes, and Venice since TNC's inception. Apart from Lin Cheng-sheng's 2001 Silver Bear for Best Director for Betelnut Beauty (Ai ni ai wo, 2001), the quartet has garnered over a dozen awards at these festivals, including those for Ang Lee's English-language films (Sense and Sensibility, Golden Bear, 1996;

Brokeback Mountain, Golden Lion, 2005).[18] As we can see in Table I.1, a comparison with similar awards won by Hong Kong and China (both of which have much larger film industries and higher production figures) illustrates that, not only is size not the sole factor in assessing the status of a nation's cinema, but this status can also rest almost exclusively on the shoulders of a few giant-sized auteurs whose consistent winnings have maintained the international profile of Taiwan cinema over the past 40 years.

By measuring success based on number of awards won at the three major international film festivals, where the currency of authorship is highly valued, my account would appear to concur with Udden's premise that "decades of government policy eventually produced a cinema now almost entirely predicated on art and culture at the expense of any industry whatsoever" (2007, 144). Yet, while Udden rightly critiques the Taiwan government's treatment of cinema as being merely "a tool of the state: either for propaganda purposes or as an endless source of tax revenue" (157), he fails to acknowledge the same government's role in wielding cinema as its most effective soft-power tool. As Udden claims, the government's submission of Taiwan films to international film festivals was initially undertaken "more as an afterthought than as a clear-cut strategy" (152), but a strategy has nonetheless been developed over the years to encourage participation in and to reward success at these festivals. Udden's focus on domestic production is understandable given the remit of the edited book in which his chapter appears, but it gives only half the picture if government policy on international film festival participation has not also been taken into account.

Policy formulation indicates that the Taiwan government has long been aware, predating the popularization of the notion of soft power in academic discourse, that cinema can be mobilized as a diplomatic tool to compensate for what the island lacks in hard power.[19] In February 1992, the Government Information Office (GIO) published the "Enforcement Directions Governing the Provision of Incentives and Guidance to the Motion Picture Industry and Industry Professionals Participating in International Film Festivals," which had undergone numerous revisions since. The 2018 version groups film festivals into four categories, with the top tier comprising the three European festivals mentioned and the Academy Awards ("Dianying shiye" 2018). Under the scheme, a Best Film Award (Golden Bear at Berlin, Palme d'Or at Cannes, Golden Lion at Venice, Best Picture or Best Foreign-Language Film at the Oscars) would bring the director and the production company each a cash prize of NT$10 million (New Taiwan dollars) in 2010, as would a Best Director Award.

These figures can be put into perspective when compared to government policies to support domestic filmmaking. The Domestic Film Production Subsidy and Assistance scheme provided, in 2010, funding for no more than half of the production cost for a domestic feature-length film and a cap of NT$20 million

("99 niandu" 2010), that is, only double the cash prize for a Best Film or Best Director Award at a top-tier festival. As the only source of government subsidy for film production, the scheme opens itself up each year to a scramble for money, resulting in endless controversies among individuals, companies, and factions while leaving other structural problems of the industry (in particular, the crippled distribution system) intact. Nevertheless, Taiwan filmmakers, including those among the world-renowned quartet, continue to rely on the scheme for part of their films' funding. For instance, Hou received NT$9 million for his 2005 film, *Three Times* (*Zuihao de shiguang*), and NT$15 million for *The Assassin* (*Cike Nie Yinniang*, 2015), whereas Tsai received NT$9 million for his 2005 film, *The Wayward Cloud* (*Tianbian yiduo yun*), and NT$8 million for his 2006 film, *I Don't Want to Sleep Alone* (*Heiyanquan*).[20] From the viewpoint of the filmmakers, however, given the amount of a cash prize they would receive if they or their films were to win a prestigious award at a top festival, not to mention the opportunities presented at these sites for the sale of overseas rights of their films, the incentive to have their films selected for competition at these festivals is obvious.

It would be fair to say that the Taiwanese government has devoted resources, however limited, to both domestic film production and international film festival participation. The landscape for both aspects has, however, changed beyond recognition in the twenty-first century, even for the quartet of auteurs. After his first three Chinese-language films co-produced with Taiwan's Central Motion Picture Corporation (CMPC, the cinematic arm of the then ruling Kuomintang government) and sponsored by the GIO's production grant, Ang Lee has had virtually no relation to Taiwan's film industry, having gone on to make a string of English-language films and to become the first Asian director to win the Best Achievement in Directing Award at the Oscars (first for his 2005 film *Brokeback Mountain*, then for his 2011 film *Life of Pi*)—becoming, in fact, almost an all-American filmmaker. Yang's *Yi Yi* (also known as *A One and A Two*, 2000), for which he was crowned Best Director at Cannes, was not released theatrically in Taiwan until the 10th anniversary of Yang's death in 2017. Meanwhile, the careers of Hou and Tsai have taken them to far-flung places where their films are produced by foreign institutions and sometimes feature little or no use of any Chinese languages—including works such as Hou's Musée d'Orsay–sponsored *Le voyage du ballon rouge* (*Flight of the Red Balloon*, 2007) and Tsai's Musée du Louvre–commissioned *Visage* (*Face*, 2009). Taiwan cinema, even without the aid of its government's soft-power strategies, appears to be increasingly produced and consumed beyond the island's shores.

As such, I have chosen to tell in this book, using soft power as a lens, the story of Taiwan cinema's foreign reception in the twenty-first century. To recast the chapter outline through this lens, Chapter 1 posits, through the discussion of a

2014 documentary on TNC, that soft power can manifest in the form of cross-cultural cinephilic discourses, produced in this case by interviewees who include filmmakers, festival programmers, critics, and artists from Europe, South America, and East Asia. Chapters 2 to 4 show that Taiwan cinema's soft power is now increasingly engineered by foreign forces (coming from Japan, France, and the United States, among others) attracted to the three auteurs' (respectively, Hou, Tsai, and Lee) translingual, transmedial, and transnational abilities, although local-level government initiatives in Taiwan also contributed to Lee's making of *Life of Pi*. Chapter 5 looks at the scaling down of soft power from the global to the regional via a cultural imaginary called "little freshness" (*xiao qingxin*), which describes films such as *Cape No. 7* and Giddens Ko's *You Are the Apple of My Eye* (*Naxie nian, women yiqi zhui de nühai*, 2011) as well as other cultural products from Taiwan that have become hugely popular in China and Hong Kong. The Epilogue details how TNC and Taiwanese cinematic institutions (such as the Golden Horse Awards) have transformed into a source of soft power attraction for budding filmmakers from East and Southeast Asia at both textual and extra-textual levels to the extent that these alien filmmakers and their films now constitute a kind of Taiwan cinema's afterlife that perpetuates TNC's legacy.

This book is, therefore, a historiography not about a national cinema but about a cinematic new wave powered by the cachet of authorship and opportunities for transnational collaborations. Often emerging out of an urgent response to their own nations' tumultuous sociopolitical changes, new wave cinemas across the world have been led by innovative auteurs and accompanied by critical reflection and a concomitant experimentation in form and style. From Truffaut and Godard to Wender and Fassbinder, from Rocha and dos Santos to Hou and Tsai, these filmmakers have offered us not just "another kind of cinema" but also another way of looking at cinema. Soft, small, and perfectly formed, this kind of cinema delivers qualitative pleasure derived from a deep and penetrating investment on the aesthetic, emotional, intellectual, and political levels. The qualification or quantification of such cinematic pleasure, however, is not an easy task, and I would like to spell out, in the final two sections of this Introduction, some methodological issues relating to the deployment of the concept of soft power in this book.

Soft Power as Method

Three decades have passed since Nye proposed the notion of soft power,[21] and scholarship building on the notion has grown to the extent that a separate article is needed simply to account for that body of literature. A recent anthology, at nearly 500 pages and with sections dedicated to theoretical and methodological considerations, as well as to case studies drawn from across the world, provides a glimpse into the current state of such scholarship. In the Introduction to the anthology, Naren Chitty notes from the outset that the term has had a "mixed reception, especially in academia," partly because the effects of soft power "in the hard sense of so many bucks producing so much soft bang are tantalizingly difficult to prove" (2017, 1). It is clear the study of soft power—currently conducted mainly by social scientists—is predominantly interested in tracing the effect of soft power generated by agents' initiatives. Nye, for example, places emphasis on the source of the soft-power flow, that is, the role of agents, particularly institutions (both governmental and nongovernmental), thus lending itself comfortably to research fields, such as policy studies. Despite its aims and claims, one critique I would make of Nye's work is that it does not trace the soft-power flow of any single cultural product, political value, institution, or policy from start to finish; as such, the randomness of and lack of causality in its examples reinforce the impression about the rather slipshod use of the notion of soft power.

Beyond the disciplines of international relations and political science, the specific role that cinema has played (or can play) in the exercise of soft power has only begun to receive academic attention. In 2015 the international network "Soft Power, Cinema and the BRICS" was formed in the United Kingdom,[22] and in 2018 an edited volume, *Screening China's Soft Power* (Voci and Luo 2018a), was published. The questions to ask then: Why soft power? To what extent and in what ways does the notion of soft power lend a new analytical angle to the study of cinema? In other words, what can the notion of soft power explain and explicate where previous concepts, approaches, and methodologies could not? What insights into the production, distribution, exhibition, consumption, and reception of films does it offer that have been missing elsewhere? What are the advantages and limitations in using this notion? Given that the difficulty of measuring effect is foregrounded as one of the chief methodological discontents in the study of soft power, how can the deployment of the concept improve on existing approaches to audience research and reception studies in the disciplines of film, media, and communication studies?

I find soft power a useful conceptual holder for a thorough tracking from agent (institutions of production) to affect (interfacing the encounter between text and audience during consumption) and effect (audience response) so that a fuller picture of a film's trajectory from inception to reception can be painted. In her overview chapter of the section on "methodological problems" in the aforementioned anthology on soft power, Li Ji calls for a two-directional evaluation of soft-power effectiveness that encompasses "agents' resources, capabilities and behaviors, along with subjects' perceptions, affections and behaviors towards soft power exerted by agents" (Ji 2017, 78). Counterbalancing an overemphasis on agents, Ji's model complements Nye's work by bringing into play the reception end of the equation. Here I propose a three-pronged approach to the study of soft power by introducing affect as a missing but crucial factor in mediating soft-power transactions. Across the chapters and with varying degrees of emphasis on each, my three-pronged model will trace the following: (1) the agents, institutions, policies, and mechanisms that set out or are deployed to shape different forms of preferences for Taiwan cinema; (2) the affective environment governing the preponderance for certain preferences; and (3) the ways in which such preferences are materialized, and their effects detected and measured.

By bringing the notion of affect into the equation, my contribution—from a humanities perspective—is to raise the awareness that soft power cannot be studied purely in instrumental and quantitative terms. I place affect as a distinct category not only because it differs in meaning from what Ji calls "affections," but, more important, because, as a form of mediating environment, it also underpins the conversion process from agents to effect in a fundamental manner, which I shall explain in the next section.

Among the three aspects of soft-power flows, effect needs to be addressed first and foremost because it is, as noted, the main source of discontent about the employment of soft power as a methodological tool for academic investigation. Two questions immediately stand out: What counts as effects, and how can effects be detected or measured? For Ji, effects of soft-power practices manifest "on two parameters (cognition and behavior) of actors at three levels (individual actors, institutional actors and state actors)" (2017, 83). She further suggests three scales for evaluating soft-power effects, namely emotion/sentiment measured by empirical evidence such as a poll, survey, and/or questionnaire; perception/opinion revealed through content and discourse analysis; and behavior studied via big data and framing analysis (84–85). While Ji maps out a rather comprehensive model for evaluating soft-power effects, any study of a soft-power strategy, policy, or product cannot possibly demonstrate all the evidence corresponding to the myriad parameters, levels, and scales she proposes. Scale can become an unwieldy tool, and, in any case, each study often picks and chooses whatever evidence it can (or prefer to) find. For example, a political scientist such as Nye clearly favors hard data: the 10 bullet-point social indices he lists as examples of US soft-power resources are all quantifiable numbers (2004, 33–34); on the other hand, sociologist Chua Beng Huat, in his book *Structure, Audience and Soft Power in East Asian Pop Culture*, argues that the effectiveness of soft power "can only be verified and substantiated by empirical evidence of audience behavior subsequent to reception; there should be evidence of changes in attitude in the audience towards the exporting nation" (2012, 121).

The emphasis on hard data and empirical evidence betrays a methodological inclination that demands rethinking as the notion of soft power is adopted for cross-disciplinary use. On that front, even Ji's application of Erving Goffman's framing analysis (Ji 2017, 85–89) strikes me as too schematic and instrumentalist, as if every discourse can be explained (away) by a framework and every effect indicated—with remedies recommended, no less. Claims about (or, at least, gestures toward) certainty of findings and credibility of methodologies seem to be the hallmark of many social science disciplines, whereas scholarship in the humanities is typically marked by ambivalence, ambiguity, and speculation. As Yingjin Zhang notes in his afterword to *Screening China's Soft Power*, "contrary to social scientists, cultural studies scholars prefer close textual analysis to data collection and compilation, and their attention to questions of multiplicity and heterogeneity . . . frequently reveal meanings in excess of the intended message in China's soft power projects" (Zhang 2018, 255)—a spirit of inquiry I follow in this book.

I propose, therefore, affect as an alternative method for appreciating the operation of soft power. If, according to Nye, "in behavioral terms soft power is attractive power" (2004, 6), which can then be concretized as "*likable features*" that include a country's cultures and values (Voci and Luo 2018b, 2, emphasis in original), there is arguably a "mismatch between soft power's stated goals (i.e. succeeding in world politics) and some of the key means through which soft power is developed and deployed (cultural practices and values)" (Voci and Luo 2018b, 2). As Paola Voci and Luo Hui insightfully point out, "cultures and values are neither simply containable nor fully controllable by the state; they are shaped by hybrid local and global belongings that transcend a country's national borders" (2). Thus, understanding how cultures and values are transmitted from country to country, indeed, how likable features pass from body to body, is key to unpicking the underlying working mechanisms of soft power.

Affect as Method

I believe the notion of affect can help us explain the mediating environment that fundamentally undergirds any cultural flow and communicative process. As such, we can shift the focus of analysis from specific strategies adopted by agents or the measurement of effects to an understanding of affect, that is, how and why people are moved by certain objects. On the notion of affect, Eric Shouse (2005) suggests that "the pleasure that individuals derive from music has less to do with the communication of meaning, and far more with the way that a particular piece of music 'moves' them." In many cases, affect rests upon the fact that "the message consciously received may be of less import to the receiver of that message than his or her non-conscious affective resonance with the *source* of the message" (Shouse 2005, emphasis mine). That is to say, for example, it is not a film's message but rather the environment (including the object, its source and communicative events, its bodies of transmission, and so on) in which the message is carried that ultimately embodies, emits, and transmits affective intensities to the extent that the message itself can often be ignored. To misappropriate a famous construction by media theorist Marshall McLuhan, we might say that it is not the medium, but the affect, that is the message.

I draw my inspiration of affect as mediating environment from Weihong Bao's notion of cinema as an affective medium, wherein affect serves as "a platform/ interface of experience produced by media technology and media aesthetic in interaction with the perceptual subjects" (2015a, 12). Starting with questions such as "what constitutes the medium of cinema" and "what has affect got to do with it," Bao develops her thesis of "the medium as a *mediating environment*" (5; emphasis in original) insofar as perception (here she draws on Henri Bergson), while "not immediately our own but external," can only be reclaimed through "affection, conceived as a spatial terrain allowing the extensity of the body to reach the object and prepare for action" (13). In Bao's study, this affective medium enables the conversion of "spectators into the crowd" in modern China (6); in my case, Taiwan cinema's affective medium transforms foreign spectators into willing agents of Taiwan's soft power.

Because of this understanding of affect as mediating environment, I argue, throughout this book, my case for Taiwan cinema's soft power from the *reverse* direction of the cultural transaction, prioritizing (and using as a starting point) the effects Taiwan cinema has had on foreign audiences and institutions rather than actions taken by local agents, thus treating the former instead of the latter as originators of soft-power flows. Indeed, I would go as far to say that because affect, however "unformed and unstructured" (Shouse 2005), is nonetheless palpable, penetrating the entire cinematic flow from production, distribution, and exhibition to consumption and reception; it is, perhaps more than anything else, its intangible, unquantifiable, and unverifiable intensities that may eventually undermine or determine the efforts of agents and render the measurement of effects a moot point. Failure to appreciate the mediation of affective atmosphere in the soft-power conversion process would fundamentally thwart agents' strategies, in turn impacting the effect whose measure is always already circumscribed by affect.

Agency, for me, does not stem from Taiwanese governmental and nongovernmental actors devising strategies to promote Taiwan cinema's soft power. Rather, agency emanates from foreign bodies (both individual and collective, personal and institutional) that, precisely because of their affective resonances with Taiwan films and auteurs, have initiated schemes, processes, and expressions that now stand as concrete manifestations of such a soft power. Or, to put it differently, this book traces the soft power of authorship in transforming Taiwan cinema into a transnational operation that reconfigures Taiwan film historiography.

As such, it grants primacy to the discourses of foreign filmmakers, critics, and cinephiles who express their love for TNC in a documentary (Chapter 1), the Japanese and French institutions commissioning Hou to make non-Chinese-language films (Chapter 2), the European and other sources of funding enabling Tsai's slow walk from the cinema to the museum (Chapter 3), the collaboration between a Hollywood studio and Taiwanese local government to produce Lee's *Life of Pi* in Taiwan (Chapter 4), and the regional appeal of the "little freshness" imaginary in China and Hong Kong (Chapter 5), presenting them as "evidence" and effects of Taiwan cinema's soft power, exercised unevenly and intermittently over four decades.

By employing the notion of affect as a method for studying soft power, this book seeks to find the right tool for analyzing its research object and, in the process, inadvertently raises some fundamental questions about disciplinary boundaries. For the sake of convenience, I made references earlier to the humanities and social sciences as if they were distinct and mutually exclusive disciplines when many research fields within those two categories actually straddle them. If cinema can be regarded as a form of soft power (whether as strategic resource for state and nonstate agents or as affective source of attraction for audiences), and if affect is the most effective and productive way of understanding the operation of soft power, there is no reason, it seems to me, not to marry a notion originating from the social sciences (in this case, soft power from international relations, or IR) with the notion of affect (in which there are cross- and inter-disciplinary interests) for the examination of a cinematic new wave (TNC) that has transmuted into a transnational cinema. In this I find a kindred spirit in Andrew A. G. Ross, whose book *Mixed Emotions: Beyond Fear and Hatred in International Conflict* draws literature from two fields beyond IR (namely, microsociology and neuroscience) to "derive an account of how emotions both generate and are generated by social interactions" (2014, 3), thereby offering "a timely challenge to some conventional assumptions in IR theory" (7). My book demonstrates, however unwittingly, that no single discipline has monopoly over the complex answers to any research question and object and that the search for the right analytical tool should trump parochial territorialism, disciplinary or otherwise.

To return to the occasion of the 2018 Golden Horse Awards that opened this Introduction, the IR maneuvers from the PRC attest to the operation of an affective environment in which China is widely perceived as a bully in its cross-Strait relations with Taiwan.[23] I have discussed elsewhere how China's efforts to deploy cinema as a soft-power tool in films such as Zhang Yimou's *The Great Wall* (*Changcheng*, 2016) had been undermined by affective resonances toward the emergence and the march of China in the twenty-first century (Lim 2021). As Brian Massumi (1995, 106–107) reminds us in his reading of the US ex-President Bill Clinton's failure to sell his healthcare plan to the public because Clinton was deemed to have lost his "presidential" feel, "this fact about affect—this matter-of-factness of affect—needs to be taken seriously into account in cultural and political theory. Don't forget." By complementing the more empirical and quantitative inclination of social-science-oriented methodologies with an understanding of affect in all its ontological invisibility, metaphorical complexities, cultural resonances, and economic and political imperatives, this book offers an alternative transnational historiography of Taiwan cinema's authorship in the hope of contributing to a better appreciation of why and how soft power works—because affect is intrinsic, rather than external, to agent, atmosphere, text, and effect.

1

The Historiographical Turn

Documenting Taiwan New Cinema
as Cross-Cultural Cinephilia

In his 1997 documentary on Hou Hsiao-hsien, the French critic-turned-director
Olivier Assayas interviewed the Taiwanese critic-turned-director Chen Kuo-
fu in Taipei. As early as 1984, Chen had urged Assayas to visit Taiwan because
he felt that what was then happening in Taiwan (referring to the Taiwan New
Cinema movement, hereafter TNC) "was clearly much more significant than
what was happening in Hong Kong" (referring to the Hong Kong New Wave).
Speaking in English, Chen recounted his first meeting with TNC directors at
Edward Yang's house:

> The first night I met them, everybody was there. Everybody. I mean, Hou
> Hsiao-hsien, Chang Hwa-kun, [Edward] Yang De-chang, Ko I-cheng, Wan Jen.
> Everybody. . . . The feeling was absolutely incredible. I mean, it really doesn't
> matter how good their films are. You know, there is a white board where every-
> body used to just put on things; there are titles for his films to come, ideas, and
> friends will put on some of their own ideas. The board was there for everybody
> to see. So, you definitely sense that something is happening, and is going to
> happen, but you don't really know what.[1]

Entitled *HHH: Portrait de Hou Hsiao-hsien*, Assayas's documentary is much
more than an intimate portrait of a major Taiwan filmmaker. Rather, it can be
claimed it is one of the first historiographical accounts—in the form of documentary film—of the TNC movement, indicated here by the other directors
mentioned in Chen's recollection and elsewhere by the multifarious players
interviewed by Assayas. Two features about the TNC immediately stand out in
the documentary: camaraderie as a hallmark of the movement's early days, and,
as James Tweedie points out in the context of new wave cinemas, the rise of youth
as "the principal agent of social and cultural change" (2013, 19).[2] Wu Nien-jen,
who worked at the Central Motion Picture Corporation (hereafter CMPC), the
state-run studio credited for producing the movement's first films, explained that
they wanted to give new directors the chance to make a film as soon as possible,
thus leading to the portmanteau film *The Sandwich Man* (*Erzi de da wan'ou*, dir.

Taiwan Cinema as Soft Power. Song Hwee Lim, Oxford University Press. © Oxford University Press 2022.
DOI: 10.1093/oso/9780197503379.003.0002

Hou Hsiao-hsien, Zeng Zhuangxiang, and Wan Ren, 1983). Hou, at the time of the early 1980s already a relative veteran, remembered the new directors as full of vibrancy, as if ready to start a revolution like Sun Yat-sen did in the final years of the Qing dynasty. Chen, then playing the role of the US-trained film critic, reminisced about how he, Hou, and Yang used to meet every other day to "exchange our ideas about film, filmmaking," an arrangement that lasted about five to six years. In a rare intervention, Assayas asked, "Do you miss it?" Chen became visibly emotional in his reply: "Of course. Of course. I would exchange all the films that I've made to get back the feeling again."

Assayas's documentary is significant, I believe, for the reconstruction of TNC's historiography on at least two fronts. First, it foregrounds the documentary as a historiographical form, here rendered more self-reflexive as one about a movement based on the medium of film. In particular, the talking-head interview format not only invites intimate self-reflection on the part of the interviewees but also allows multiple perspectives on the same subject to be given by different interviewees and the building of a larger narrative in the editing process later. In the examples cited earlier, the interviews of Chen, Hou, and Wu were, in fact, conducted separately, but they were crosscut tightly in a segment to stage a conversation that never actually took place among the three—a conversation at once private and public, individual and collective, spontaneous and directed. Moreover, as a form of historiographical record, the documentary film can register information at audio-visual and affective levels that are perhaps unique to its own. Chen said he nearly burst into tears when he saw on TV news that Hou's *A City of Sadness* (*Beiqing chengshi*, 1989) had won the Golden Lion award at Venice; he sent Hou a fax to say that "I was very proud of him," fighting back tears as he spoke. This affective expression is all the more powerful given the contrast between Chen and Hou on the audio-visual level: Chen, the US-trained sophisticate, was speaking in English, at night in a bar where glasses of red wine were scattered on the table across from which Chen and Assayas sat; Hou, plain-talking and plainly dressed, was showing Assayas and an interpreter in broad daylight around the neighborhood where he grew up, mingling comfortably with the locals like a boy next door. These everyday details—profilmic indexicality captured on screen—add textures and flavors to agents and events, details that would otherwise disappear from other forms of historiographical writing because they would have been considered too insignificant to be recorded.

Second, and more important, Assayas's documentary highlights a network of trademarks—namely, authorship, transnationality, and soft power—that I am proposing in this book as key organizing principles for the weaving of an alternative historiographical account of the TNC movement and its legacy. It is clear, in the documentary segment cited earlier, that the movement's birth was induced, in part, by a transnational consciousness, inspired by the Hong Kong New Wave and facilitated by a willingness to give young turks recently trained in the United States a chance to make films that, in turn, challenged local veterans such as Hou to reconsider the film medium at the most fundamental level.[3] Even the young turks' translingual ability was put to good use as Chen suggested the English title for Hou's *A Time to Live, A Time to Die* (*Tongnian wangshi*, 1985) after visiting Hou's film set. As the saying goes, the rest is history, but, I would argue, it is a history of TNC's soft power cast as cross-cultural cinephilia. This soft power was manifested, above all, by Taiwan cinema's winning streak at top European film festivals after Hou's triumph at Venice in 1989, leading Chen, citing Ang Lee and Tsai Ming-liang as auteurs following in Hou's footsteps, to joke that the "disruptive side" of TNC's impact was that every Taiwan film was now expected to get an award of some sort.[4] Winning top prizes also had the effect of turning a director from a small nation into a bankable global brand name, thus helping Hou, as he revealed in the documentary, to more easily attract international and domestic funding so he could pay back his debts and invest in equipment on behalf of the sound engineer Tu Duu-chih. Taiwan cinema, therefore, was, and remains, a transnational phenomenon powered by the currency of authorship.

The Soft Power of Taiwan New Cinema

In this chapter I want to provide, through the notion of soft power, a historiographical account of the TNC movement by constructing a story about Taiwan cinema's reception in foreign lands. I ask the following questions: What makes Taiwan cinema attractive to foreigners, and what makes such receptive reception possible? I will examine the various agents, institutions, and mechanisms that have facilitated this cross-cultural cinephilia as well as the actual objects (directors and films), processes (including cultural translation), and discourses involved. This historiography is not meant to be a comprehensive or chronological account of a nation's cinema; rather, it is a transnational lens cast upon that cinema's most significant new wave movement as deemed by alien agents.

I am acutely aware that my sole focus on TNC in this chapter risks reinforcing what Guo-Juin Hong (2010) has forcefully argued against and termed a "historiography of absence," wherein Taiwan films made before 1982 do not appear in English-language scholarship.[5] I hope to demonstrate in this book, however, that TNC, despite its dominance in this body of scholarship, could have been interpreted differently—in particular, not as a national cinema but as a cinematic new wave. In his typographical survey of major models in Chinese film historiography, Yingjin Zhang (2000) modifies Charles Altman's categorization (whose context is American film) to posit 10 models, including film personality and auteur, film audience, film genre, and film industry, among others. What is missing from this survey is precisely a historiography of new waves, a phenomenon that is prominent in postwar European art cinemas.[6] As Tweedie states in his book *The Age of New Waves: Art Cinema and the Staging of Globalization*, the "proliferation of new waves on the international art house and film festival circuits is one of the few cinematic phenomena from the past half century with a global reach that rivals the geographical range and ambition of Hollywood" (2013, 1–2). While Tweedie's book admirably analyzes and compares three new waves (French, Taiwanese, Chinese) across three periods (respectively, the 1960s, the 1980s, the 1990s), this chapter explores instead the ways in which an account that focuses on Taiwan cinema's soft-power legacy beyond the island's shores might contribute to and constitute a historiographical turn about TNC as well as how, by situating TNC in the global context of cinematic new waves, this historiography is invariably transnational rather than nation bound.

This chapter, therefore, seeks to illustrate the ways in which and the extent to which a documentary proffers a historiographical account of Taiwan cinema as a form of soft power that travels transnationally through the notion of authorship. The historiography of new waves is especially amenable to my focus on the interplay among authorship, transnationality, and soft power. As Joseph S. Nye suggests: "All power depends on context—who relates to whom under what circumstances—but soft power depends more than hard power upon the existence of willing interpreters and receivers" (2004, 16). This chapter uses a documentary, *Flowers of Taipei: Taiwan New Cinema* (*Guangyin de gushi: Taiwan xindianying*, dir. Hsieh Chin-lin, 2014; hereafter *Flowers of Taipei*), to look at how willing interpreters of TNC, who include filmmakers, festival programmers, critics, and artists from Europe, South America, and East Asia, share personal stories that attest to Taiwan cinema's far-reaching soft power across three continents and after 30 years.[7] *Film in Our Time: Taiwan New Cinema on the Road* (*Guangyin zhi lü: Taiwan xindianying zai lushang*, Wang 2015a), the book that accompanies the release of the documentary on DVD, will also be brought into discussion to contextualize the documentary's conditions of production, exhibition, and consumption.

Why make a documentary about a cinematic movement that started over 30 years ago? To put it differently, what affective resonances toward TNC can be captured in a documentary made not too long after its birth and alleged death (such as the one by Assayas) compared to *Flowers of Taipei*, which unavoidably invites, because of the 30-year time lapse, not just an account of TNC but also a reflection on its legacy? It is easy to forget, when appraising TNC's canonical films and key directors today, not so much the sociopolitical context from which the movement was born in the early 1980s (because the context would form the backdrop to many of the films) but rather the affective resonance of TNC films for the island's citizens who had just lived through a traumatic decade when

Taiwan suffered a string of diplomatic setbacks, from its withdrawal from the United Nations in 1971 to its severing relations with the United States in 1979.[8] One only needs to be reminded of the political upheavals of the Diaoyu/Senkaku Island movement and the Formosa incident in the 1970s to appreciate the desperation of Taiwanese citizens—both at home and abroad, and still living under martial law on the island—to forge a sense of national identity in the face of ostensible governmental impotence in international relations.[9] At the same time, while Taiwan had been partially compensating for its diplomatic isolation by flooding the world with mass-produced products carrying the label "Made in Taiwan," in what was to become known as an economic miracle that would earn the island a place in the rank of the "four little dragons" in the early 1990s,[10] this economic prowess could not satiate a yearning among the island's young artists and intellectuals to put Taiwan on the international stage through the soft power of cultural representation. In the view of Wang Keng-yu, producer of *Flowers of Taipei*, it was precisely the visibility of Taiwan cinema at major European film festivals in the 1980s that helped alter the global image of Taiwan as a mere sock-and-umbrella-producing kingdom (He 2015).

It is thus an inspired move that *Flowers of Taipei* opens with an unlikely interviewee: Lin Hwai-min, founder of Cloud Gate Dance Theater, arguably the earliest and most prominent soft-power resource in postwar Taiwan. Lin's speech sketches the geopolitical context of the 1970s, just described, and places TNC's emergence within the genealogy of a host of cultural interventions during that period, from the nativist literature movement and the founding of Cloud Gate to the folk song movement and the little theater movement. More important, Lin sees TNC's cinematic form as possessing an ability to perform the task of intellectual reflection about the island's political predicament and economic change on a much larger scale, thereby contributing to lifting martial law in 1987, the subsequent liberalization of cross-Strait relations, and the freedom and democracy enjoyed in Taiwan today. While Lin regards cinema's potential mainly in terms of its scale, I would suggest that cinema's mobility and translatability are why, among the different kinds of cultural interventions he lists from the period, TNC was and Taiwan cinema remain the best-known Taiwanese art forms across the world.

The Stakes of Historiography

What, then, are the stakes of exhibiting Taiwan cinema on an international stage, and how does *Flowers of Taipei* negotiate its own stakes in constructing such a historiography? When Assayas was interviewed in *Flowers of Taipei*, he cited an anecdote provided by Marco Müller, who curated a retrospective of Chinese film

at the Torino film festival in 1981; apparently, it was virtually impossible to feature films from both the People's Republic of China (PRC) and the Republic of
China (ROC, Taiwan's official title) at the same event, and Taiwan cinema was
banned "for political reasons." Although, in Müller's appearance in *Flowers of
Taipei*, he revealed that it was the veteran PRC director Xie Jin who, at the Venice
film festival in 1989, convinced the jury to give Hou's *A City of Sadness* a major
award because he believed the film would "make history in Chinese cinema" and
would mark "a new chapter in cinema history." As a result of the triumph of Hou's
film, Taiwan's flag was hung on the Palazzo del Cinema, though it had to be taken
down following an official PRC protest. Müller, in turn, welcomed the Taiwanese
delegates with their national flag at the hotel, as we can see in Figure 1.1, so they
could meet the press and do television interviews "without losing their identity
as a nation."

As a documentary-as-historiography, *Flowers of Taipei* provides valuable
insights into how geopolitical dynamics can change with time at the site of the
institution of film festivals, with a little help from the goodwill of agents (both
Xie Jin and Müller) whose affective affiliation with Taiwan cinema, in the latter
instance, transcended political divides and circumvented official interference.
By inserting the archival photograph shown in Figure 1.1 into the Müller's account, the documentary evinces how the soft power of cinema can raise Taiwan's
international profile—and, literally, Taiwan's flag—in spite of the diplomatic

Figure 1.1 Flying Taiwan's flag in Venice in the documentary *Flowers of Taipei*
Copyright Department of Cultural Affairs, Taipei City Government, 2014

hard power exerted by China. In fact, the timing of the Venice film festival, usually held in September, meant that the producers of Hou's film (about Taiwan's February 28 incident in 1947) could promote it as "Taiwan's June 4 incident" (Chi 1991, 95), thus tapping into the fresh memory of the Tiananmen massacre that took place only months earlier in Beijing, generating an affective response among jury members and audiences that would be more likely to identify with Taiwan's soft power rather than China's hard power.[11]

Such insights into the behind-the-scenes machinations of an international film festival would not have been possible if not for the candid accounts by foreign agents in *Flowers of Taipei*. The benefit gained from the documentary's inclination toward a soft-power approach raises questions about the stake of historiographical writing, the scale of the object's impact, and the scope of the stakeholders—questions I alluded to when I mentioned earlier that the choice to have Lin Hwai-min open the documentary is both inspired and unlikely. The fact that Lin (not a filmmaker, by the way) together with Hou and Tsai, who both appear at the end, are the only Taiwan-based interviewees has become a bone of contention in the documentary's reception in Taiwan.[12] The main body of the documentary consists of journeys to Beijing, Buenos Aires, Chiang Mai, Hong Kong, Paris, Rotterdam, and Tokyo, featuring interviews with, among others, filmmakers Apichatpong Weerasethakul, Jia Zhangke, and Hirokazu Kore-eda; actor Tadanobu Asano; artist Ai Weiwei; and film critics Tony Rayns and Sato Tadao. One reviewer regards *Flowers of Taipei* as "a largely pointless exercise in celebrity endorsement, a parade of international names drawn from the festival circuit who, despite their considerable intelligence, appear to have little of interest to say on the subject" (Elley 2017). Awarding the documentary a mere 3 out of 10 points, the reviewer asks, "who, honestly, really cares whether Ai Weiwei was 'blown away' when he first saw Hou's films?" (Elley 2017).

Here, a detour to the documentary's production background puts the question of the stake of historiography in context before we return to discuss its implications. At the 2012 Taipei film festival, a series of four forums were held to commemorate the 30th anniversary of the TNC movement.[13] At one of the forums, the then commissioner of the Taipei City Government's Department of Cultural Affairs (DOCA) and Hsiao Yeh, who worked with Wu Nien-jen to support the movement at CMPC during TNC's founding days, mooted the idea for a documentary. Because the documentary was subsequently commissioned by DOCA, a governmental body, *Flowers of Taipei* can be considered "an exercise of soft power in a cinematic form" (Chan 2015). Indeed, the producer Wang Keng-yu explained, "I'd often wondered why these [TNC] films had such a big impact overseas," and "I wanted to discover how foreigners perceived these works," noting that a 2002 documentary, *Our Time, Our Story* (*Baige jihua*, dir. Hsiao Chu-chen), had already adequately covered local perspectives on the movement

(Gao 2015).[14] Determined that *Flowers of Taipei* was not intended merely for domestic consumption, the documentary had its world premiere in 2014 at Venice, and an international public relations company managed its participation at film festivals.

At stake in the writing of historiography, then, is whether there is space for more than one perspective, and whether different approaches must be regarded as necessarily competing rather than complementary. Gian Piero Brunetta has argued in the context of Italian cinema that "for the film historian, historiographic truth does not consist so much in the ability to produce a *history*, but rather in his ability to keep in mind that there are *many histories*, and in knowing how to bring them to light in a net of new, unforeseen relations" (1982, 13, emphasis in original, qtd. in Casetti 1999, 311). In the light of a new set of relations between cinema and soft power in the twenty-first century, in what sense is *Flowers of Taipei* "revisionist," and why is an account by the movement's domestic participants deemed as "the true story" whereas one by foreign agents is considered a "limited perspective" (Elley 2017)?[15] Moreover, if the making of the aforementioned documentaries on TNC had been occasioned by the movement's anniversaries (one in 2002 for the 20th, and the other in 2012 for the 30th), what purposes did these documentaries serve at the time of their production and for whom? In the case of *Flowers of Taipei*, besides possibly addressing a perceived lack of knowledge about TNC's history among a younger generation of students today (Chen R. 2015, 276; Wang 2015b, 23–25), in what ways can it help us rethink the relationship between film historiography and soft power?

Taiwan New Cinema as Transnational Historiography

It is my intention in this chapter to propose a historiographical turn for TNC so that it is no longer conceived as part of a national cinema or a constituent of transnational Chinese cinemas but *singularly* as a form of transnational cinema. While new wave movements have typically arisen from a shared vision by filmmakers from a particular nation at a certain historical juncture (Chen R. 2015, 276), the history of new waves across the world also tells us that such cinematic movements are always already cosmopolitan in outlook, transnational in nature, and globalized in effect, often eschewing the limitations of a nation-based film industry as much as reacting against native (if not nativist) filmmaking traditions and ideologies. Hence, new wave movements are best understood "not as isolated events but as a series of interlaced moments, as an alternative vision of global modernity, and as an opening onto the 'world' promised in the phrase 'world cinema'" (Tweedie 2013, 2). The appearance of each new wave is itself "a symptom" (Tweedie 2013, 6), at once wielding "the threat and promise of transnational film movements to confront the inertia of its home in-dustry" and "a product and an account of globalization" (Tweedie 2013, 5).

If, for Chia-chi Wu, TNC's "historiographical significance . . . lies in its dual tendency in inscriptions of the 'nation' " (Wu 2007, 76),[16] I contend, instead, that Taiwan cinema can be understood singularly as a transnational site in which transactions of film production, distribution, exhibition, and consumption have been taking place both at home and abroad to the extent that its historiography cannot be contained by an account of its domestic agents and audiences alone. That is to say, the new wave that is TNC must be situated in the context of world cinema and its global circulation via the institutions of international film festivals and art house circuits, involving foreign programmers, critics, and scholars, as well as mobilizing discourses of authorship and art cinema. Because the cate-gory of the new wave "either remains a formless and oceanic metaphor without history or substance, or it falls under the rubric of particular national cinemas" (Tweedie 2013, 5), "the most revealing transnational dimensions of these cine-matic movements" have often been ignored (Tweedie 2013, 6). However, if the emergence of alternative or multiple histories, to recall Brunetta's earlier argu-ment, invites not peaceful coexistence but competing claims to "truth," transna-tional film studies similarly do "not exist in a vacuum" but must carve out a space for itself within scholarship in its departure from the national cinema model (Higbee and Lim 2010, 18). Moreover, a "critical transnationalism," proposed by Will Higbee and myself, "refuses to see the flow or exchange within transna-tional cinema as taking place uniquely between national cinemas" and wishes to "pay attention to the largely neglected question of the audience" (Higbee and Lim 2010, 18).

The notion of soft power comes into the purview of transnational histori-ography precisely because its focus (or "evidence") is on the ability of a nation's cultural product (in this instance, TNC) to shift "its audience's perception, preferences, interpretative frameworks and emotions . . . towards a generally pos-itive disposition and attraction to the exporting country, which is the applicant of soft power" (Chua 2012, 121). As such, soft power engenders a narrative that extends the scale of a cinema's impact beyond its national borders and expands the scope of its stakeholders to transnational agents and audiences. *Flowers of Taipei* serves as a useful lens to examine Taiwan cinema's soft power because its interviewees include not only foreign agents who have helped promote TNC on various platforms but also a wider range of artists who, despite practicing in dif-ferent art forms, have drawn on Taiwan films as inspiration for their own cre-ative work. It is in this light that, to return to the aforementioned query by the reviewer of the documentary, one might actually care about Ai Weiwei's feelings toward Hou's films. To cite the Taiwan film critic Ryan Cheng, *Flowers of Taipei* "casts a broader look at the movement and focuses on its influence and status in

global film history" (Gao 2015). The stakes of constructing a transnational historiography is worth taking because "others have already taken that risk, including
generations of filmmakers whose sense of their own universe is infinitely larger
than the carefully delimited domain of the state" (Tweedie 2013, 6).

Cross-Cultural Cinephilia as Soft Power

I read *Flowers of Taipei* as documenting private moments of cross-cultural
cinephilia as a form of collective historiography and as an expression of TNC's
soft power. Cinephilia (literally, a love of cinema), as Sarah Keller proposes, is
"*an affect*, something that derives from feeling and is therefore personal and
subjective" (2020, 15, emphasis in original). For Keller, cinephilia "*depends on
displacements in time and space*" (2020, 15, emphasis in original), and whereas
her focus is on the role of time in negotiating the cinephile's relationship to
cinema's past and future (2020, 24), my attention is drawn instead to space precisely because the love object concerned (TNC) is foreign—hence crossing
cultural and national boundaries—to the cinephiles interviewed in *Flowers of
Taipei*. As I have suggested elsewhere, cinephilia raises a set of questions, for example, "What is the relationship between an individual and his or her love of film
as artefact and as viewing experience? What drives an obsession with particular
films, directors, stars, periods, genres, costumes, mise-en-scène, technologies,
themes, representations, and cultures?" (Lim 2014a, 58), the list on which we
may now add the item "new waves."

While studies employing the notion of soft power have tended to place the
emphasis on the roles played by state and nonstate actors from the country
of origin of soft power, here I shift the locus of agency to the sites of reception where audiences, rather than being passively under the influence of a
foreign soft power, have actively appropriated this affective identification to
serve their own agendas and needs. Indeed, Keller also highlights cinephilia
as "*an extension of affect into actions*" (2020, 15; emphasis in original) to the
extent that a central action of the cinephile is "writing and seeking a mean-
ingful conversation about cinema" (2020, 20). The documentary under examination provides abundant evidence not so much for what Taiwanese agents
and institutions have done to promote Taiwan cinema's soft power as for how
transnational audiences express their affect for TNC through the interviews.
I discuss in this chapter two forms of this affective conversation—TNC as a
reflection of lack in the audiences' home environments, and TNC as an inspiration for the interviewees' own creative endeavors—before moving on to
the third dimension of postcolonial guilt, which complicates the notion of
cinephilia as soft power.

Taiwan New Cinema as Reflection of Lack

In the 1980s, TNC, alongside the Hong Kong New Wave and the PRC's fifth-generation directors, caught the attention of international film festivals; hence its historiographical writing using the approach of soft power invites comparison by filmmakers, artists, and critics from the other two cinemas. Among the key soft-power resources identified by Nye (2004, 11)—culture, political values, and foreign policies—interviewees from the PRC are particularly prone to admiring Taiwan cinema's cultural values of pluralism and humanism while lamenting their absence in China. For Jia Zhangke, TNC's inspiration as a movement lies in demonstrating cinema's close relationship to reality, personal experience, and memory, an approach to film and literature that had been interrupted in China during the Cultural Revolution (1966–76). In Ai Weiwei's view, the spirit of humanism, thoroughly destroyed in China but fully embodied by TNC directors such as Hou Hsiao-hsien and Edward Yang, arouses one's respect for the geopolitical entity of Taiwan because its ability to produce such filmmakers says a lot about China. These interviewees, therefore, see in Taiwan films and auteurs a reflection of what was missing in China during their formative years when the antithetical values of authoritarianism and collectivism held sway (and arguably still do). By positing TNC as providing a connection to cinematic and literary traditions in China in the 1920s and 1930s, Jia, in effect, critiques the official dogma on film and literature imposed by the Chinese Communist Party (CCP) since the founding of the People's Republic in 1949, an ideology rooted even earlier in Mao Zedong's famous 1942 Yan'an talk on the role and function of literature. Furthermore, the PRC documentary filmmaker Wang Bing regards China's fifth-generation films by Zhang Yimou and Chen Kaige (first made in the relatively open political climate of the early 1980s) as remaining a form of collective cinema whose achievement is limited compared to the realistic, individual, and fleeting historical sense displayed in films such as Yang's *A Brighter Summer Day* (*Gulingjie shaonian sharen shijian*, 1991).

The sense of "wonder" and "astonishment" (two examples listed by Keller as "powerful feelings attached to the cinema"; 2020, 3) about TNC's humanistic qualities is shared by Hong Kong interviewees through their reflection on a different lack in their own environment: The courage to confront reality in film and camaraderie between filmmakers. For Shu Kei, then chair of Film and Television at the Hong Kong Academy of Performing Arts, Taiwan cinema completely fulfills the two criteria he holds in the best of films—a record of and response to the epoch. For him, Taiwan films have realistically captured the spirit of the times, with a clear point of view that expresses concern for the characters and society. Stating matter of factly that Hong Kong cinema is "decidedly commercial" (his words in English), Shu wonders where TNC directors, despite the immense political pressure they faced at the time, got their courage, persistence, and determination, values that, Shu claims, are very remote for Hongkongers. On the subject of camaraderie, film critic Law Wai-ming notes that Hong Kong New Wave directors knew each other well from their days of working in television, but it was difficult for them to collaborate on filmmaking the way TNC directors did, citing the astonishing example of Hou mortgaging his house to bankroll Yang's making of *Taipei Story* (*Qingmeizhuma*, 1985). For these Hong Kong interviewees, the absence of commercial consideration and mercenary calculation among TNC directors provides a stark contrast to the capitalist ethos embraced by Hong Kong society at large, the latter translating into what Shu calls "a natural condition of survival" that marks Hong Kong cinema as inescapably commercial in nature.

Cinephilia as Filmmaking Inspiration

As a form of receptive (that is, positive) reception, cinephilia does not have to be a merely passive activity (film appreciation) but can also be actively incorporated into one's creative practice. As Keller also notes, "Nostalgia in the form of allusions and creative reworkings is even more pertinent to the *filmmaker* as cinephile" (2020, 9, emphasis in original). I have argued before that Tsai Ming-liang's inclusion of François Truffaut's *The 400 Blows* (*Les quatre cents coups,* 1959) and the actor Jean-Pierre Léaud into the diegesis of his own film *What Time Is It There?* (*Ni nabian jidian*, 2001) is testament to "the productivity of cinephilia, a love of films by other auteurs that can become the driving force of one's own filmmaking practice" (Lim 2014a, 62). After all, the hallowed auteur is simultaneously, if not first and foremost, a devoted fan, whose love of the works of previous auteurs underpins his or her own filmmaking, regardless of whether such cinephilia has been expressed, implicitly or explicitly, in one's works or words. Moreover, such cinephilia is often cross-cultural because the circulation and consumption of films, especially those belonging to the categories of new wave and art cinema, are typically transnational. However, if Taiwan filmmakers, such as Tsai, had drawn inspiration from past European masters such as Truffaut,[17] TNC has, in turn, become a source of affiliation for a younger generation of directors in East and Southeast Asia (see more discussion in the Epilogue). Such cross-cultural cinephilia within East and Southeast Asia "arguably heralds a new era that moves away from the East-West binary that has dominated intellectual discourses throughout the twentieth century," and re-orientates our attention instead to "intra-Asian cultural exchanges, though the geopolitical histories of the region present different sets of power dynamics to be negotiated" (Lim 2011b, 22).

In *Flowers of Taipei*, this intra-Asian cinephilia as productive filmmaking appropriation is evident in the Thai director Apichatpong Weerasethakul, the first alien agent to appear in the running order of the documentary. This cinephilia is presented in true cinematic fashion, beginning with a montage of clips from early TNC films (all uncredited), then unsuspectingly suturing, as Figure 1.2 illustrates, the memorable shot of a train entering mountain tunnels in Hou's *Dust in the Wind* (*Lianlian fengchen*, 1986) before emerging, as we can see in Figure 1.3, in the documentary's diegetic space, in Chiang Mai, Thailand, where Apichatpong would be interviewed. Accompanying subsequent shots of a train journey along rural landscapes followed by shots from a vehicle of winding country roads (and before the sequence ends at the destination that is his home) is Apichatpong's voice-over, uttering a list of his snapshot memories of TNC films (without naming the film titles): "in the corridor of a hospital, a nurse is running; in the corridor of a hospital, light flickers; a mosquito net; on a train, a man who can't speak; a young student is stabbed by her lover." This vocalized list, like the visual montage of unidentified TNC film clips that preceded it, presupposes a cinephilic audience that can recognize the films from the clips shown or brief descriptions given without the aid of on-screen credits. In so doing, *Flowers of Taipei* can be said to be cinephilic in both form and content, interpellating an audience that has already embraced

Figure 1.2 Taiwan New Cinema as soft power: Shot of train entering the tunnel from Hou's *Dust in the Wind* in *Flowers of Taipei*
Copyright Department of Cultural Affairs, Taipei City Government, 2014

Figure 1.3 Cinephilia as soft power: Apichatpong's voice-over reminiscing about Taiwan films in a shot of a train emerging from the tunnel in Chiang Mai in *Flowers of Taipei*
Copyright Department of Cultural Affairs, Taipei City Government, 2014

the often-challenging form and content of the documentary's very own subject matter (TNC films).

For his part, Apichatpong's contribution illustrates intra-Asian cinephilia in at least three aspects. First, a deeply personal reflection on how he was stunned by the novelty of the different film forms in Taiwan and Iranian cinemas when he first encountered them while studying in Chicago about 20 years ago, leading to his decision to return to work in Thailand. In particular, Hou's films reminded him of home and his experience of growing up in Thailand, making him realize that "film is about memory," that "film *is* memory." Second, a retrospective awareness of TNC's influence on his filmmaking, especially in relation to framing, including the use of flat composition, windows and doors, and frame within a frame. Third, the book that accompanies the release of the documentary on DVD contains an anecdote on how TNC auteurs had served as a kind of moral support in Apichatpong's filmmaking. Apparently, when Apichatpong met some TNC directors for the first time in Taipei, he was so star-struck he asked to take a photograph with them, a photograph, he claimed, he would subsequently take out to look at when he needed inspiration for filmmaking (Wang 2015a, 52). Taken together, Apichatpong has drawn on TNC as inspiration for filmmaking on personal, formal, and cinephilic fronts.

Cinephilic Encounters of the Postcolonial Kind

The title of Keller's book, *Anxious Cinephilia: Pleasure and Peril at the Movies*, suggests that a love for cinema can be both an enjoyable and a dangerous business. Crucially, Keller points out that cinephilia is an object of a "one-way exchange," and, as such, it "would seem to tell us more about lovers than about the beloved" (2020, 14). Cinephilia could be perilous because lovers of cinema might see in the beloved object something about themselves that they have been suppressing deeply, feelings too personal or painful to be revisited, much less shared in public. The tension between peril and pleasure is manifest in the Japanese interviewees in *Flowers of Taipei* owing to the postcolonial relationship between Japan and Taiwan.

If French New Wave filmmakers of the 1950s had used American cinema as a tool "to confront a lifeless 'tradition of quality' that dominated their domestic industry" (Tweedie 2013, 5), the Japanese director Hirokazu Kore-eda similarly signaled his departure from Japanese cinema of the 1980s via his affection for Taiwan cinema. He confessed that even though there were some Japanese directors working in the 1980s whom he respected, there was no one in whose footsteps he wanted to follow. It was not until he had seen Hou's *A Time to Live, A Time to Die* that he finally found the kind of film he wanted to shoot, "the match" he'd been waiting for. Yet, Kore-eda's relationship to TNC is more personal and complex, as his father was born in Taiwan's southern city of Kaohsiung (the setting of Hou's aforementioned film) and lived there until his youth. While his father, who only stepped onto Japanese soil for the first time as an adult, would reminisce about how pineapples always tasted much better in Taiwan, Kore-eda's feelings toward Hou's aforementioned film are more mixed as he could not see Taiwan merely through the rose-tinted lens of his father's memory after he had learned about the colonial relationship between Japan and Taiwan. In fact, Kore-eda revealed that he has been brewing, for 15 years, an idea for a film about Japanese history (specifically, Japan's role in World War II) that would be his own version of *A City of Sadness* (Yang and Xie 2020), a sign that Hou's films had staged a cinephilic encounter that prompted the Japanese director to reflect on the colonial legacy of his country of birth.[18]

This postcolonial dynamic adds a twist to the notion of cross-cultural cinephilia, for cinephilia is here intertwined with guilt because the soft power of films from the ex-colony cannot be divorced from an acknowledgment of the hard power of historical occupation by the ex-colonizer. Tadao Sato, the eminent Japanese film critic, delves into this dynamic in some detail in the documentary, which deserves more discussion for the complication it brings to the notion of cross-cultural cinephilia as soft power. Three aspects in Sato's interview are especially pertinent: the pain of cinephilia, mixed emotions in colonial memory, and appreciation of the ex-colony's situation.

I believe Sato's contribution is significant in bringing about a more sophisticated understanding of cinephilia beyond its more obvious manifestation as a love of a cinema's form, content, or spirit. Confronted by a cinema originating from one's ex-colony, how could this attraction be possibly free from colonial guilt, regardless of one's personal role (or lack thereof) in the historical enterprise of colonial rule? Sato, for example, felt an acute pain watching Wan Jen's *Super Citizen Ko* (*Chaoji da guomin*, 1995), a film about Taiwanese intellectuals who were educated during the Japanese occupation period (1895–1945) and persecuted during the Kuomintang's White Terror campaign of the 1950s because their reading of Japanese political essays and their academic activities conducted in Japanese had led to a charge of treason.[19] The film's final scene, in which the protagonist goes looking for the grave of a friend who was executed in the campaign and, having found it, kneels down and begs for forgiveness—in the Japanese language—was particularly hard for Sato to watch. Hearing a Taiwanese character capable of expressing his innermost feelings only in Japanese struck a chord with Sato, as these traces of colonialism in aural and linguistic forms in a film from an ex-colony bespeak as much about the complex historical formation of subjectivity of the colonized as about the colonizer's role in its formation. In this case, an attraction to TNC is inextricable from pain, the pain of having to face up to the collective guilt of the political occupation imposed by one's country on another, and the pain of empathizing with a character from an ex-colony whose most private language of affective expression is the same as one's own.

This postcolonial encounter in cinematic form is bittersweet for Sato since such traces of colonialism abound in Taiwan films, engendering at once a sense of familiarity and a sobering reminder of the situation of the colonized. The Japanese-style house in Hou's *A Summer at Grandpa's* (*Dongdong de jiaqi*, 1984), for instance, is immediately recognizable to Sato as a typical historical building in Japan and hence evidence of how "Taiwan has inherited Japanese culture." Yet, for Sato, it is "difficult to feel delight" in such a form of nostalgia because, he says, "colonial history is always dark" and "the locals must have suffered." Sato's mixed emotions toward and identification with the ex-colony's situation enrich the notion of cinephilia as soft power because they subvert the hierarchy of attraction, which, in the logic of colonialism, would place the center/metropole above its peripheries/colonies as the object of desire. If the spread of Japanese pop culture to other parts of Asia in the 1990s can be claimed by Japanese nationalists as proof of Japan's "cultural superiority through asserting commonality with other Asian nations" (Iwabuchi 2002, 66), thus summoning the specter of the rhetoric of an Asian "co-prosperity sphere" propagated by Japan during its imperial expansion in the Second World War (Chua 2012, 127), Sato's love of Taiwan cinema signals the potential for the ex-colonizer to launch a broader reflection on its historical role in geopolitics to which it has yet to face in an honest manner.

Documentary as Historiography

Hsiao Yeh, executive producer of *Flowers of Taipei*, published a collection of essays entitled *The Beginning of a Movement* (*Yige yundong de kaishi*) during TNC's heyday in 1986. The book's title sounds like a manifesto, and the book's publication indeed predates the "1987 Taiwan Cinema Manifesto."[20] Yet the book hardly mentions the term "movement" in its pages, and its title, in fact, appears only as a subtitle to an essay that unwittingly reveals that the very notion of a movement was not mooted by TNC filmmakers but suggested by international critics who regarded the film *In Our Time* (*Guangyin de gushi*, dir. Tao Te-chen, Edward Yang, Ko I-cheng, and Chang Yi, 1982) as marking the beginning of a movement (Hsiao 1986, 104). In another essay entitled "A Friend from France," Hsiao Yeh tells the story of a Frenchman who could not forget his experience of watching *The Boys from Fengkuei* (*Fenggui lai de ren*, dir. Hou Hsiao-hsien, 1983) in Taiwan and who kept telling his friends about Taiwan cinema after he had returned to France. That Frenchman is, of course, Assayas, who subsequently produced a seven-page special feature on TNC in the December 1984 issue of *Cahiers du Cinéma* back in Paris (Hsiao 1986, 148–149), and who would return to Taiwan more than a decade later to make the documentary on Hou with which I started this chapter's discussion.

These two vignettes from a book purportedly about the TNC movement foreground the role of alien agents in the "romantic fairytale" (Chang 2015) into which TNC has now evolved in the history of world cinema. I have opted to focus on historiographical accounts of TNC in the form of documentary film over the written word partly because *Flowers of Taipei* lends itself comfortably to my reading of Taiwan cinema's soft power owing to its choice of foreign interviewees, and partly because written accounts, especially those published in the Chinese language in Taiwan, tend to be more (if not exclusively) concerned with TNC's position within rather than outside Taiwan. This chapter, therefore, does not enter debates about the termination date of the movement nor does it deal with the voluminous archive accumulated about TNC since the movement's inception. Its ambition is modest in scale, confined to an examination of TNC's impact on a select group of foreign audiences only. It is, however, provocative in intent on two fronts: It promotes an alternative mode of film historiography that interrelates transnationality and soft power rather than providing a nation-based account; it also favors the documentary film over the written word as a mode of historiography.

Distinguishing between documentary (which provides meaning) and docu-ment (in the form of the actuality film), Philip Rosen suggests that part of the stake in making documentary film, like the "most culturally prestigious, disci-plined versions in the practice of historiography," is about the "control of past-ness in the register of meanings" by controlling documents, "the indexical traces of the presence of a real past" (2001, 234). Rosen locates the medium of cinema as "a kind of threshold" in the history of historiography (2001, xix), a claim echoed by Jeffrey Skoller who posits that "still and moving pictures are among the most important ways our society comes to understand its past" at the end of the twen-tieth century (2005, xxi). Such a claim calls for a medium-specific analysis of what documentary cinema brings to the historiographical form that is unique to its own, and the answer is indexicality, which designates "the presence of camera and sound recording machinery at the profilmic event, which in turn guarantees that the profilmic really did exist in the past" (Rosen 2001, 259). The status of a shot as "document of a real that preexists the spectators' viewing" is undeniable (as long as no mechanical manipulation has taken place, one hastens to add), and what is at stake in any debate about the state of the concepts of document and documentary "remains, precisely, a referent" (Rosen 2001, 259).[21]

I want to propose that *Flowers of Taipei* pushes Rosen's argument further to show us that the documentary film form does not merely document the index-ical real of the past; rather, it also possesses a distinct capability to revisit past re-corded sites in the present time, not so much to re-enact past events as to register another moment of the profilmic as though historiography itself, in the medium of cinema, is a palimpsest upon which it can be infinitely layered. This effect is achieved in *Flowers of Taipei* via several means, from the staging of interviews at past shooting locations and the recreation of shots in Taiwan films, to intertex-tual references (both implicit and explicit, textual and extratextual) to directors and their works. The overall effect of the documentary is akin to what Sing Song-yong (2010a) has called, in his discussion of Hou's homage films *Café Lumière* (*Kôhî jikô*, 2003) and *Flight of the Red Balloon* (*Le Voyage du ballon rouge*, 2007), "the phantom-effect of cinema revisited."[22] These palimpsestic and phantasmal effects also attest to "film's immateriality and the very material force of its affec-tive impact on the body and mind that renders cinema such a powerful medium for the making of history" (Skoller 2005, xvi).

Affective Cinema Revisited

Let me elaborate on the means by which *Flowers of Taipei* generates the effect and affect of such cinematic revisits, and the implications they have for an apprecia-tion of the uniqueness of documentary cinema as a mode of historiography. The most direct of these methods of (re)visitation is by forging a sense of familiarity in the audience through conducting interviews at shooting locations in Taiwan films, whether or not the interviewees had previously appeared in the diegetic space of those locations (Tadanobu Asano in the secondhand bookshop where he played its owner in *Café Lumière*; Sato in the café where the female protagonist does her writing in the same film; Assayas and Jean-Michel Frodon discoursing by the pool in the Jardin des Tuileries in Paris where Tsai filmed *What Time Is It There?*). More spectacularly, *Flowers of Taipei* evinces the illustrative power of the film medium when it cuts, following an interview with Shôzô Ichiyama (producer of several Hou films) in the hotel room, shown in Figure 1.4, where Hou would usually stay when he visits Tokyo, to a clip of the final scene of Hou's *Millennium Mambo* (*Qianxi manbo*, 2001), which is set in the same room, shown in Figure 1.5. The editing together of these two shots provides both an evidence for the real-life existence of such a hotel room in Tokyo and an indexical trace of the very same room in a *fiction* film. Hence, what this editing pieces together is not so much, as a conventional documentary would have it, a profilmic document of the real past as well as a profilmic document of the real present. Rather, it stitches an indexical trace of the real present (Ichimaya), the diegetic space of a fictional past (the final scene of *Millennium Mambo*), and a mental image of Hou staying in the same room through Ichimaya's verbal account. In this instance of suture, one plus one equals three, which, in cinematic language, we can regard as

Figure 1.4 Profilmic indexicality: Ichiyama interviewed in *Flowers of Taipei* in a Tokyo hotel room where Hou usually stays and where *Millennium Mambo* was shot
Copyright Department of Cultural Affairs, Taipei City Government, 2014

Figure 1.5 Diegetic space of a fictional past: Shu Qi in the same Tokyo hotel room in the final scene of Hou's *Millennium Mambo*, as shown in *Flowers of Taipei*
Copyright Department of Cultural Affairs, Taipei City Government, 2014

montage, though the Eisensteinian notion of a third meaning arising from two conflicting images is absent here.

Indeed, Skoller uses the term *montage* to describe an understanding of history as "not simply a story of events unfolding but rather a set of *relations* between events, memories, temporalities, geographies, cultures, and objects that move outward beyond the events themselves, creating new forms of knowledge," thereby producing "new ideas in the mind of the viewer that don't necessarily exist in the images themselves" (2005, xxxvi, emphasis in original). As I indicated earlier in the chapter, *Flowers of Taipei* achieves a similar effect through a different method because the images juxtaposed do not have an uneasy relation with each other (Eisenstein's notion of montage), instead they resemble or layer upon each other (palimpsest) to the extent that one is almost indistinguishable from the other. A shot that exemplifies this effect appears in the opening segment of the documentary's journey to Tokyo, showing trains coming in and out of a railway station reminiscent of similar shots in *Café Lumière*. However, because many film clips (including this one) shown in the documentary are not framed or credited on-screen, it is difficult to ascertain if this shot belongs to *Flowers of Taipei* or is taken from Hou's film—that is, its status as documentary or document. In so doing, it unhinges any secure sense of meaning in historiography. If context should be regarded, in film historiography, "as a force field in which multiple and contradictory temporalities and forces operate simultaneously"

(Vitali 2010, 142), here the ambiguity of the shot's status further complicates spatiality and temporality to the extent that the distinction between text and context becomes untenable.

In this light, documentary as historiography undermines the ontological and epistemological bases of meaning and "truth" at the same time as it affords cinephilic pleasure and affect. Like the intratextual elements permeating Tsai's oeuvre, sensing intertextuality at play in the aforementioned shot of trains arriving at and departing from a railway station "raises questions about the validity and reliability of memory, and rewards a kind of spectatorship and viewing position that, rather than challenge such inconsistency [or, in the shot described, ambiguity], would find pleasure . . . precisely because of it" (Lim 2007, 229).[23] It is in the sense that *Flowers of Taipei* was probably made with a cinephilic audience in mind (K. S. 2015), not only does it pay homage to TNC in explicit ways (through interviews with alien agents), it also presumes a spectatorship that is familiar with Taiwan cinema in its refusal to credit the film clips inserted as well as through implicit references only identifiable—and at times enjoyable, at times affectual—by devoted cinephiles. This documentary's cinephilic tendency even extends to extratextual connections that are somewhat circuitous by, for instance, placing Kore-eda in the hotel room where Yasujirô Ozu and his collaborator Kogo Noda used to write their scripts (including the one for *Tokyo Story*). In the early years of his TNC career, Hou had been endlessly compared to, if not regarded as an imitator of, Ozu. Hou's film *A Time to Live, A Time to Die*, as noted earlier, has, in turn, been declared by Kore-eda as instrumental in turning him into the kind of filmmaker he is today. The loop from Ozu to Hou to Kore-eda and back to Ozu's workplace completes a circuit—a genealogy, indeed—that is decidedly cross-cultural and cinephilic.

As a documentation of TNC's legacy, *Flowers of Taipei* is at once personal for the interviewees and the audiences as well as collective as a shared memory of a cinematic movement that has exerted its soft power for about three decades at the time of the documentary's making. Its cinematic properties record profilmic textures and gestures that enrich the historiographical form as well as generate effect and affect through its suturing of images and sounds. It tells the story of a transnational attraction in which alien agents pay touching tribute to Taiwan auteurs and their films. It is a historiography of presence, a presence that lives in the minds and bodies of viewers whose cross-cultural cinephilia has expanded into a deep respect for an island-state whose lack of hard power continues to be compensated by the global reach of its cinema as soft power.

2

The Aural Turn

Hou Hsiao-hsien's Gendered and Material Voices

At the 2015 Cannes film festival, Hou Hsiao-hsien received the Best Director award for his *wuxia* film, *The Assassin* (*Cike Nie Yinniang*, 2015), 15 years after the same award had been bestowed upon his Taiwan New Cinema (hereafter TNC) pioneering counterpart Edward Yang for what would turn out to be Yang's final film, *Yi Yi: A One and a Two* (*Yi yi*, 2000). In Hou's case, there was a sense of belatedness because both the award and the film had been long in coming. The first director to have demonstrated Taiwan cinema's soft power by clinching a top award (Golden Lion) at one of the top-three international film festivals (Venice) way back in 1989 for *A City of Sadness* (*Beiqing chengshi*, 1989), Hou's subsequent achievement at this level had only been a Jury Prize at Cannes in 1993 for *The Puppetmaster* (*Ximeng rensheng*, 1993), his legacy overshadowed, from the 1990s onward, by TNC newcomers Ang Lee and Tsai Ming-liang.[1] On the one hand, the 2015 prize, therefore, can be regarded as more akin to a lifetime achievement award for the then 68-year-old director. On the other hand, news that Hou had been planning for years to make a *wuxia* film might have been greeted with an equal measure of trepidation and anticipation. Trepidation, because the rush to capitalize on Ang Lee's phenomenal success with his reinvention of the *wuxia* genre, *Crouching Tiger, Hidden Dragon* (*Wohu canglong*, 2000), had already produced a slew of rather dismal flicks within transnational Chinese cinemas; anticipation, because Hou's austere authorial style, when brought to the *wuxia* film, might serve as an intervention in, if not a corrective to, the revamped genre's overwrought digital aesthetic.[2] Long in gestation—eight years separate Hou's *wuxia* offering and his previous feature-length film *Flight of the Red Balloon* (*Le voyage du ballon rouge*, 2007)—*The Assassin* is, to say the least, a baffling film, leading critics to swoon over the stunning images while acknowledging their difficulty in following the elliptical plot.[3]

The Assassin opens this chapter not only because it evinces the soft-power appeal of Hou's cinema evidenced by the conferment of top international film festival awards over a period of nearly three decades but also because it points to two important features in Hou's films made in the twenty-first century, namely aurality and gender. Prior to *The Assassin*, Hou had only made four films in the new millennium, two predominantly in Mandarin (*Millennium Mambo/*

Taiwan Cinema as Soft Power. Song Hwee Lim, Oxford University Press. © Oxford University Press 2022.
DOI: 10.1093/oso/9780197503379.003.0003

Qianxi manbo, 2001 and *Three Times/Zuihao de shiguang*, 2005) and two in non-Sinophone languages (the Japanese-speaking *Café Lumière/Kôhî jikô*, 2003 and the French-speaking *Flight of the Red Balloon*).[4] Hence, with two films *sounding* distinctly alien over this period, *The Assassin* marks Hou's return to Chinese-language filmmaking after a gap of 10 years. Moreover, with the exception of *Three Times*, which consists of three stories about three couples (played by the same actor and actress who carry equal weight in the film), all other films made after the year 2000 foreground women as the chief protagonists—most notably in *The Assassin* in which a female character's name becomes the Chinese title of the film, a first in the transnational *wuxia* film.[5] More important, Hou's aural turn, registered as much by the use of non-Sinophone languages as by a privileging of aural over visual elements in the mise en scène, is inextricably bound to gender, indeed, quite literally, to gendered voices in these films. Focusing on the two non-Chinese-language films, *Café Lumière* and *Flight of the Red Balloon*, as my objects of analysis, I argue that these female voices draw on earlier instances of Taiwan's cultural soft power to displace the centrality of visuality and to showcase material aspects of gendered aurality.

The Soft Power of Hou Hsiao-hsien's Cinema

In terms of the overarching framework of this book, the chosen films illustrate the intertwining relationship between soft power and the three keywords in the book's subtitle, namely authorship, transnationality, and historiography. To begin with authorship, Hou, as TNC's elder statesman, has always been the most well-known Taiwan director among international cinephiles, with volumes dedicated to the study of his films in various languages and a documentary made about him, as early as 1997, by the French critic-cum-director Olivier Assayas.[6] Since the dawn of the new millennium, Hou's auteur status has increasingly been mobilized—both by himself and by the Taiwanese authorities—as a soft-power resource to promote film culture at home and abroad. An example of outreach efforts is Hou's founding of the Golden Horse Film Academy (under the aegis of the Golden Horse Awards) in 2009 to train 10 to 12 emerging directors, scriptwriters, and cinematographers from Chinese-speaking regions each year.[7] As for domestic consumption, Hou headed, in November 2002, Spot-Taipei Film House, an initiative to turn the derelict former residential building of the ambassadors of the United States to Taiwan into a cultural venue. Effectively an art house cinema with a shop and two cafés, the venue benefits from Hou's authorial stamp insofar as the two cafés were renamed Spot Café Lumière and Spot le ballon rouge. That preference had been given to the titles of Hou's two non-Sinophone films in the renaming exercise attests to the cosmopolitan image the venue was eager to project, tapping into the potential (reverse) soft-power attraction generated by Hou's foray into foreign-language filmmaking.

The second keyword, transnationality, aptly accounts for the production background of Hou's two non-Chinese-language films. To mark the centenary of the director Yasujirô Ozu in 2003, the Japanese studio Shochiku commissioned Hou, long famed for the affinity of his films to those of Ozu, to make a film that would turn out to be *Café Lumière*.[8] An unexpected bidding war, however, apparently broke out in the process. As Hou disclosed in an interview, Shochiku had initially planned to engage a few directors who would each make a 20-minute short to be combined into one film; the project was then shelved as the studio's business department felt it "would be difficult to market" an omnibus film. The broadcaster NHK subsequently invited Hou to make a 60-minute film instead, triggering Shochiku to counter-offer Hou the opportunity to make a feature film (Lupke 2016, 255).[9] Like *Café Lumière*, *Flight of the Red Balloon* is also the result of a transnational commission, this time by Musée d'Orsay in Paris to celebrate its 20th anniversary in 2006. Its production background, as it happened, was similarly tortuous. Musée d'Orsay's original idea was to make a portmanteau film comprising shorts by four directors, the brief being that at least one scene in each short had to be filmed in the museum (Klawans 2008). In the end, Hou and Assayas made two feature-length films instead (both starring the French actress Juliette Binoche), whereas Raoul Ruiz and Jim Jarmusch dropped out of the project altogether (Wen 2010, 73–74).[10] Hou's completion of both foreign-commissioned projects, which can also be understood as a form of "internationally recognized subcontracted art cinema" (Wu 2007, 76), cements his status as a transnational auteur capable of working in alien environments and unfamiliar languages.

Hou's making of non-Sinophone films (and similar efforts by Tsai Ming-liang and Ang Lee, see Chapters 3 and 4 respectively) demands a rethinking of film historiography (the third keyword), in particular one that is organized along national and linguistic lines. Using these two Hou films as examples in an article entitled "Six Chinese Cinemas in Search of a Historiography," I draw upon Prasenjit Duara's notion of "rescuing history from the nation" (1995) to make a case for films that "resist participation in the myth of nationalism" (Lim 2011a, 41); I also offer a critique of Shu-mei Shih's model of the Sinophone (Shih S-m. 2007) which, as a lingua-centric model rooted in postcoloniality, cannot speak fully on behalf of polyphonic realities, expressions, and subjectivities that are not bound by a single linguistic family or a postcolonial logic.[11] In another article, "The Voice of the Sinophone," I echo Jing Tsu's call to take the "phone" in Sinophone seriously (Tsu 2010, 94) by asking specifically: "If film is a medium of image and sound, and placing the emphasis here on the latter rather than the former, what does—and might—the Sinophone sound like in cinema?" (Lim

2014b, 63). It is against this context that this chapter marks Hou's aural turn. The two chosen films, I would argue, upend lingua-centric and nation-based models of film historiography as much as they bank on the currency of Hou's auteur status as soft power.

The Aural Turn

Within the discipline of film studies, it has been widely acknowledged that film sound still exists "in the shadow of the image" (Beck and Grajeda, 2008, 2) and that "the cinematic voice is difficult to write about" (Whittaker and Wright 2017b, 1). In Chinese cinema studies, more attention has now been paid to the aural dimension, from the use of music in Wong Kar-wai's films (Biancorosso 2013; Chen 2017) and the prominent role of the songstress (Ma J. 2015) to aspects of diegetic sound and silence in Tsai Ming-liang's films (Lim 2014a) and the intersections of film, media, music, and popular culture in postsocialist China (Xiao 2017). As for the study of Hou's films, David Bordwell has noted how Hou's soundtrack mixes "sentimental love tunes, Japanese-flavored ballads, hard rock, MOR pop, and plaintive synthesizer Orientalism" (2005, 189). Indeed, Hou has collaborated with a broad range of musicians on his film scores, from Chen Ming-chang who won the Best Film Score for *Dust in the Wind* (*Lianlian fengchen*, 1986) at the 1987 Nantes Festival of Three Continents, to Japanese group S.E.N.S. on *A City of Sadness* and Taiwan indie musicians such as Summer Lei and especially Lim Giong from the 1990s onward.

If the pleasure of narrative cinema, to recall the title of Laura Mulvey's famous essay (1975), lies in the visual, what, asks Mary Ann Doane in relation to the voice in the cinema, is "the specificity of the pleasure of hearing a voice with its elements escaping a strictly verbal codification—volume, rhythm, timbre, pitch?" (1980, 43) My turn to aurality in this chapter participates in a wider interest in sound studies within academia since the early 1990s, distinguished by a "self-consciousness of its place in a larger interdisciplinary discussion of sound" that "takes sound as its analytical point of departure or arrival" (Sterne 2012b, 1, 2). Scholars have noted the domination of ocularcentrism across many disciplines as well as a recent shift, in anthropology for example, in favor of "the increasing use of aurally evocative metaphors" (Sui 2000, 323) and toward the development (per James Clifford) of "the ethnographic ear" (Samuels et. al. 2010, 330).[12] Sound, in fact, can be situated in relation to script and in a longer historical context in which, as Walter J. Ong argues in his seminal book *Orality and Literacy*, the "basic orality of language" is regarded as permanent insofar as "oral expression can exist and mostly has existed without any writing at all, writing never without orality" (2002 [1982], 7, 8). For Ong, the study of language and literature has shied away, for centuries, from what he calls "purely oral art forms" or "verbal art forms" (14), forms of a "primary orality" rooted in peoples and cultures totally unfamiliar with writing (6). Ong further notes a "secondary orality" emerging from "present-day high technology culture," a new orality "sustained by telephone, radio, television, and other electronic devices" (11). This "secondary orality" has arguably driven the expansion of the scope of research objects in sound studies to include soundscapes of all kinds (from human utterances to environmental noise), an expansion paralleled by artistic practices such as sound art, sound installation, and recorded soundscapes (Samuels et. al. 2010, 334), a polyphony of what Jonathan Sterne (2012b) calls "sonic imaginations."

In her discussion of the seemingly unremarkable (because commonplace) film technique of visually showing a character silently reading a text (say, a letter) and aurally broadcasting the voice of the (unseen) writer of the text, Rey Chow suggests that such instances of hearing a character's voice-over are really a "multifaceted semiotic relay of traces involving writing, reading, reading aloud, and other activities, a relay of which the audible voice is, recognizably, an arrangement, a rendition," mediated further by "technical and mechanical issues such as dubbing, postproduction recording, sound editing and mixing, and so forth" (2017, 25). As such, Chow contends, contra Doane, that the question about the voice in the cinema "should not and cannot be confined to the cinematic frame" (17), and that the writing voice demands to be "reconceptualised in intersemiotic, intermedial, and perhaps intercultural terms" (28). Hence Ong's account, which regards the coexistence of literacy and orality as "transitional, and therefore fugitive, and therefore unimportant" (Coleman 2007, 69–70), must be challenged on both medial and historical fronts. Defining orality as "the shared hearing of texts" and literacy as "the private reading of written texts," Joyce Coleman highlights instead the concept and practice of aurality, "the shared hearing of written texts," which combines aspects of both orality and literacy (68–69). According to Coleman, aurality was "the predominant means of experiencing written texts throughout the Middle Ages," and people "kept reading books aloud to each other until they got radios," a practice now reinvented in the form of audiobooks (71). Chow, on the other hand, explains how similar forms of aurality might be reformulated on screen.

Departing from Coleman's use to refer to a specific reading practice and heeding Chow's call for an intermedial approach to the study of sound and voice, I use the term aurality in its broader sense, according to the *Oxford English Dictionary*, of relating to ears and the sense of hearing, however a sound is "captured" or "represented." More important, I ask what is at stake in a turn to aurality in film studies in particular and in academia in general. As we have seen, the relationship between sound and script is more complex than Ong's evolutionary account in which "orality giving way to literacy as dinosaurs gave way to mammals"

(Coleman 2007, 69) would allow for. In fact, script did not replace sound but was used (or even partially invented) precisely to "record" sound, as different types of "inscriptive practices that involved musical notation and words about sound and aural perception" existed before the advent of modern recording technology (Samuels et. al. 2010, 332). This raises the question about where to "look" for traces of sound. Ana María Ochoa Gautier, in her book *Aurality: Listening & Knowledge in Nineteenth-Century Columbia*, delineates how "lettered men (and it was mostly men)" constantly struggled to put down in writing "sounding and listening practices that differed from their own" (2014, 4). By "reading the archives against the grain," she proposes, the aural will emerge as "a formation and a force that seeps through [the archive's] crevices demanding the attention of its listeners" (4–5). A sound object, as it turns out, could well be in the form (or in the crevices) of script.

The Gendered Voice in Cinema

By drawing our attention to the taken-for-granted gender of "men of letters," Ochoa Gautier highlights an important stake in the aural turn in both critical theory and cultural practice. Sterne emphasizes the importance of reflexivity in sound studies vis-à-vis the stakes of its own knowledge production because "hearing requires positionality" (2012b, 3–4). Indeed, any approach to aurality must consider the "condition that must be given for something to become recognized, labeled, and valorized as audible in the first place" (Erlmann 2010, 18). To take an example, accounting for a shift from visuality to aurality in the discipline of geography in late twentieth century, Daniel Z. Sui provides a sociological explanation: "the increasing participation of women in general and the contributions by feminist geographers in particular" (2000, 325).

Zooming in (or, should I say, booming out) on the film industry, it is common knowledge that men tend to dominate the position of the director whereas women play a slightly bigger role in production and screenplay. According to the Women and Hollywood website, even though women make up 51 percent of moviegoers in the United States in 2018, of the top-100 grossing films of 2019, they constituted only 12 percent of directors, 2 percent of cinematographers, 20 percent of writers, and 26 percent of producers ("Statistics," n.d.). Moreover, a larger proportion of male (59 percent) than female characters (43 percent) were seen in their work setting, actually working ("2019 Statistics," n.d.). These statistics tell us that, in Hollywood at least, women are overwhelming underrepresented behind the camera and that, in front of the camera, they are less likely to be seen as financially independent or possessing an identity beyond the domestic realm. In light of the #MeToo movement that swept through Hollywood since the end of 2017,[13] these figures—and the, no doubt, huge crevices among them—are a sobering reminder that women's voices often remain unheard in an overtly sexist and misogynist industry, with dire implications on the gendered voice in cinema. The two films by Hou under discussion provide a contrast to this situation, as one female protagonist is a working and de facto single mother with a young son, whereas the other, a freelance writer who has just discovered that she is pregnant, is determined to bring up the child on her own.

Among the range of objects available for study as soundscapes, both music and film (as much as music *in* film) have had a history, often conservative if not reactionary, of marking the female gender through form and genre, whether by associating a Romantic style of music with gender and emotion (Laing 2007, Chapter 1) and developing gendered theories, discourses, narratives, and use of music (McClary 1991, Chapter 1) or by designating specific film genres as female (musicals, melodrama, the woman's film; see Gledhill 1987). Such bias in the use of music is unsurprising if we consider that, of the top-250 grossing Hollywood films of 2019, women comprised a mere 6 percent of composers ("Statistics," n.d.). These gendered practices and biases can be traced to a longer and broader history, in the Western cultural tradition at least, in which the subject of the European Enlightenment identified himself by "differentiating *his* language—rational language, purified of unnecessary associations and suited to expressing 'universal' concepts—from the language of the lower-class folk, which was mired in custom and superstition" (Weidman 2015, 234, emphasis in original). This idea would subsequently become the basis of a binary system that includes contrasts such as "human versus animal; language versus music; male versus female," a corollary of which is a repeated staging of the female voice as "an excessive but powerless vocality that is controlled by authorial male voices" (Weidman 2015, 234). Sound and voice, therefore, have gendered as much as class inflections.

Yet, the very notion of the voice is a tricky one. There is a tendency, in Western philosophy, of what Jacques Derrida (1976) has called phonocentrism, which attributes to voice qualities of an inner meaning: "spirit, soul, mind, consciousness, and the like" (Chow 2017, 19). Because the voice is the carrier of speech and can be distinguished (in both senses) from utterances such as sound and noise, it is presumed to possess an "inner relationship to meaning," thus implying "a subjectivity which 'expresses itself' and itself inhabits the means of expression" (Dolar 2012, 540). This presumption not only bequeaths the idea of voice as "guarantor of truth and self-presence" but also treats "the sonic, material aspects of voice as secondary and as potentially disruptive to the sovereignty of the subject" (Weidman 2015, 233). The reason for the latter presumption, as Michel Chion notes, is because we confuse voice with speech, as if "the voice is there to be forgotten in its materiality; only at this cost does it fill its primary function" (Chion 1999, 1).

Furthermore, metaphorical imaginations of the voice are often more potent that the voice's literal manifestations to the extent that it has become a cliché that everyone owns a voice or is entitled to one (Chow 2017, 20), conflated as the figurative uses of the voice are with "ideas of agency in political theory and some strands of feminist- and Marxist-influenced writing" (Sterne 2012b, 9). Therefore, while the narrative voice (in particular, the use of voice-over) has been analyzed in the study of films, the notion of the voice is typically taken less literally and more metaphorically to signify the conferring of representation to an oppressed group, be it ethnic minorities, women, queer, or other subjects. More clichés abound in the contrast between audio and visual metaphors— "hearing immerses its subjects, vision offers a perspective" (Sterne 2012b, 9), for example—that we would do well to bear in mind these pitfalls in our discussion of the gendered voice in cinema.

However, even when dealing with the literal voice in film, a *vococentrism* prevails insofar as the presence of a human voice "instantly sets up a hierarchy of perception" and *"structures the sonic space that contains it"* (Chion 1999, 5, emphasis in original). As such, even though "there is much more to the voice than dialogue" (Shingler 2006), most conventions of classical cinema "were implicitly calculated to privilege the voice and the intelligibility of dialogue" (Chion 1999, 6). Hence, any interest in "overhearing film dialogue" (Kozloff 2000) or analysis of how speech or sound is delivered through the actor's voice should not forget that "sonic and material experiences of voice are never independent of the cultural meanings attributed to sound, to the body, and particularly to the voice itself" (Weidman 2015, 232). It is for these reasons that I will explore later in the chapter the literal materiality of the female voice in Hou's non-Chinese-language films. As a bridge to that analysis, I locate, in the next section, two historical instances of Taiwan's cultural—indeed, sonic—soft power, that form the premise on which gendered aurality is projected in *Café Lumière* and *Flight of the Red Balloon*.

Taiwan's Historical Sonic Soft Power

The first historical instance relates to Jiang Wenye (Koh Bunya in Japanese; 1910–1983), who was born in Taiwan during the Japanese occupation period (1895–1945) and moved as a child with his parents to Xiamen in China's Fujian province, which was then also under Japanese rule. Jiang traveled with his older brother to receive secondary school education in Japan in 1923 and subsequently completed his education in a technical college whilst taking music lessons in the evenings. His greatest musical success at the international level was to represent Japan in the 1936 Berlin Olympic Art Competition with his piece "Formosan Dance," which won the fourth prize in the category of Compositions for Orchestra of All Kinds, the only prizewinner among the five entries from Japan. He became a professor of music in 1938 at the Beijing Normal University, and he suffered under both the Kuomintang (KMT) regime after the end of World War II and the Chinese Communist Party before and during the Cultural Revolution (1966–1976). He passed away in China in 1983 and remained practically unknown in Taiwan for over 40 years.[14]

During KMT's rule in Taiwan, especially before the lifting of the martial law in 1987, it is unsurprising that Jiang's sonic success at the 1936 Olympics would be hardly mentioned, never mind celebrated, in public. Hou's 2003 film *Café Lumière*, then, goes some way toward bringing Jiang's legacy to light by designating the film's female protagonist (Yoko) as a freelance writer researching Jiang's musical career. The postcolonial imperative behind this cinematic maneuver is unmistakable: Jiang, a real-life colonial subject subjected to the project of "becoming Japanese" (Ching 2001), is revisited, in postcolonial time and at the site of the metropole where he once lived, by a fictional writer from the land of the ex-colonizer.[15] With Taiwan having experienced the change of government between two ruling parties (the other being the nativist-leaning Democratic Progressive Party) not once but twice,[16] today, not only Jiang's "Formosan Dance" was performed, on the 80th anniversary of its Olympic success by the National Taiwan Symphony Orchestra in 2016, Jiang's music could also serve as a soft-power export even to Japan, where a lecture performance and workshop based on his work was held at the Taipei Economic and Cultural Representative Office in Japan in 2019.[17]

There is, however, another twist to this story: Yo Hitoto, who plays Yoko in *Café Lumière*, is a pop singer with a Taiwanese father and a Japanese mother. Hitoto and her older sister (Tae) were both born and raised in Taiwan, and they took their mother's family name when they moved to live in Japan following their father's death.[18] Hitoto's biography adds another layer of texture to the already complex postcolonial fabric of Hou's film in relation to its production background (commissioned by a Japanese studio as a homage to Ozu), composition of cast and crew (Taiwan director, Japanese cast), and plot element (Yoko studying Jiang's work). The twist to this story demonstrates that the voice (both Jiang's and Hitoto's) is never pure—in linguistic as much as in national terms—given the historical entanglements among Taiwan, Japan, and, in the case of Jiang, China. Besides, while *Café Lumière* marks Hitoto's debut in film acting, it acknowledges Hitoto's established music career and projects a literal gendered voice via a song written and sung by her, which runs alongside the film's end credits. The link from the fictional Yoko to the historical figure of Jiang to the singer-songwriter

Hitoto comes full circle in Hou's interweaving of historical and contemporary sonic elements that variously bespeak a hybridized Taiwanese-Japanese soft power as much as a polyphonic phenomenon engendered precisely because, not in spite, of a postcolonial relation.

The second historical instance of Taiwan's sonic soft power relates to Li Tien-lu (1910–1998), the subject and actor of Hou's 1993 biopic of Li, *The Puppetmaster*, which forms the second part of Hou's Taiwan trilogy.[19] In 1931 (that is, during the Japanese occupation period), Li formed his puppetry troupe I Wan Jan, whose reputation was so widespread after World War II that a Frenchman, Jean-Luc Penso, came to Taiwan to study with Li in 1974. However, Li had to disband his troupe in 1977 owing to financial difficulties, partly as a result of the then KMT government's Mandarin policy that imposed a limit on puppetry troupes performing in the Hoklo language on television channels (Chen 2010, 101). Penso, who subsequently formed in Paris a similar troupe (Théâtre du Petit Miroir) whose Chinese name Hsiao Wan Jan salutes the name of Li's troupe (Chiu 2010, 108; Chen 2010, 102), invited Li to France in 1978, thus giving Li and Taiwanese puppetry a second lease on life, with disciples and troupes spreading in quite a number of foreign lands until this day (Chiu 2010, 6, 108–118).

More than a decade after making *The Puppetmaster*, Hou's 2007 film *Flight of the Red Balloon* picks up on this legacy of Taiwan's cultural soft power by casting Li's second son, Li Chuan-tsan, in the role of a Taiwanese puppet master (Ah Zhong) invited to work with the female protagonist (Suzanne, played by Juliette Binoche) in France.[20] While *Flight of the Red Balloon* is, ostensibly, Hou's homage to Albert Lamorisse's *The Red Balloon* (*Le ballon rouge*, 1956), the staging of Taiwanese puppetry and the genealogical link—both personal for the Li father and son and cinematic for Hou's oeuvre back to his 1993 film on Li senior—attest to how Hou has repeatedly given voice, quite literally, to an art form formerly censured in its own country yet possessing soft-power appeal in a faraway land. In *Flight of the Red Balloon*, by having both the vocal performer (Suzanne) of the Parisian puppetry troupe and the interpreter (also nanny of Suzanne's son and a film school student, played by Song Fang) between Suzanne and Ah Zhong as female, Hou's film boldly (albeit in a fictional world) changes the gender of the genealogies of Taiwanese puppetry and filmmaking, elevating women to the status of heir(ess) apparent in art forms more typically dominated by men.[21]

Hou's two non-English-language films and their material conditions of production, therefore, exemplify a world in which boundaries—geographical, linguistic, gendered—have become increasingly porous as a result of the transnational circulation of capital of all kinds, including the soft power of authorship (Hou, Jiang, Li), art forms (cinema, orchestra music, puppetry), cultural institutions (Shochiku Studio, Musée d'Orsay), and stardom (Hitoto, Binoche). Situated in the context of the 1990s when Hou's career was confronted with the wane of TNC in the domestic market, Hou's auteur status has allowed his filmmaking to flourish in the new millennium thanks, in no small part, to commissions from such overseas institutions. In these two films he made in languages he does not speak, Hou, through the respective historical instances of sonic soft power delineated here, grants primacy to female gendered voices that articulate their material dimensions in ways that displace visuality at the same time as they reconfigure aurality in cinema.

Displacing Visuality in *Café Lumière*

In his book *Cinesonica: Sounding Film and Video*, Andy Birtwistle defines sonic materiality as "the specific qualities, states, forms and structures" of sounds, including the qualities of "timbre, duration and development over time" (Birtwistle 2010, 15–16).[22] *Café Lumière* introduces the material dimensions of the gendered voice from its very beginning.[23] Following the opening credits, which include a brief establishing shot of a passing train and the film's title, the fade-in first shot of the film is a long take of Yoko in her Tokyo flat.[24] It first shows her hanging her laundry, and soon after the phone rings. From her one-sided conversation with the caller, identified as Hajime (played by Tadanobu Asano) but not seen or heard through cross-cutting, we know that Yoko has just returned from Taipei the night before. Yoko is still on the phone when her landlady comes to the door, so she puts Hajime on hold and continues the conversation after a brief exchange with the landlady (whom we hear off-screen but do not see on-screen). Yoko tells Hajime a weird dream she has been having, about an unhappy mother and a baby with a wrinkly face, though the fact of her pregnancy has yet to be revealed at this point in the diegesis. The long take, which lasts three minutes and twenty seconds, ends with the phone conversation.

This opening shot foregrounds the materiality of female voices not just by denying the sound of Hajime's voice from the telephone conversation, but, more important, it also displaces the centrality of visuality in cinema when Yoko steps out of the room (and the screen) twice to speak to the landlady. As Figure 2.1 illustrates, by showing us an empty room while we listen to the off-screen dialogue between Yoko and her landlady (each time lasting around eleven seconds), Hou's film privileges aurality, making us "look" for—and failing to find—these gendered voices. If "we never see the same thing when we also hear; we don't hear the same thing when we see as well" (Chion 1994, xxvi), the combination of film sound and image, or what Michel Chion calls audio-vision, is further problematized—and reconfigured—in these moments because we see at the same time as we hear, but what we see is *not* what we hear. By staying in the same place, Hou's camera preserves the unity of both time and space in Yoko's room,

Figure 2.1 Voice without visuality: Yoko exits the room to speak to her landlady in *Café Lumière*

Copyright Shochiku Co. Ltd., The Asahi Shimbun Company, Sumitomo Corporation, Eisei Gekijo Co. Ltd., and Imagica Corp., 2003

but the soundtrack directs us to an unseen space while the 11 seconds on each of the two occasions when Yoko leaves the room present duration as a "material piece of time" (Gidal 1975, 191, qtd. in Birtwistle 2010, 14), a temporal materiality in sync with the material aurality of the spectator/audience.

Audaciously, given the general dominance of visuality in cinema, *Café Lumière* repeatedly makes us listen to the sonic materiality of its characters precisely by blocking them from view, a filmic strategy that can be described as a "cinema of obstruction" (Higbee and Lim 2010, 17). One example is a slow mobile pan of Yoko on the phone following her visit to a bookshop Jiang apparently used to frequent in Tokyo; in this long take, Yoko keeps disappearing behind pillars and built structures to the extent that the final 13 seconds of her one-sided conversation with Hajime is completely visually concealed by a pillar. In another example, Hajime and Yoko have arranged to meet to visit a café where Jiang used to be a regular customer when Yoko suddenly suffers from morning sickness on her train journey; Yoko then tells Hajime about her pregnancy at the exact moment when they are visually obstructed by a pillar while crossing the road, so that Hajime's immediate reaction is only captured aurally. In these sonic encounters, even when meaning and signification are conveyed through the contents of the monologue or dialogue, the affect behind the characters' speech-acts is not registered through visual means such as facial expression but via the material qualities of the voice. The spectator/audience is thus invited to imagine or identify with the characters' state of being not through what is shown but via what is heard. Regardless of the meaning of the monologue/dialogue, the tone, timbre, volume, rhythm, and so forth of the characters' uttered sounds become crucial aural cues which, in turn, might trigger in the spectator/audience "non-cognitive responses" that we now call affect (Birtwistle 2010, 6).

Affect, as Barbara M. Kennedy argues via Gilles Deleuze, "operates beyond subjectivity within the materiality of the film itself, through an immanence of movement, duration, force and intensity, not through a semiotic regime of signification and representation, but in sensation" (Kennedy 2002, 101). Rather than offer a metaphorical reading of the gendered voice by discussing Yoko's determination to bring up the child on her own as a burgeoning form of feminist subjectivity,[25] I want to focus instead on another source of secondary orality—this time the sound of moving trains—that is related to gender via Yoko's pregnancy. From the outset, Yoko's body seems to be a reluctant vehicle of maternity, haunted by the weird dream about an unhappy mother and a baby with a wrinkly face. For Yoko, the fetus her womb is housing is like a kind of alien object, an invasion from outer space, suggested by the title of the book *Outside Over There* by Maurice Sendak, which Hajime told her about and subsequently got her a copy after hearing her describe her dream. As it happens, fetuses are unable to see, but they can recognize sound. In a drawing that Hajime shows Yoko when she notices it on his laptop during his visit to her flat following the morning sickness incident, the close-ups of the drawing depict a fetus with a watch round its neck and holding a boom microphone, immersed in deep red blood and surrounded by chains of green carriages that look like an umbilical cord. Claiming that the central figure is himself, Hajime describes the drawing (done, incidentally, by Asano himself) as "a womb of trains," vividly shown in Figure 2.2.

Yoko's interest in Hajime's drawing of the fetus leads us to a consideration of what constitutes gendered and material voices that, *Café Lumière* suggests as it moves swiftly from visuality to aurality in its penultimate shot, could well be the sounds of passing trains that a fetus might hear—and sense—in the mother's body. While Yoko's pregnancy has hitherto been expressed variously as fear (weird dream), discomfort (morning sickness), and hesitation (delayed disclosure to Hajime until she could no longer hide it), the couple's shared interest in aurality—Jiang's music for Yoko and recording sounds of trains for Hajime—hints at a possible futurity fostered in the figure of the fetus. The film's penultimate shot sees the couple at a railway station and Hajime recording sounds of passing trains and station announcements with his boom

Figure 2.2 The maternal voice: Drawing of a fetus holding a boom microphone in *Café Lumière*

Copyright Shochiku Co. Ltd., The Asahi Shimbun Company, Sumitomo Corporation, Eisei Gekijo Co. Ltd., and Imagica Corp., 2003

microphone. With amplified sounds of train carriages running on tracks, this shot favors the aural-temporal dyad of rhythm and speed, sounds that the fetus might register, remember, and even revisit through Hajime's recordings. For the first time in the film, it is no longer Hajime who is aiding and following Yoko's trail of Jiang Wenye, but rather Yoko keeping Hajime company in the pursuit of his sonic interest. It is also the first time that Yoko is slowing down and standing still instead of always on the trot, a stillness and silence that might allow her to finally find—and hear—her own maternal voice, which exists within her body in the form of the fetus.[26]

Hou's aural turn, represented by a displacement of visuality and a materialization of gendered voice and sound, is epitomized in *Café Lumière*'s penultimate shot, shown in Figure 2.3, in which trains cross the screen horizontally from right to left, obscuring the silent couple standing on a station platform in the background. This shot downplays the visibility of the image and spoken words to amplify sounds of moving trains so we can practice what Pierre Schaeffer calls "reduced listening," which, Chion explains, "focuses on the traits of the sound

Figure 2.3 Practicing reduced listening: Recording sounds of passing trains in *Café Lumière*

Copyright Shochiku Co. Ltd., The Asahi Shimbun Company, Sumitomo Corporation, Eisei Gekijo Co. Ltd., and Imagica Corp., 2003

itself, independent of its cause and of its meaning" (Chion 1994, 29). Moreover, this aural turn is inflected by gender, not through an easy, metaphorical under-standing of what it means to own a gendered voice, but via a sophisticated, lit-eral engendering of voices obstructed by visuality and of train sounds—at once material and devoid of signification and meaning—registered by a fetus in a mother's corporeality. The yet-to-be-born fetus, whose ability to hear but not see, echoes Hou's privileging of aurality over visuality and a yet-to-be-realized promise, within film studies, of more devoted listening to sound. Hou may have been hailed (alongside Tsai Ming-liang) as masters of the long take and painterly composition, but the long take of *Café Lumière*'s carefully composed penultimate shot testifies that he does not hesitate to render visibility a blur to make us hear more intently and intensely. *Café Lumière* reminds us that, rather than painstak-ingly crafted images, it may well be the unintelligible, meaningless, and repetitive sounds of passing trains whose rhythm and materiality, like the unseen but sen-sible heartbeat of the fetus, that resonate in and with us, and that ultimately *move* us in our film-watching—and film-listening—experience.

The Corporeal Voice in *Flight of the Red Balloon*

In a useful survey of the state of scholarship on the human voice in film, Martin Shingler (2006) issues a call to arms in his conclusion:

> The received wisdom on what film is and why people love it may well take something of a bashing when one of the conceptual cornerstones of film studies is undermined. For when the profound power, subtlety and appeal of the dramatic human voice in film is more fully understood, the established notion of film as primarily a visual medium is likely to give way in favour of film as an audio-visual medium where audio really does come first. Something fundamental is at stake here and, consequently, the debate within (and across) film studies may become heated and polarised. Now might be a good time for film scholars to fasten their seatbelts and prick up their ears.

Shingler proposes that an appropriate place to begin an investigation into the uses and effects of the voice in the cinema would be "the fundamental question of what is a 'pure voice,' divorced from language and linguistic meaning" (2006). *Flight of the Red Balloon* gestures toward such an investigation by, on the one hand, presenting instances of Taiwanese puppetry shows in which the linguistic meaning of the spoken text is arguably less important than qualities (such as timbre, tone, pitch, and rhythm) of the performing voice and, on the other hand, visualizing the corporeal body without which the pure voice cannot be enunciated. For Shingler, the value in studying timbre is that "it inscribes a sense of musicality into the speaking voice and forces us to conceive of the voice as essentially musical" (Shingler 2006).[27] In the puppetry sequences in *Flight of the Red Balloon*, however, the performing voice is always already musical when Ah Zhong demonstrates Taiwanese puppetry and when Suzanne rehearses a show based on a story from a Yuan dynasty Chinese opera. In this story, Zhang Sheng (also known as Zhang Yu) falls in love with the daughter of the Dragon King, who opposes their marriage and imprisons his daughter at the bottom of the sea. Zhang then decides to boil the sea dry with a big pot in an attempt to reach his wife.

As Suzanne, Binoche's vocality is most spectacular in the film's third and final puppetry sequence in which she provides the voice for both Zhang Yu and a transfigured being called Maonü (the hairy woman). As is shown in Figure 2.4, Zhang is represented by a glove puppet in human form and looks like a Chinese monk; what cannot be shown or, rather, heard (thus inadvertently alerting us to the limitation of illustrating a book with film stills but not film sounds), is the way in which Zhang speaks in a fairly normal voice but in a slightly hurried pace as he is busy scooping sea water into a pot using a ladle. Maonü, on the other

Figure 2.4 The third and final Taiwanese puppetry sequence in *Flight of the Red Balloon*

Copyright Margofilms & Les Films du Lendemain, 2007

hand, is presented merely as two elongated arms on rods; she speaks in a falsetto voice, with extended cadences and an exaggerated tone. Suzanne switches effortlessly between these two characters, ensuring no confusion between them and granting Maonü's voice an ethereal quality.

How does Suzanne perform such vocal virtuosity? If *Café Lumière* deliberately prevents us from seeing the source of the human voices to make us hear more clearly, *Flight of the Red Balloon* instead unveils visuality because the art form central to the diegesis—Taiwanese puppetry—is one in which aurality is, by its very own design, hidden from view.[28] Whereas the visible glove and rod puppets serve as extensions of their human manipulators, their movements indicating the latter's presence beneath the stage, the voice artists (and musicians) are completely disembodied (from the puppets, at least) and physically separated on stage from the supposed speaking objects. This unseen source of the voice is a manifestation of a concept that Chion has famously revived: the acousmêtre, "a sound that is heard without its cause or source being seen," modern-day examples of which include the radio, telephones, and phonograph records (Chion 1999, 18), similar to Ong's examples of secondary orality. However, if in a real puppetry show we will only hear but not see Suzanne's performance, Hou's film allows us visual access to the body of the vocalizing subject, thus deepening our understanding of the relationship between visuality and aurality, image and sound. The first two-and-a-half minutes of the long take of the puppetry sequence under discussion show the puppets and their manipulators in action when Suzanne's son (Simon) enters the room with his nanny (Song). Despite Suzanne's visual absence over this duration, we recognize, from the first puppetry sequence set in the same rehearsal room, that this voice-off, "the already visualized acousmêtre" (Chion 1999, 21), belongs to her. The rise and fall of Suzanne's tone of voice is matched throughout by the movement of the camera as it circles round the stage to reveal the puppeteers, then wanders downward to Simon's eye level to capture his look of wonder.

The materiality of the voice, according to Amanda Weidman, encompasses the sound itself as well as the "bodily process of producing and attending to voices" (2015, 235), a process expressed in the second part of the long take, which begins with the camera drifting toward Suzanne, as illustrated in Figure 2.5, as she utters the line, "I was transfigured. They call me Maonü, the hairy woman." The next 80 seconds visualize how Suzanne's vocal performance involves not just her voice but also her body, the "'internal choreography' involved in shaping the vocal tract each time a singer sings or a person speaks" (Weidman, 2015, 235). In particular, Suzanne's right arm never ceases to gesticulate, lifting and dropping in tandem with the pitch of her voice as if to exteriorize how the bodily movements help her express her vocality. Enunciating the dialogue between Zhang Yu and Maonü, Suzanne visibly straightens her back every time she delivers the latter's lines because they are in a much higher pitch and much more theatrical. As such, we not only hear Suzanne's voice in terms of volume, rhythm, timbre, and pitch

Figure 2.5 Visualizing the corporeality of the voice in *Flight of the Red Balloon*
Copyright Margofilms & Les Films du Lendemain, 2007

but also *see* the materiality of her middle-aged, blond, glamorous, female, star body from which the French dialogue emanates, her vocality buttressed by physical gestures and movements.[29]

What preparation did Binoche undertake for voicing a Chinese story in the form of Taiwanese puppetry, albeit in French dialogue? According to an interview with Hou, Binoche was assigned a vocal coach (Martine Viard) once it was decided that she would participate, as part of her role in the film, in the performance of an actual puppetry troupe, Le Théâtre aux Mains Nues-Paris. The eventual performance, however, did not make it into Hou's film because of the timing, and the two sequences featuring Binoche as a puppeteer were culled from recordings of the troupe's rehearsals (Wen 2010, 78). As Binoche revealed in an interview, the rehearsal was already underway when Hou arrived and started shooting without informing the puppeteers (Chu 2009, 619).[30] This was partly because Hou's shooting schedule with the troupe had to be cut by half to a week owing to budget constraints (Wen 2010, 78).

Binoche's voice in *Flight of the Red Balloon* articulates the film's material condition of production, an economy that demands spontaneity and premises on serendipity, echoed in Hou's free-floating camera. Similarly, the instances of cinema of obstruction in *Café Lumière* are likely to have been improvised solutions to filming restrictions in Tokyo, thus necessitating the use of extreme long shots whose visual concealment may or may not include considerations about sound recording.[31] Conditions such as these, therefore, strike highly on what Chion calls "materializing sound indices" because they lay bare "the concrete process of the sound's production" and make us "'feel' the material conditions of the sound source" (1994, 114). That is to say, Hou does not shy away from, to return to *Flight of the Red Balloon*, displaying the more constrained materiality of its own condition of production, including the stumbled lines uttered by Suzanne in a voice that is still a work in progress. The decision to reinforce or erase materializing indices, as Chion extrapolates, "contributes toward the creation of a universe, and can take on metaphysical meaning" (1994, 116). In this light, I will conclude this chapter by examining the material conditions of aurality in Hou's cinema, using examples from these two films to draw out the wider stakes of Hou's gendered voices in relation to the key concerns of this book, namely authorship, transnationality, historiography, and soft power.

The Materiality of Gendered Aurality

In this chapter I have used the term materiality to refer to both the literal, sonic properties of female voices (and other nonhuman sounds) in Hou's filmmaking and the conditions (film production as much as sociopolitical) under which gendered voices can be heard, indeed, can materialize. In relation to the notion of authorship, Hou's aural-cum-gender turn must be credited, in no small part, to the role of Chu Tien-wen, one of the most acclaimed novelists in Taiwan. Up to and including the making of *The Assassins*, Chu has been the sole screenplay writer on six and co-writer on nine films by Hou since Hou's TNC days.[32] Chu was, however, not listed as screenwriter for *Flight of the Red Balloon* because the funding model demanded a certain percentage of the crew being French, and thus the (male, French) producer was credited as the screenwriter instead (Bai 2014, 265). The key role that Chu has played in transforming Hou into the director he is today troubles the notion of sole authorship in a collaborative art form such as film;[33] it also implies, as I have stated elsewhere (Lim 2016b, 38), that Hou's films can be claimed as a form of *écriture feminine*, which, in Hélène Cixous's conception, is not biologically determined and thus not confined to female writers.[34] Moreover, the role of female stardom deserves special mention not simply for its aural materiality but also for the added value of soft power it brings. Indeed, if Hou's signature filmmaking style is cherished for the credence he lends to the French notion of the auteur,[35] Binoche's vocal performance of the French dialogue in "Zhang Sheng Boils the Sea" gives voice, vicariously, to Chinese and Taiwanese cultural forms of theater and puppetry that date as far back as the thirteen and fourteenth centuries.

In terms of historiography, Hou's oeuvre occupies a position way beyond the realm of cinema to serve as a form of record for Taiwan's long twentieth century, bringing obscured and hitherto taboo historical subjects to wide public attention often via gendered voices. Christopher Lupke employs the musical term *sotto voce* (sound lowered for added dramatic effect) to account for the way the female voice in Hou's films is suppressed and "can only communicate its message through refracted and oblique means" (2016, 53). In Hou's earlier films such as *A City of Sadness*, the first film to touch upon the February 28 incident of 1947, we can already hear a female voice providing not only a "diaristic voice-over" whose "alterities position [the speaker] outside the 'official' discourse of the KMT" (Haddon 2005, 56) but also a counterpoint to the recorded disembodied male voices heard on radio broadcasts announcing the official position on the incident.[36] Hou's female voices, whether projected in a subdued manner or refracted through other means, signal different modes of knowledge and understanding, as well as of engagement and evaluation, alerting us to the inherent materiality of their voices as much as the external material conditions under which they have remained unheard.

Here I want to explore a little more the materiality of the voice before drawing out its implications for our understanding of transnationality and soft power in cinema. In his essay "The Linguistics of the Voice," Mladen Dolar raises a provocative question—"Can hiccups be a philosophical statement?"—to highlight the ways in which "the non-articulate itself becomes a mode of the articulate" (2012, 547). The hiccup challenges an obsession with perfectly fluent and correct articulation, a myth that can take on material consequences and, as Chion argues above, metaphysical meanings. For example, compared to the imperfect enunciation in Suzanne's vocal performance of Taiwanese puppetry in *Flight of the Red Balloon*, Ang Lee's *Crouching Tiger, Hidden Dragon* adopts a diametrically opposite approach to the execution of voice. Two of the leads, Michelle Yeoh and Chow Yun-fat (both Cantonese rather than Mandarin speakers), were given five months of elocution classes in Mandarin prior to the shoot and three voice-recording sessions in post-production, the latter involving the director himself coaching the actors on their accent and emotive expression. Moreover, the enunciation of these actors in the final product was pieced together word by word by the American sound engineer, even to the extent that sometimes a word was apparently amalgamated from three separate phonemes (Zhang 2005, 205). Lee even joked that the process was so exhausting that he wanted, at the time, to kill the actors before ending his life by biting off his tongue (Zhang 2005, 205).

Lee's joke, I contend, must be taken seriously because it reinforces, however unwittingly, a myth about linguistic articulation that is married to cinematic practice as much as to notions of ethnicity/race.[37] Rather than the pure voice in Shingler's construction, it is a different kind of purity—linguistic "authenticity"—that prevailed in the production of Lee's film, which devoted a laborious and, no doubt, costly process of mechanical composition in post-production because the language spoken was not the actors' so-called mother tongue and because the director refused to compromise on the standard of "native" pronunciation. Michelle Yeoh, a Malaysian-born ethnic Chinese whose first languages are English and Malay, only learned Cantonese as a spoken language when she went to Hong Kong to kick-start her acting career in the 1980s. For her role in *Crouching Tiger, Hidden Dragon*, Yeoh had had to memorize the Mandarin dialogue phonetically. In an interview following the release of the film, Yeoh claimed that "Mandarin is one of the most complicated languages in the world to study" and that her task was made even more difficult because the Mandarin used in the film was "so stylized and so formal" and "the passages [in the dialogue] were long" (Blair 2000). She went on to qualify:

> Obviously it's your *tone* that imparts the meaning to your audience. At the end of the day, regardless of what language we were speaking, you could feel what we were trying to tell you, from our *voice* and the little subtle movements. (Blair 2000, emphasis mine)

To the director's credit, despite audiences laughing at Yeoh's and Chow's articulations in test screenings of *Crouching Tiger, Hidden Dragon* in Taiwan, rather than choosing to dub the dialogue in "standard" Mandarin (a convention that would have been more familiar to domestic audiences in their reception of Hong Kong cinema), Lee decided to keep the actors' original voices because he believed that "the emotion conveyed by the quality of the voice is more touching than dubbed standard Mandarin" (Zhang 2005, 206). Both Yeoh's and Lee's accounts, therefore, concur with the main argument I have been developing in this chapter: it is not so much the content of the dialogue (meaning); rather, it is the materiality and the manner in which the dialogue is delivered (timbre, tone, etc.) that matters in our study of the human voice in cinema.

This understanding of the materiality of the voice—in spite of or precisely because of its imperfection in enunciation—prompts us to rethink the terms of transnationality and soft power. To return to Binoche's vocal performance in *Flight of the Red Balloon*, I want to propose a radical interpretation of the puppetry sequences to argue that the language of her delivery does not matter as much as the conventions by which dialogue is delivered in puppetry, Taiwanese or otherwise.[38] That is to say, if a non-French-speaking-audience like myself were to ignore the subtitles during screenings or to turn off the subtitle function on the DVD, what I would be listening for in Binoche's performance is the expressivity of the pure voice, a voice devoid of the meaning of words but not of meaning itself, because meaning can be conveyed through modes of the voice that are "seemingly recalcitrant to the signifier: the accent, the intonation, and the timbre" (Dolar 2012, 544), here modulated by conventions of vocal articulation in puppetry theater. In fact, in the film's second puppetry sequence, Li Chuan-tsan's demonstration at a master class is similarly unintelligible to me because the form of Hoklo language spoken is highly formal and rather archaic. This incomprehensibility, however, is welcome because it foregrounds the materiality rather than the meaning of the voice; the voice is, in this sense, "*what does not contribute to making sense*" (Dolar 2012, 541, emphasis in original).

For me, this understanding of the materiality of the voice implies that soft power—in the context of this book, what makes a new wave cinema attractive to foreign audiences—does not necessarily depend on nation-bound features such as the meaning of spoken languages (even "accurate" ones that Ang Lee insisted upon) but on transnational qualities such as the seemingly meaningless but utterly articulate hiccup and the affective resonances transmitted via the timbre, tone, pitch, and rhythm of an expressive human voice or even sounds of trains. Soft power can operate through transnational pure voices that do not—even refuse to—make sense. The aural turn in Hou's cinema, then, broadcasts gendered and material voices as something to be sensed rather than to make sense of. This refusal to privilege the imperative of making sense (meaning), I would posit, highlights the potential political value of the materiality of the voice. Hou's two non-Chinese-language films have given voice (in both literal and metaphorical senses) to languages (including the language of music) that have been suppressed for political reasons, languages (regardless of their content and meaning) whose materiality has been at odds with the ideologies of different ruling regimes over Taiwan's long twentieth century. If aurality in Taiwanese music, puppetry, and cinema was, over many decades, caught up in the politics of language, the sonic soft power of Jiang Wenye, Li Tien-lu, and now Hou himself epitomizes an openness to an aural turn that embraces the transmutation of languages within their own chosen art forms, leading to the exercise of their soft power in these transnational, cross-cultural exchanges. Divorced from language and meaning, the materiality of gendered voices in Hou's cinema has indeed projected a soft power so loud it makes us turn our heads to listen more closely to aurality.

3

The Medial Turn

Tsai Ming-liang's Slow Walk to the Museum

At the 2013 Venice film festival where his tenth feature film, *Stray Dogs* (*Jiaoyou*, 2013), won the Grand Jury prize, the Malaysia-born, Taiwan-based director Tsai Ming-liang declared that this would be his last film, joining Béla Tarr, another master of slow cinema, as filmmakers who had recently announced their retirement.[1] Tsai's announcement did not come as a surprise to those who have followed his career closely; he had been disillusioned by filmmaking as a practice for quite some time. As he said in an interview at Venice: "If you look back at the old films you have the feeling among all these products there were also some very good products and some very poor ones. Now we seem only to have the low quality and somehow we lost the quality of film" (Roddy 2013). Besides, with the completion of his previous feature-length film, the Louvre-commissioned *Visage* (*Lian*, 2009), Tsai claimed that the future of cinema was in museums and galleries. Indeed, since the start of the twenty-first century, Tsai has, with increasing frequency, ventured into the realm of expanded cinema, an "elastic name for many sorts of film and projection event" (Rees 2011, 12). For example, in an installation piece entitled *It's a Dream* (*Shi meng*) and exhibited at the 2007 Venice Biennale, 54 salvaged seats from an old cinema in Kepong (a district in Kuala Lumpur, Malaysia) were displayed alongside a 22-minute version of an eponymous film (Sing 2014, 105), which has its origin in Tsai's 3-minute contribution to the portmanteau film *To Each His Own Cinema* (*Chacun son cinéma . . .*, Tsai Ming-liang and 32 others, 2007), in celebration of the 60th anniversary of the Cannes film festival in 2007.

Tsai's declaration of retirement from feature-length filmmaking opens this chapter not so much to undermine this book's overarching thesis about the relationship between soft power and the medium of cinema. Rather, precisely because Tsai's retirement from one form of filmmaking would free him to develop other modes of artistic practice—what I shall call a medial turn—his new endeavors demand an expanded definition of cinema at the same time as they index the permeability of an auteur's soft power across different fields. This redefinition of (expanded) cinema as (inter)mediality will impact the functions of the three keywords in this book's subtitle, namely, authorship, transnationality, and

Taiwan Cinema as Soft Power. Song Hwee Lim, Oxford University Press. © Oxford University Press 2022.
DOI: 10.1093/oso/9780197503379.003.0004

historiography. More important, it will shift our focus from the more commonly discussed question about the ontology of the cinematic image in the digital age to one about the relocation of cinema's exhibition space—away from the movie theater and into art galleries and museums.

The Soft Power of Tsai Ming-liang's Expanded Cinema

With regard to the three keywords, soft power is manifested, to begin with the notion of authorship, not only in the form of another prestigious award for Tsai at the European film festival circuit, but also in the ways in which directors could wield such power beyond their established realm. Whereas Tarr will continue as producer at his Budapest film company alongside his new role as president of the Hungarian Filmmakers Association (Rapold 2012) and open a film academy at the University Sarajevo School of Science and Technology (Brooks 2012), Tsai has been carving out a new career as an intermedial artist and returning to his roots in theater.[2] That is to say, while this book primarily studies the relationship between soft power and cinema, the soft-power currency attached to the label of authorship can, in effect, be transferred from the world of filmmaking to undertakings by auteurs in new arenas. Such currency crosses borders that are both national (the Hungarian Tarr's film school located in Bosnia and Herzegovina) and artistic (Tsai's installation piece in the Venice Biennale), thereby highlighting the dimension of transnationality (a premise for the operation of soft power) while complicating the notion of film historiography (with intermedial practices).

Moving on to another keyword (historiography), Tsai's intermedial practices call for an understanding of an expanded notion of cinema and, in turn, an expanded form of film historiography. As Ginette Verstraete suggests, intermediality "asks difficult questions not only about art and media—and their interrelations—but also about the institutional boundaries we draw around them" (2010, 11). Within Anglophone academia, expanded cinema is typically studied and practiced under the discipline of fine arts whereas film is usually housed in departments of film studies, English, and modern languages. Funding, whether for practitioners or researchers, also tends to come from disparate sources, represented institutionally by distinct national bodies such as, in the case of the United Kingdom, the England Arts Council, and the UK Film Council respectively. Furthermore, publication outlets, professional bodies, conferences, and events relating to both media forms are more likely to be mutually exclusive than overlapping. In terms of exhibition spaces for works created in their names, the demarcation between film and expanded cinema is captured vividly as that between the black box and the white cube.

The two media forms, therefore, have distinct historiographies, genealogies, practices, and disciplinary boundaries that underpin the very notion of intermediality, which I shall examine in a later section with reference to Tsai's works. Here I want to foreground the soft-power dimension that marks Tsai's slow and gradual drift from the movie theater to the museum. The Louvre's commissioning, in 2005, of Tsai to make a film that would become the museum's first collection in feature-length film was as much a recognition of the French connections in Tsai's previous films (such as the 2001 film *What Time Is It There?/Ni nabian jidian*, set partly in Paris) and of his conscious mobilization of the French discourse of *la politique des auteurs* (see Lim 2014a, 60–65) as it was a testament to Tsai's soft-power appeal at both transnational and transmedial levels. Crucially, this new soft-power resource from the Louvre, which resides unequivocally in the realm of high art, was offered at a time when Tsai had been bemoaning the commercialization of international film festivals that had become, for him, "nothing more than oversized auction houses where everything [came] down to business and money" (Berry 2005, 394). While the transfer of cinematic soft-power resources can also take more popular forms, such as Disneyland's and Universal Studios' theme parks across the world and location tourism to "Middle-earth" in New Zealand thanks to the success of the *Lord of the Rings* trilogy (Peter Jackson 2001, 2002, 2003),[3] Tsai's turn to the museum as a source for film production and a site of film collection and film exhibition (and later, a location for intermedial practices) adheres to his staunch belief in cinema (in both its conventional and expanded forms) as art. The cultural signification and symbolic capital that an institution such as the Louvre hold for Tsai cannot be overstated in relation to his decision to cross over from the movie theater to the museum.

Transnationality, as the final keyword to be discussed here, may turn out to be insufficient in capturing the new sites of Tsai's intermedial practices. The commission by the Louvre kick-started the gravitational pull of Tsai's walk toward the museum, represented by a series of short films entitled "Slow Walk, Long March" (hereafter the Walker series), which will be my main object of analysis in this chapter. The series casts Tsai's muse Lee Kang-sheng as the character of Xuanzang (a Buddhist monk who made a pilgrimage from China to India in the seventh century) walking in a deliberately slow pace in various urban landscapes and artificial structures, a literal and corporeal rendition of slowness that has long been a hallmark of Tsai's full-length cinematic oeuvre (Lim 2014a).[4] Five installments from the series were made during the four-year gap between *Visage* and *Stray Dogs*, the longest break in Tsai's career of over 20 years in feature-length filmmaking, and, at the time of this writing (late 2020), three more had been completed since the release of *Stray Dogs*. While the production background and sites of exhibition of this series are distinctly transnational, some aspects of its distribution and consumption can be said to have taken place, so to speak, in the non-places (Augé 1995) of digital screens and the World Wide Web. Two installments, "Walker" (*Xingzhe*, 2012) and "No No Sleep" (*Wu wumian*, 2015), were commissioned by the Hong Kong International Film Festival Society and Youku as parts of a portmanteau film project (China's leading online video network);[5] "Walking on Water" (*Xing zai shui shang*, 2013) was included in a series of short films commissioned by China's Phoenix New Media.[6] Both initiatives set out to release short films primarily for online consumption, which arguably has the effect of deterritorializing both national and transnational spaces.

Finally, it is noteworthy that Tsai's medial turn is simultaneously a digital turn as these online platforms for exhibition facilitated his transition to digital filmmaking, which he had resisted in his feature-length filmmaking until *Stray Dogs*, his supposed swansong. This digital turn made possible even more extended long takes for which Tsai is famed, resulting in a 15-minute long take of Lee descending the steps to an underpass in Marseille in "Journey to the West" (*Xiyou*, 2014) as well as the penultimate shot of *Stray Dogs* lasting over 13 minutes. In 2017, Tsai even released a virtual reality (VR) film, *The Deserted* (*Jia zai Lanruosi*), defying popular expectation by positioning himself at the forefront of cinematic technological experimentation.[7] In what follows, I will demonstrate how Tsai's slow walk to the museum challenges us to expand our notion of cinema and to rethink the boundary between various sites of exhibition for the cinematic image. My aim in this chapter is to trace the flow of soft-power resources across different artistic realms through Tsai's intermedial practices in order to reflect upon the state and status of the cinematic image in the post-media era.[8] I begin by mapping out the medial turns in Tsai's career.

The Medial Turn

While Tsai is known across the world mainly as a film director, to speak of him *only* as a filmmaker is to disregard the fact that the adoption of the medium of cinema was, for Tsai, already a medial turn. Born in Malaysia in 1957, Tsai went to Taiwan to pursue his college education in the late 1970s where he obtained a degree from the film and drama section of Chinese Culture University's drama department in 1982. He first made his name in Taiwan as a theater director, playwright, and actor who caught the wave of the "little theater movement" at the time of his graduation. Some elements from his early plays, such as his Genetesque second play, which is completely without dialogue and in which an old male inmate rapes his younger male cellmate (Lim 2006, 132), can be seen to have prefigured the sex scene between the father and son in his third feature-length film, *The River* (*Heliu*, 1997). Following his spell in theater, Tsai moved on to write screenplays for established film directors such as Wang Tung and Wang Hsiao-ti in the early to mid-1980s before turning to directing television dramas from the late 1980s onward (Sing 2014, 242). In the early 1990s, Tsai was included, alongside Ang Lee, Yee Chih-yen, and Chen Yu-hsun, in a scheme by the Central Motion Picture Corporation (CMPC) to promote new directors; this cohort would sometimes be referred to as second-generation Taiwan New Cinema (hereafter TNC) directors.

Tsai's debut film, *Rebels of the Neon God* (*Qingshaonian Nezha*), appeared in 1992. His medial turn to cinema was unfortunate in its timing as the Taiwan film industry was then in sharp decline, hence CMPC's last-ditch effort to resuscitate itself via the new directors' scheme. While the scheme had had considerable success in catapulting directors such as Ang Lee and Tsai to global fame with their almost immediate success at winning top awards in the international film festival circuit (see Table I.1 in the Introduction), the performance of films by TNC directors (whether first or second generation) and of the dwindling number of Taiwan-produced films in general at the domestic box office remained dismal, a phenomenon I have described elsewhere as a paradoxical "bifurcation between high international prestige and low domestic production" (Lim 2013, 160).[9] Tsai, in particular, became a controversial figure as he came under scrutiny about his eligibility for governmental subsidy schemes given his Malaysian citizenship and under attack for the portrayal of homosexuality in his films (Lim 2007, 238). To gain greater control over the production and distribution of his films, Tsai set up Homegreen Films in 2000 and devised various strategies to boost the box-office performance of his films, albeit with limited success (Lim 2014a, 49). His *What Time Is It There?* was one of only 16 Taiwan films released in 2002 (Wang 2003, 63); its meager box-office intake of just over NT$1.2 million already enough to be ranked ninth among top-grossing Chinese-language films (i.e., including those made in Hong Kong, China, and Singapore) released in Taiwan that year (Wang 2003, 64).

It was during this sustained period of industrial decline and hostility when Tsai started to receive invitations from a different realm—the art world—to produce works beyond the medium of cinema.[10] In 2004, the performance artist Cai Guo-Qiang invited Tsai to participate in a festival he was curating in Kinmen (the frontline of Taiwan's defense against the People's Republic of China during the Cold War era and site of the August 23 artillery battle in 1958), for which Tsai installed a bronze statue of Chiang Kai-shek, ex-president of Taiwan, looking onto mainland China from a gun embrasure (Lin and Tsai 2016b, 10). In 2007, Tsai exhibited an installation piece *It's a Dream* at the Venice Biennale (described in the opening page of this chapter) upon the invitation of a curator from the Taipei Fine Arts Museum (Lin and Tsai 2016b, 10), which subsequently acquired the piece for its collection. More invitations—both local and overseas—followed, culminating in two solo exhibitions at the Museum of National Taiwan University of Education in 2014 and 2016 as well as two multi-media retrospectives in Brussels and Vienna in 2014 (see Table 3.1 for a selected list of Tsai's intermedial work).

For me, the key point in Tsai's medial turn came in 2005 when the Louvre commissioned him to make a film. The Louvre is, of course, a cultural institution with super global soft power—the most visited museum in the world in 2018, attracting a record number of 10.2 million visitors of whom foreigners accounted for nearly 75 percent ("Paris Louvre" 2019). Indeed, it was the additional rev-enue generated by soaring annual visitor numbers between 2001 (5.6 million) and 2008 (8.5 million) that allowed the Parisian museum "to commission works from contemporary artists to reflect on its permanent collection" (Bruyas 2009, qtd. in Bloom 2016, 214n29). With 20 percent of its nearly 4 million euros budget contributed by the Louvre (Heurtebise and Lin 2015, 6), Tsai's *Visage* not only became the museum's first commission in the medium of film but its making, I would argue, also had a fundamental impact on Tsai's outlook on his career. In particular, Tsai began to regard film as a collectable objet d'art, and he decided not to release *Visage* on DVD in Taiwan.[11] Rather, he would produce 10 limited-edition copies of the film in both celluloid and digital forms, encased in a cypress box decorated with his own oil painting of images from *Visage*, each priced at NT$1 million and containing a contract stipulating conditions of use, barring further sales to broadcasting agencies or for DVD release (Sing 2014, 143, 226). By May 2017, Tsai had sold three copies and was in the process of painting the fifth box (Chiu 2017).

Following his collaboration with the Louvre, coupled with other factors (such as his deteriorating health), Tsai was clearly in no hurry to make another feature-length film, exploring instead other media forms for his creative expression. These endeavors range from, among others, an exhibition of his paintings and installations at a creative industry institute (2010) to designing a room, as shown in Figures 3.1 and 3.2, as part of an exhibition in a historical building converted into a hotel in Tainan in southern Taiwan (2012).[12] For Tsai, the bottom line for the production of his work—in whatever medium—is this: "I need money. I need freedom and I need Lee Kang-sheng" (Vagenas 2013). A standout example is "No Form" (*Wu se*), the first installment in the Walker series, which started life as a product-image advertisement for a cellphone company. The fact that the com-pany simply wanted to capitalize on his brand name did not seem to bother Tsai, and he confessed to not even knowing the name of the company or what the cell-phone looked like (Yu 2012). A more recent example is the VR film, which was commissioned by the cellphone company HTC to the tune of USD$1.6 million (Frater 2017). To sum up, Tsai's work in the twenty-first century has not only

Table 3.1 Tsai Ming-liang's intermedial works (selected)

Work (duration, year)	Commissioned or sponsored by	Premiere
"Slow Walk, Long March" series		
"No Form" (20 mins., 2012)	Product image for a cellphone company in Taiwan	International Film Festival Marseille[a]
"Walker" (25 mins., 2012)	"Beautiful 2012" project by Youku and Hong Kong International Film Festival (HKIFF)	HKIFF[b]
"Diamond Sutra" (20 mins., 2012)		Venice Film Festival[c]
"Sleepwalk" (20 mins., 2012)	Taiwan Ministry of Culture and National Taiwan Museum of Fine Arts	Venice Architecture Biennale[d]
"Walking on Water" (30 mins., 2013)	Phoenix New Media	Phoenix New Media (online)[e]
"Journey to the West" (56 mins., 2014)	Centre National de la Cinématographie (CNC) and Centre National des Arts Plastiques	Berlin Film Festival[f]
"No No Sleep" (34 mins., 2015)	"Beautiful 2015" project by Youku and HKIFF	HKIFF[g]
"Sand" (79 mins., 2018)	Zhuangwei Dune Visitor Center, Yilan, Taiwan	Zhuangwei Dune Visitor Center, Yilan, Taiwan[h]
Theater productions		
Only You (2011)	National Theater, Taipei	National Theater, Taipei[i]
The Monk from the Tang Dynasty (2014)	Taipei Arts Festival, Kunsten Festival des Arts, Wiener Festwochen, and Asian Culture Complex-Asian Arts Theatre (Gwangju)	Kunsten Festival des Arts, Brussels[j]
Installation Art Pieces		
It's a Dream (2007)	Taipei Fine Arts Museum	Venice Biennale[k]
An Erotic Space II (2010)		Aichi Triennale, Nagoya[l]
Solo Exhibitions		
Stray Dogs at the Museum (2014)	Museum of National Taipei University of Education	Museum of National Taipei University of Education[m]

Table 3.1 *Continued*

Work (duration, year)	Commissioned or sponsored by	Premiere
No No Sleep At MoNTUE (2016)	Museum of National Taipei University of Education	Museum of National Taipei University of Education[n]
Multimedia Retrospectives		
March–May, 2014	Kunsten Festival of Arts, Brussels	Kunsten Festival of Arts, Brussels[o]
May 2014	Wiener Festwochen, Vienna	Wiener Festwochen, Vienna[p]

[a] All online sources listed were accessed September 22, 2020. https://www.scmp.com/lifestyle/arts-culture/article/1299497/filmmaker-tsai-ming-liang-says-his-work-should-be-appreciated.

[b] http://hkiffcollection.org.hk/beautiful-2012-2016/.

[c] https://taiwantoday.tw/print.php?unit=10,23,45,10&post=19626.

[d] https://www.taiwannews.com.tw/ch/news/1985644.

[e] http://v.ifeng.com/program/yingshi/yxyls/.

[f] https://www.berlinale.de/en/archiv/jahresarchive/2014/02_programm_2014/02_Filmdatenblatt_2014_20147028.html#tab=filmStills.

[g] http://hkiffcollection.org.hk/beautiful-2012-2016/.

[h] https://www.upmedia.mg/news_info.php?SerialNo=46170.

[i] http://www.funscreen.com.tw/feature.asp?FE_NO=145.

[j] https://www.kfda.be/en/archive/detail/the-monk-from-tang-dynasty-2.

[k] http://www.funscreen.com.tw/headline.asp?H_No=333.

[l] https://aichitriennale2010-2019.jp/2010/en/artists/contemporary-arts/tsai-ming-liang.html.

[m] https://montue.ntue.edu.tw/straydogs/; Lin and Tsai 2016a.

[n] https://montue.ntue.edu.tw/nonosleep/.

[o] https://www.kfda.be/en/archive/detail/walker; https://www.kfda.be/en/archive/detail/the-monk-from-tang-dynasty-2.

[p] https://screenanarchy.com/2014/05/melons-love-and-emptiness-tsai-ming-liang-retrospective-in-vienna.html.

ventured beyond the realm of cinema but also sought to expand the very notion of cinema.

Cinema Expanded

Expanded cinema, a term first used in the mid-1960s, was aimed at breaking down the barrier between artist and audience and at challenging "existing notions of cinema as a commercialised regime of passive consumption and entertainment" (Rees 2011, 12, 13). While practitioners of expanded cinema in those days were not filmmakers in the conventional sense, what they discovered when they

Figure 3.1 Entrance level of hotel room designed by Tsai
Photo by author

took up the technology of cinema was that it was "comparatively easy to make different kinds of films, but much more difficult to change the way in which films were seen" (Uroskie 2014, 12). They soon realized it was "no longer sufficient to change the form of cinema"; rather, "one needed to change the total situation within which the moving image was exhibited and seen as well as the context within which it was understood" (Uroskie 2014, 12). Thus, "beyond the confines of the single screen and the black box" (Rees 2011, 19), expanded cinema sought to, precisely, expand the notion of cinema—from single to multiple screens; from

Figure 3.2 Mezzanine level of hotel room with Tsai's screenplays and related items displayed for sale
Photo by author

scheduled to looped projection; from passive consumption to active interaction; from eventful narrative to nothing much happening. In the process, it also relocated cinema's site of exhibition to the white cube of "the gallery," a term that encompasses both the public museum and the private gallery (Rees 2011, 19). If we were to follow Andrew V. Uroskie's call to take seriously "the metaphor of spatial dislocation that lies at the heart of the term 'expanded cinema'" (2014, 12), then, as Chris Dercon (2002) argues, "the question posed by the famous film theoretician André Bazin, *'Qu'est-ce que le cinéma?'* (what is cinema?) now seems less relevant than the question *'Où est le cinema?'* (where is cinema?)."

Otherwise called moving image art, expanded cinema's gesture was to "recontextualise cinema" (Newman 2009, 88). Institutional boundaries and spectatorial practices, however, can be tenacious and resistant to change. Between the movie theater and the gallery, the former, being the more industrialized, mechanized, and commercialized, is probably less versatile and thus less responsive to the demands of expanded cinema, which were voiced mainly by those in the art world. Indeed, since the 1990s, the idea of moving-image installation has "become the norm rather than the exception within contemporary art galleries and museums" (Uroskie 2014, 5) to the extent that a "cinematization of the gallery" can be discerned (Sing 2014, 101). Indeed, the boundary between the two institutions—and that among the different forms of cinema, expanded or not, that could be housed within them—remains arbitrary but porous. Tsai's 2018 work, *Your Face* (*Nide lian*), which won the Best Documentary at the 2019 Golden Horse Awards, yet described elsewhere as an "experimental gallery film," had its world premiere not in a gallery but at the Venice film festival as an out-of-competition entry (Pollacchi 2019, 131), a sign of its defiance of generic and medial categorization.

While Tsai's drift from the black box to the white cube can be situated within the discourse and practice of expanded cinema, rooted in "an emerging consciousness of the paradoxical site specificity of cinematic practice" (Uroskie 2014, 11–12), in the context of Taiwan cinema, Tsai's awareness of—and dissatisfaction with—the institutional conditions structuring his cinematic practice can be pinpointed exactly at the site of the movie theater, increasingly dominated by Hollywood fare after the Taiwan government relaxed its quota for domestic release of foreign films in the mid-1980s (Lu 1998, 322).[13] On his first solo exhibition, *Stray Dogs at the Museum*, Tsai said: "In fact, in the beginning, I did not imagine what it would be like to bring *Stray Dogs* to a museum. I only knew that I don't want to be restrained by box office and theater schedule anymore, neither do I want to worry about bad box office that would make my movie excluded from theater screening" (Fan 2014). Despite his disavowal of any links between his filmmaking and the TNC movement, Tsai's sentiments about the institutions of the Taiwan film industry echo those expressed in the "Taiwan Cinema Manifesto," penned by TNC pioneers in 1987.[14] In this sense, Tsai can be said to be a true heir of the TNC movement, devoted to the notion of cinema as art and bemoaning the entertainment- and market-driven tendencies of the domestic film industry.[15]

Even though Tsai did not initially intend to have the theatrical release for *Stray Dogs* in Taiwan, he relented to scheduling 50 screenings after requests by fans following the film's winning the Venice prize as well as of the Best Director award for him and the Best Actor award for Lee Kang-sheng at the Golden Horse Awards (josephine 2014). More significantly, his decision to incorporate the full screening of *Stray Dogs* in his solo exhibition resonates with the "*situational perspective*" within expanded cinema practices, which shifts the focus from the "specificity of a work's *medium* toward a newfound importance of thinking about the specificity of a work's *site*" (Uroskie 2014, 6, emphasis in original). That is to say, whereas TNC pioneers called on, in the aforementioned manifesto, governmental organizations, the mass media, and film critics to bring about the changes they wished for (Zhan 1988, 116–117) and whilst their practices remained tied to the medium of film, Tsai took matters into his own hands and voted, quite literally, with his feet by walking out of the movie theater and into the museum, upstaging the institution of the film industry by relocating the site for his film's exhibition and by situating the cinematic image within a larger intermedial environment.[16] While I had not been able to visit Tsai's intermedial work staged in museums outside of Taiwan to assess its extent of soft-power appeal, my following discussion of his solo exhibitions held in Taiwan nonetheless raises general questions concerning Tsai's drift from the black box to the white cube, an institutional relocation that reformulates the affective relationship between cinema (now expanded) and its audience.

Museum as Affective Experience

In her book *The Museum as a Cinematic Space*, Elisa Mandelli notes the centrality of the notion of "experience" in contemporary museology and defines the term as entailing "an intense, multi-sensory, affective, and often interactive involvement" (2019, 77). In a chapter entitled "From the Museum Experience to the Museum as an Experience," she draws on Tom Gunning's notion of the cinema of attraction to argue that the use of films and moving images as museographic tools "engage visitors on an emotional and embodied level, stimulating visceral and sensory reactions" (2019, 80). Tsai's first solo exhibition, held at the Museum of National Taiwan University of Education from August to November 2014, went way beyond the use of cinematic images in his reimagination of an affective experience for the museum audience. In the notes he wrote for the exhibition catalogue, Tsai disclosed how the museum altered its practices to fulfill his wishes, from extending the museum's closing time from six to ten in the evening and adding late-night talks that would end at midnight, to organizing sleepover sessions in tents that saw the museum open for 36-hours nonstop over the weekend for three consecutive weeks (Tsai 2016, 96–102). While these initiatives were driven by the less-than-satisfactory audience figures when the exhibition opened, they had had the unwitting effect of generating new modus operandi for the museum as well as for Tsai.

What has been expanded in Tsai's staging of *Stray Dogs* in this museum, then, goes beyond the medium of film and its mode of spectatorship or the spatial dislocation of the movie theater. Rather, Tsai's exhibition advances new conceptions about what a museum might achieve in terms of a wider agenda of arts education, how the public could use the space of a museum, what events might be held in conjunction with an exhibition, and what and who a cultural figure like Tsai could mobilize to turn the notion of intermediality into almost a kind of carnival. The installation of the exhibition itself—with both scheduled and looped screenings of the complete version of, as well as excerpts from, *Stray Dogs* over three floors of the museum's space, the incorporation of fallen branches and leaves salvaged near Tsai's residence from a recent typhoon—might be fairly standard practice. The recruitment of fine arts students to paint 150 cabbage-patterned cushions a week before the exhibition's opening, the late-night storytelling and singing sessions by Tsai, the invitation of musicians to perform alongside him, and the family-friendly atmosphere of camping overnight at the museum's premises (both indoors and outdoors) combine to mark Tsai's intermedial practice as a complex and multifaceted operation; at the same time, it is a simple return to the folk ritual of street theater so common during the seventh month of the lunar calendar in Southeast Asia (where Tsai grew up) when the ghosts are believed to be released from hell and need to be appeased with the offering of food and burning of incense whilst being kept at a distance through boisterous operatic performances.[17]

Here we witness not only a continuation from his filmmaking days, both of Tsai's modus operandi (such as selling tickets in public) and of a "camp" (*song* in the Taiwanese dialect of Hoklo, *su* in Mandarin) aesthetic (Yeh and Davis 2005, 218–219) that mixes highbrow art cinema with folk rituals and practices, but also a re-signification of the cultural meaning of a museum even as Tsai's own entry into this space has transformed the symbolic value of his cinematic work. In her book *Exhibiting Cinema in Contemporary Art*, Erika Balsom notes how cinema has had to grapple with its changing cultural status "as it both persists and even expands its reach as mass spectacle but simultaneously metamorphoses into an object worthy of the protection of the sanctified spaces of the museum and the gallery" (2013, 17). For Balsom, "The presence of film in the museum and the gallery prompts important questions about the contemporary status of cinema as a cultural institution and a mass medium" (2013, 17). Tsai's carnivalesque staging of his cinematic and intermedial work in the museum, however, raises a different set of questions about the contemporary status of the *museum* as a cultural institution and a mass medium as public space. By introducing elements of *song*—described as "gaudy, vulgar, tawdry, saucy, loose, ersatz, smelling of the street if not the gutter" (Yeh and Davis 2005, 234)—such as playing songs from CDs and singing Mandarin pop songs dating from the mid-twentieth century that have made frequent appearances in his films, Tsai has effectively, in Sing Song-yong's reading, turned the museum into "something quotidian and common," "a karaoke, or more precisely, a site for community gathering" (Sing 2016, 188).

If Tsai's programming of storytelling, song sessions, overnight camping, and so on had combined to provide a multisensory, embodied, and affective experience for the museum audience, I would argue that this affectivity had also been achieved through Tsai's own cinematic images installed at the exhibition. To be more exact, Tsai's medial turn allows him to extend the duration of his famed long takes thanks to the adoption of digital technology. As mentioned, Tsai had resisted using the digital camera for his feature-length filmmaking until *Stray*

Dogs, though he had earlier shot shorter pieces digitally. Embedding his cinematic work in an intermedial exhibition in a museum necessitates the use of digital projection, particularly for screening clips in a loop. If Tsai's cinematic oeuvre has been known for narratives in which nothing much happens (Lim 2014a, 13–22), the popular use of the loop in moving-image art in the gallery "opens up the possibility of transforming [cinema's] normally linear narrative trajectory" (Newman 2009, 90) to an even greater extent. Indeed, precisely because, in moving-image art, "the temporality of cinema is not constrained by the habits of narrative," narrative becomes "no more than one option within a range of temporal conceptions" (Le Grice 2011, 170). That is to say, relocating cinema in the gallery frees the medium of film from the tyranny of linear narrative so beholden to mainstream cinema so that a new—and perhaps more critical as much as affective—relationship between the spectator and the image can be formed.

The relationship between the spectator and the image has become the focus of much scholarship within film and media studies in recent decades because of the advent of digital technology that drastically changes the modes of production, distribution, exhibition, consumption, and reception of audiovisual products, with Tsai's feature-length films, in particular *Goodbye, Dragon Inn* (*Busan*, 2003), having contributed to a wider discourse on the death of cinema (Lim 2014a, 65–76). However, with regards to Tsai's medial-cum-digital turn, my concern here is not about how digitality impacts the question of the ontology of the film image or the convergence of media forms and the process of remediation through digital means.[18] Rather, Tsai's digital turn affords an opportunity to expand my previous examination of his feature films as a cinema of slowness (Lim 2014a) to a new exploration into the extension of temporal duration in his intermedial work and the extent to which this reformulates the relationship between the spectator and the image, complicated, in this instance, also by the spatial relocation of the moving image to the site of the museum. Using the Walker series (in particular, "Journey to the West") as an example, I examine the ways in which the relationship between the spectator (both on-screen and off-screen) and the image might be changed on an affective level through the staging of the spectacle of walking slowly in the city. This spectacle, I argue, is multiply registered on the foreignness of the spectacle (it's set in Marseille) and on the extended duration afforded by digital technology; it also creates affective situations that demonstrate the soft power of Taiwan cinema (here represented by Tsai's filmmaking) in transforming the dynamics of the everyday practice of walking.

The "Slow Walk, Long March" Series

Among the new endeavors that Tsai embarked upon in the twenty-first century, the Walker series deserves special attention as one that has the most sustained thematic concern as well as the most varied intermedial manifestations. The inspiration for this series betrays Tsai's status as a multimedia artist as it originated from a theater production directed by Tsai in 2011 for the National Theater in Taipei. Entitled *Only You* (*Zhiyou ni*), the production was made up of three "monodrama" performed by Tsai's regular actors (Yang Kuei-mei and Lu Yi-ching besides Lee) and marked Tsai's return to theater after a 27-year break. In an interview Tsai said he was profoundly touched by Lee's extremely slow walking for 30 minutes over a short distance on stage, with no plot, sound, dialogue, or action (Vagenas 2013). Tsai decided to isolate this walking process and develop it into a series of short films, designing a scarlet robe for Lee's reincarnation as Xuanzang. This characterization, in turn, became the source of a new theater production entitled *The Monk from Tang Dynasty* (*Xuanzang*), which premiered at the Taipei Arts Festival in August 2014, thus bringing the Walker series full circle to its theatrical beginning.

The Walker series can be seen as an exercise in performing slow walking as a spectacle, especially in the installments set in real places where Lee's appearance becomes an attraction to the public eye. The series begins with "No Form," a 20-minute short film set in and around a Taipei street market and in an all-white space; the second, "Walker," is 25 minutes and set in various locations across Hong Kong. In the third, "Diamond Sutra" (*Jingangjing*), another 20-minute short, Lee walks slowly past a steaming rice cooker encased in a constructed wall; the fourth, also 20 minutes and entitled "Sleepwalk" (*Mengyou*), features Lee moving among the architectural models of Taiwan's 2012 entry in the Architecture Biennale in Venice. Two longer pieces followed. The 30-minute "Walking on Water" sends Lee wandering in the neighborhood in Kuching, East Malaysia, where Tsai spent his formative years. The 56-minute "Journey to the West" references Wu Cheng'en's Ming novel that fictionalized Xuanzang's pilgrimage and sees Lee's character making the journey to the West, this time Marseille, where he is mimetically followed, in equally slow motion, by the French actor Denis Lavant. In 2015, Tsai produced the seventh installment of the series, "No No Sleep" (34-minutes long), in which Lee spends less time walking in a wintry Tokyo and more time soaking and sleeping in a sauna. The eighth, "Sand" (*Sha*, the longest so far at 79 minutes), was made in conjunction with the opening, in April 2018, of the Zhuangwei Dune Visitor Center in Yilan in northeast Taiwan, where the entire Walker series was exhibited. The Visitor Center, designed by renowned architect Huang Sheng-yuan, does not contain neat exhibition spaces in the form of white cubes; rather, it uses gray, fair-faced concrete slabs (to echo the black sand dunes from the area) to build curved walls onto which Tsai's short films are projected in rooms and linking spaces, a selection of which can be seen in Figures 3.3 and 3.4.[19]

Figure 3.3 Not a white cube: Lee Kang-sheng as Xuanzang in Tsai's Walker series, projected onto a curved wall of a corridor in the Visitor Center
Photo by author

Figure 3.4 Tsai's "No No Sleep" projected in a room installed with sand and a shallow pool of water
Photo by author

A regular winner at European film festivals for his feature films, Tsai's soft-power appeal extends to securing funding sources and exhibition sites for his new venture into expanded cinema. The first three and the sixth installments of the Walker series were shown in European festivals, namely "No Form" at Marseille, "The Walker" at Cannes, "Diamond Sutra" at Venice, and "Journey to the West" at Berlin. In his plenary speech delivered at the annual meeting of the Consortium of Humanities Centers and Institutes held at the Chinese University of Hong Kong in June 2014, Tsai mentioned that the International Film Festival Marseille (FID) struck a deal to sponsor his production of "Journey to the West" in exchange for showcasing "No Form" in its 2012 festival.[20] Moreover, invitations have come from film festivals as well as art and other festivals, providing multiple platforms on which Tsai's intermedial works could be displayed. The third and fourth films in the Walker series, made under the auspices of Taiwan's Ministry of Culture and the National Taiwan Museum of Fine Arts respectively, were included as part of the Taiwan pavilion in the 2012 International Architecture Exhibition at Venice. In fact, European interest in Tsai's multimedia work seems to have gathered pace since Tsai announced his supposed retirement in 2013. In Spring 2014 alone, Tsai was honored with an achievement award at the 16th Festival du Film Asiatique de Deauville in Normandy; a three-week retrospective of all his film and television work at the Cinémathèque Française in Paris; a retrospective of his films, an installation of the Walker series, and a theater production of *The Monk from Tang Dynasty* at the Kunsten Festival of Arts in Brussels; and a similar program subsequently at the Wiener Festwochen in Vienna ("Europe Celebrates Tsai" 2014). In the rest of this chapter, I focus on a 15-minute long take in "Journey to the West" to argue that the Walker series, on the one hand, marks Tsai's medial turn through the use of digital filmmaking that affords even more extended duration and, on the other hand, evinces Taiwan cinema's affectivity through the figure of Xuanzang's journey to Marseille.

"Journey to the West": The Power of Walking Slowly

The Walker series can be regarded as a form of late cinema in Tsai's career as its production period coincided with Tsai's decision to retire from feature-length filmmaking, although it also paradoxically returns to the very beginning of the medium in its resemblance to the genre of actuality film, documenting the flows of everyday life in the city where the human objects recorded on-screen were often also spectators of the spectacle of the filming process itself. I argue that, through this series, Tsai demonstrates the power of walking slowly by reformulating the praxis of walking in the city as a means for questioning the speed of everyday life via the politics of temporality. The main distinction between Tsai's Walker series and film history's early cinema, however, lays in the object of spectacles staged, in Tsai's case a slow-moving corporeal being. If Eadward Muybridge and Etienne-Jules Marey had had to find ways to capture movement because it was too quick for the naked eye, Tsai reconstitutes the relationship between movement and temporality by rendering movement visible through physical slow motion. Whereas at the turn of the twentieth century the cinema itself was an attraction and what audiences went to see was "machines demonstrated" (Gunning 1986, 66), Tsai shifts the dimension of temporality from the technical properties of the film medium to the technology of the human body. That is to say, temporality in the Walker series is not only manifested by the ability of the cinematic apparatus to capture duration (as in early cinema, and now extended thanks to digital technology) but also embodied in the capacity of the human body to perform slowness.

By displaying the power of slow walking as a spectacle in the cityscapes, the Walker series foregrounds corporeality rather than technology as the vehicle for slowness in order to open up a rethinking of the relationship between visuality and mediality as well as the politics of temporality. The Walker series asks what is a socially acceptable temporality—specifically, the speed of walking in the city— and what kinds of effect and affect are produced by what Brian Morris calls "differentiated practices of walking" (2004, 676). In the topography of walking in the city, spatiality is typically privileged over temporality.[21] Walking in the city has also become a prominent trope in cinema since the postwar era, especially in European neorealist and modernist films. As James Tweedie (2013) observes in a chapter entitled "Walking in the City" in his book The Age of New Waves: Art Cinema and the Staging of Globalization, the heroes and heroines in early French new wave films "often have nothing more to do than walk through the city for minutes at a time" (2013, 86). Tweedie elaborates on how the corporeality of the human body highlights the temporal aspect of this practice of everyday life and sets the pace for the film medium itself:

> The city is experienced through the most deliberate of vehicles, the human body; the lugubrious pace of the pedestrian, rather than the racing automobile or careering train, momentarily set the tempo for cinema. . . . This figure in motion also becomes a support for the eyes and ears that absorb and process a welter of information present in the streets, architecture, and crowds. Like a camera traveling carefully through the city, the body serves as a device for recording the goings-on throughout town. The city is imagined as an extension of the body in motion and the body as an extension of cinema. And neither the city nor the characters appear to be going anywhere fast. (Tweedie 2013, 90)

In the Walker series, Tsai literally reduces the distance traversed in the cityscapes via Lee Kang-sheng's slow-motion walking to the extent that temporality dislodges spatiality and the tempo of cinema comes almost to a standstill. In particular, the longest take in "Journey to the West" provides an intriguing instance for scrutinizing the effect and affect of staging slow walking as a spectacle in everyday cityscapes. In a 56-minute film that contains only 14 shots, its longest take kicks in at around a third into the film and lasts almost 15 minutes. It is set at the entrance/exit of a staircase that is presumably linked to a subway in Marseille. The camera is placed below the third flight of steps from the top so that we see, as a low-angle shot, two flights of staircases (14 steps each) in the foreground and the middle ground, whereas the entrance/exit is bathed in bright sunlight in the background with another flight of seven steps or so leading to the ground level. Metal railings run along both walls and down the middle of the stairway. At the start of the shot, Lee is situated at the top right-hand corner, practically occupying the right side of the stairway over the duration of the shot, an encumbrance to other pedestrians. He descends close to the camera by the end of the shot (averaging around two steps per minute), during which time 100 people (43 going up, 57 down) and a dog pass through the stairway. Shot in natural light, the static camera tilts down gradually to accommodate Lee's descend, resulting in the shot becoming less bright over time. The long take begins with the square-shaped entrance/exit at the top of the frame and ends with its complete disappearance from the shot, Lee's figure shrouded in darkness in the final seconds.

Lee's rhythmicity becomes a sight of wonder at a site where the rite of passage tends toward speed rather than slowness;[22] Lee's figure as a Buddhist monk dressed in a rather elaborately layered costume also becomes, given its foreignness, a sign of wonder, more so in Marseille than in the other Asian locations in the Walker series. The most immediate aspect of this spectacle perhaps resides in Lee's appearance, a visual register of unusualness, an out-of-character character in the cityscape. Yet, I would suggest that Lee's spectacularity is even more pronounced in his performance of a mode of walking whose temporality is at variance with that of the city. Any initial attraction owing to Lee's appearance would very swiftly be turned into wonderment at the slowness of his movement, slowness so imperceptible it almost grinds to a halt. As Henri Lefebvre and Catherine Régulier note, "We are only conscious of most of our rhythms when we begin to suffer from some irregularity" (2004, 77). In "Journey to the West," this irregularity is embodied in the rhythm of Lee's walking and the disproportionate amount of time (almost 15 minutes) he took to descend the flights of steps, compared to that of most pedestrians who got up the steps in around 20 seconds and traveled downward in even less time.

For Tsai, a Buddhist who claims that his artistic form "possesses a spiritual component" and that the Walker series is "an actualisation" of Xuanzang's pilgrimage, Lee's slow walking "has a direction, but not a precise goal. His destination is an indefinite place he may never reach" (Vagenas 2013). Tsai's ethos echoes performance practices in Taiwan and Japan that draw on Buddhist notions of temporality, most notably *butoh*, a metamorphic form of dance founded in Japan in 1959 (Fraleigh 2010, 1).[23] According to one of its founders, Hijikata Tatsumi, *butoh* cultivates movements of transformation and healing in "the body that becomes" (Fraleigh 2010, 3). Hijikata creates his work through what he calls *butoh-fu* (*fu* meaning "chronicle"), "images in states of becoming and only seldom in states of arrival," with the primary means of *butoh* training involving "the streaming or morphing of images ever in the process of change" (Fraleigh 2010, 43). In a similar spirit, Tsai asserts that he is "not a filmmaker who tells stories" but one "who creates images." More important, he insists that "to be able to appreciate details like the transformation of the light, or the particularity of a sound, we need time" (Vagenas 2013). In "Journey to the West," the most spectacular images during the 15-minute-long take are the moments when Lee's figure is set against the bright sunlight behind him, casting a strong silhouette of electrifying glow, as we can see in Figure 3.5, that has been described in a review as "heavenly" (Fujishima 2014). Like *butoh-fu*, Tsai's long take chronicles infinitesimally small moments of constantly changing light and sound, a Buddhist temporality of slowness during which a body, as in *butoh*, not only becomes but is also "reduced to nothingness" (Fraleigh 2010, 46).

Figure 3.5 The power of slow walking: Lee's character of Xuanzang bathed in light in an entrance/exit to an underpass in Tsai's "Journey to the West"

Copyright House on Fire, Neon Productions, Résurgences, and Homegreen Films, in association with Arte France La Lucarne, 2014

A Sign Taken for Wonder: Buddhist Monk Walking

The notion of nothingness is crucial for an understanding of how narratives and events might be constituted differently between film and expanded cinema. If, in narrative terms, "nothing happens" (Margulies 1996) has become a common complaint among bored audience in global art cinema (Lim 2014a, 28–30; Schoonover 2012), its place in expanded cinema is less contentious partly because spectators are not bound to their designated seats in a black box and partly because moving-image art installations are typically of shorter durations and projected in a loop, thus jettisoning the very notion of a beginning and an end expected of conventional narratives. Moreover, as Michael Newman explains:

> Often the event presented in moving image art is the kind of event that might erupt in the viewers' lives, rather than being pre-structured by narrative . . . . Because the events of life are not (usually) subject to narrative closure (the "good death" is no longer a possibility), they maintain their enigmatic character, and, because they are unclosed, retain their capacity to give rise to unexpected turns. Moving image events may be more like this kind of "life event" than narrative events contained in an integrated story with a beginning and end. (2009, 105)

For off-screen audiences who encounter moving-image art in the gallery, the nothingness of the event in these images may remind them of similar moments in their daily lives that are simply moments, snapshots without a beginning and an end. Such a realization is arguably more acute for an on-site audience, particularly those captured on-screen, who are akin to the people who appeared in the actuality films of early cinema—workers leaving a factory in the films of the Lumière brothers, for example—unwitting "actors" as much as spectators of the profilmic event. In Tsai's "Journey to the West," the on-screen pedestrians in Marseille not only witnessed Lee's performance but were also, in many instances, conscious of their own status as actor-audience owing to the presence of the camera, at which some of them were caught glimpsing. However, more than 100 years after the birth of cinema, the passersby-actors-audiences of Marseille would be less astonished by the camera's capacity to "perfectly *represent* the contingent, to provide the pure record of time" (Doane 2002, 22, emphasis in original) and more intrigued by Lee's execution of corporeal slowness in a typically fast-paced cityscape. Yet, because there is no reason to stop in a passageway, only a few passersby paid momentary notice to Lee, with a schoolgirl expressing the most fascination with this spectacular attraction and a woman stopping to take a photograph of Lee on her mobile phone.

Marseille is, of course, one of the most culturally diverse cities in France, with a substantial portion of the population consisting of migrants who have arrived over the centuries, including, in the interwar and postwar periods, those from the (former) French colonies in North Africa and sub-Saharan Africa. This is not the place to provide a full-blown account of the postcolonial condition of Marseille, but suffice it to say that this postcoloniality, with its hallmark traits of hybridity, diversity, and difference, is visibly marked, in "Journey to the West," in the long take discussed earlier as well as in the penultimate shot of the film set on a busy street corner. Hence, if Marseille is itself distinguished by its ethnic difference within the body politic of the modern nation-state of France, this difference is upstaged here by the appearance of a pilgrim from the East in its cityscape, a sign taken for wonder.[24]

This display of displaced difference is most evident in the disproportionate attention paid, in the penultimate shot of the film, to Lee compared to Denis Lavant, who mimics Lee every infinitesimal step of the way, about four to five usual strides behind, as we can see in Figure 3.6. The camera faces a café where about seven men of African origin sit around three tables on the pavement. During the 11-minute static long take, numerous pedestrians enter and exit the frame, most of whom are simply going about their business on a bright summer's day—shopping bags in hand, pushing prams, delivering goods on trolleys, riding a bicycle or a motorcycle—casting no more than a fleeting glance at Lee and barely stopping in their strides. Visually, Lee stands out in terms of a foreignness marked by his identity as a monk and the bright scarlet robe he is wearing; Lavant, despite his status as a French film actor, dissolves into the crowd in his

Figure 3.6 A sign taken for wonder: Lee's character of Xuanzang mimicked by Denis Lavant on a Marseille street in Tsai's "Journey to the West"

Copyright House on Fire, Neon Productions, Résurgences, and Homegreen Films, in association with Arte France La Lucarne, 2014

somewhat ordinary appearance, dressed in blue denim jacket, black T-shirt, black jeans, and black shoes, his hair slightly disheveled.[25] The attention paid to Lee is most salient after he has exited from the frame while Lavant remains in it: Over the duration of almost a minute and a half, the eye line of most of the observers is directed toward the off-screen Lee, with Lavant receiving scant notice throughout.

Tsai's insertion of the figure of a Buddhist monk into the postcolonial space of Marseille could easily be read as a form of self-orientalism that parades Eastern mysticism for the consumption of the West (however hybrid the "Western" space has become in this case). Such a line of reading, however, could be applied to the careers of Tsai and other "third world" artists who have found favorable reception in the Western world, a familiar rhetoric that has already been challenged and nuanced.[26] Instead, we might recast such a postcolonial encounter as an exercise of Taiwan cinema's soft power, embodied here by the figure of a Buddhist monk whose extremely slow walking pace encourages residents of a French city to reflect upon the speed of their everyday lives and contemplate, however vicariously, the notion of nothingness. Precisely because the presence of the camera designates this as a performance, the very act of looking—whether caught on camera or not—is also itself a form of performance, a display of interest, in this case, in difference and otherness, an affective resonance that takes place at the site of cinematic encounter, flown in from Taiwan under the aegis of a French institution thanks to the currency of an auteur whose obsession with slowness crosses medial boundaries and extends with the help of digital technology. Tsai's medial turn, represented by the Walker series, expands the horizon of Taiwan cinema's soft power as much as it raises broader questions about the labor of performance and the ethics of spectatorship that are specific to the extended duration afforded by digital media and platforms.

Medial Attention: The Ethics of Spectatorship

By staging Lee's slow walking in cityscapes and documenting the process digitally, Tsai's Walker series resembles recordings of performance art pieces that emphasize corporeality as a means "to counter the potentially alienating effect of the digital moving image" (Newman 2009, 104).[27] In what can be perceived as a rejection of technological advancements to record or to slow down physical movement in ever-more precision,[28] Tsai favors, instead, the organicity of the human body to perform almost imperceptible movement whilst exploiting digitality's capacity to record the spectacle in extended duration. However, as the usually reticent Lee commented on the weight (five kilograms) of the monk's costume and the need to soak his feet in water after each performance to relieve the pain,

"I am the one who suffers" (Lin S-c 2014). By exhibiting slow motion in corporeal instead of technological form, Tsai foregrounds the labor of performance as a premise for the ethics of spectatorship, demanding as it does a corresponding labor of seeing.

Because Tsai's intermedial works are produced and exhibited in the digital mode, now increasingly consumed in the new space of the white cube and in the non-place of the World Wide Web and digital screens, this new relationship between the spectator and the image—indeed, between visuality and mediality— calls for a reflection on the ethics of spectatorship. In the context of video installation art, it has been argued that "the symptoms of distraction should be recognised as something intrinsic to the genre's structure and conditions of reception," and that a state of distraction should be understood as "an effect or a mode of response" triggered by "habitual patterns of reception that visitors bring with them into the exhibition: above all the habits of watching TV and films and the habits of browsing on the Internet or filtering information from a database" (Peterson 2010, 5). If distraction is a precondition of reception in the non-place of interactive screens—from mobile phones and tablets to laptops and desktops—the release of some installments of the Walker series online is destined to set them on a collision course with impatient netizens. After the French television company Arte made "Journey to the West" available online for seven days following the film's premiere in a Parisian cinema and public screening on TV, a so-called fan from China compressed the 56-minute film into a one-minute version and added a score before uploading it online (Hsu and Raidel 2014, 70). This, in fact, was not the first time that netizens had done this to Tsai's film, as three-minute and six-minute compressed versions of the 25-minute short film "Walker" had also been previously created and uploaded online, causing some netizens to let out a sigh of relief to claim that they had now finally finished watching the film ("Cai Mingliang" 2012).

Has the soft power of Tsai's slow cinema, whose medial turn brings with it new forms of medial attention, met its final nemesis in the speed-obsessed digital world? While there have been initiatives to promote more attentive modes of spectatorship across different art forms,[29] I am less interested in the binary opposition of attention versus distraction vis-à-vis the ethics of spectatorship. Rather, I am more concerned with how this ethics has been redefined because the object viewed has morphed from film to expanded cinema; as a result, notions of narration and event are jettisoned in this new object, the site of spectatorship has relocated to the gallery and digital screens, and the relationship governing the spectator and the image continues to mutate in tandem with both technological and social changes.

The compression of Tsai's slow-walking films into much shorter and faster versions raises the question: "Who is authorized to quantify, substantiate, or measure the labor of reception[?]" (Schoonover 2012, 67). The labor of reception, like Lee's labor of performance, needs to be situated within a broader context of the conditions of production and consumption—and not just of cultural products. The practice of walking in the city, as Lefebvre and Régulier remind us, is "simultaneously the site of, the theatre for, and what is at stake in a conflict between great indestructible rhythms and the processes imposed by the socioeconomic organisation of production, consumption, circulation and habitat" (2004, 73). Film can be understood, in Guy Debord's terms, as "'fully equipped' blocks of time" sold under capitalism, a "complete [temporal] commodity combining a variety of other commodities" (1995, 111). The museum, as the new site of exhibition in Tsai's medial turn, is also "an ideological apparatus facing distinct challenges to attract audiences and compete for consumer dollars at the beginning of the twenty-first century" (Balsom 2013, 19). If the Paris Commune in the nineteenth century pointed to the emergence of "festival-spaces where individuals and social classes could become conscious of themselves for the first time as subjects, or rather, as fully human" (McDonough 2009, 29), Tsai's carnivalesque staging of his intermedial work in the museum invites the audience to participate in a different mode of production and consumption that values and valorizes time for its own sake rather than one that views time as a commodity.

This new ethics of spectatorship has implications beyond the exhibition sites of the gallery and digital screens. In the spirit of the French new wave ideal "to render the gap between the film and urban life as indistinct as possible" (Tweedie 2013, 96), Tsai's Walker series presents what might be called "walking as a method" (Middleton 2011, 100) for reflecting upon the politics of temporality in contemporary life. By staging spectacles of the labor of performance, Tsai reformulates walking in the city as embodied slowness, reorients our attention from spatiality to temporality, and dislodges the centrality of the digital machine in favor of the human body. As a note left by a member of the audience who visited the Stray Dogs exhibition in Taipei stated: "My mind and body are completely still, to observe the most ordinary things around me."[30] Indeed, Tsai's medial turn goes against the grain by turning digital forms of spectatorship typically associated with speed into an ethos of attentive slowness imposed by the human labor of performance.

The power of walking slowly lays partly in the foregrounding of the frailty and fragility—that is to say, the softness—of the human body. Prior to the theater production of The Monk from Tang Dynasty in Brussels, Lee suffered a minor stroke but insisted on performing by lying in the center of an enormous piece of white paper on stage while the artist Kao Jun-honn drew around him (Lin S-c 2014). This softness and perishability of the body stand in contrast with the hardness and presumed durability of digital technology against which Tsai had hitherto resisted. Here a brief comparison between Tsai and Ang Lee is instructive.

Whereas Ang Lee has fully embraced, even pioneered, the use of cutting-edge technology in his filmmaking (see Chapter 4 for more discussion), Tsai has deployed the slowness and softness of the human body to counterpoint the extended durational capacity afforded by digitality. In so doing, he lays bare the decaying process of the human body, which grows old, slows down, gets sick, and will eventually die—not unlike the celluloid film he so loved to use previously. Tsai's medial-cum-digital turn shows us, ultimately, that the power that cinema (conventional or expanded) has to move us, whether in the movie theater or in the museum, remains with images that slow us down and that show us the softness and tactility of the human body, not the employment of some hard and cold technology. Tsai's intermedial works remind us that the Buddhist idea of nothingness discussed earlier in the chapter is where the human body will end, and we should take the time to walk very slowly while we are heading, however unconsciously, toward that final destination.

4

The Industrial Turn

Ang Lee's Trans-Pacific Crossings as Cultural Brokerage

At the 78th Academy Awards ceremony held in 2006, Ang Lee made history by becoming the first Asian director to win the Best Director category, for *Brokeback Mountain* (2005), a feat he would repeat in 2013 with *Life of Pi* (2012). When Lee appeared for the first time on stage at the Oscars in 2001 to receive the statuette for Best Foreign Language Film for *Crouching Tiger, Hidden Dragon* (*Wohu canglong*, 2000; hereafter *CTHD*), he fished out a crumpled piece of paper from which he read the names of people and institutions to thank. In 2006, Lee was visibly more comfortable in his own skin and with the occasion as he spoke without the aid of a written script, cracked an in-joke from the film ("I wish I know how to quit you"), and made an eloquent statement about how the film's gay protagonists taught us about "the greatness of love itself." He ended the speech by thanking his mother and family, "and everybody in Taiwan, Hong Kong, China," before adding a sentence in Mandarin, "*xiexie dajia de guanxin* [thanks everyone for your care and concern]," indicating his awareness of an audience back "home," who might be watching the live broadcast of this event, and, perhaps, also acknowledging where he and his career originated prior to his great leap onto the largest cinematic stage.

Lee's 2006 acceptance speech opens this chapter because it encapsulates the dynamic between soft power and cinema in so many respects. First, soft power never functions in a vacuum; rather, it negotiates ceaselessly with hard power precisely because it typically complements or even, in some cases, substitutes for hard power, making inroads into and occupying a space where a nation's hard-power apparatuses fail to reach. As such, every soft-power arena is also a site of contestation where the machinations of hard power may rear their heads where deemed necessary. Indeed, Lee's seemingly innocuous speech was partly censored on the state television of the People's Republic of China (PRC) for its mention of Taiwan and homosexuality. To borrow the words of Louis Althusser, "*no class can hold State power over a long period without at the same time exercising its hegemony over and in the State Ideological Apparatuses*" (2008, 20, emphasis in original). The very utterance of the word "Taiwan," the birthplace of the director who had just been crowned with glory and honor, had to be instantly silenced on PRC state television because, as an arm of the Althusserian communications

Taiwan Cinema as Soft Power. Song Hwee Lim, Oxford University Press. © Oxford University Press 2022.
DOI: 10.1093/oso/9780197503379.003.0005

ideological state apparatus, the latter functions predominantly by ideology but secondarily by repression, using the force of censorship if need be (Althusser 2008, 19). If the Althusserian repressive state apparatuses are akin to Joseph Nye's notion of hard power (i.e., military and economy prowess), the corresponding ideological state apparatuses are instruments of soft power that operate in realms such as cinema and television to fight cultural battles on behalf of the state.

Second, so-called universal values are crucial to the effective maneuvering of soft power because of "the relationships of attraction and duty" they generate and because "narrow values and parochial cultures are less likely to produce soft power" (Nye 2004, 11). Whereas the American Psychiatric Association only removed homosexuality from its official Diagnostic and Statistical Manual of Mental Disorders list in 1973, and while homosexuality was still deeply stigmatized during the heights of the HIV/AIDS crisis in the 1980s, today the rights of lesbians, gays, bisexuals, transgender, queer, and intersex persons (LGBTQI+) are increasingly regarded as a form of human rights, with same-sex marriage becoming legal across the United States in 2015—and in Taiwan in 2019. The attraction of such a form of human rights and the duty to uphold it is, however, far from universal, judging from the reaction of the Chinese authorities to Lee's speech. On this occasion, Taiwan and homosexuality were similarly regarded as renegade, the former for its defiant political status and the latter for its deviant sexuality. In fact, it was not just Lee's speech that had been partly censored; the film for which he won the award was also banned in the PRC for its homosexual theme. Even though the Chinese Psychiatric Association removed homosexuality from its list of psychiatric disorders in 2001, official attitude toward the depiction of homosexuality in cinema remains largely disapproving. Ang Lee's career, therefore, demonstrates that embracing liberal values opens doors to the Euro-American world (and beyond), having won a Golden Bear at the Berlin film festival as early as 1993 for his second feature-length film, the gay-themed *The Wedding Banquet* (*Xiyan*, 1993); *Brokeback Mountain* also captured the Golden Lion at Venice in 2005 before landing Lee the Best Director award at the Oscars.

Third, whereas Nye's model of hard and soft powers is predicated upon the nation-state as a unit of analysis, it is the very tension between nation and state that surfaces in the geopolitical context of China-Taiwan relations in this and other instances. Taiwan, isolated in international politics and excluded from membership in the United Nations, is nonetheless eligible to participate in the Academy Awards' Foreign Language Film category. Lee's award must have been a hard pill to swallow for the PRC authorities and nationalistic citizenry alike since the giant state that is China had then yet (and still has yet) to produce a film that would win a major award at the Oscars, the largest stage for the cinematic arts in terms of global media attention and coverage. At the time of Lee's 2006 award, China had only managed two nominations in the Best Foreign Language Film category for Zhang Yimou's *Judou* (1990) and *Hero* (*Yingxiong*, 2002).[1] By contrast, Taiwan edged ahead with three nominations in the same category—incidentally, all for films directed by Ang Lee—namely *The Wedding Banquet*, *Eat Drink Man Woman* (*Yinshi nannü*, 1994), and *CTHD*, the last of which singlehandedly garnered nine other nominations (including Best Picture and Best Director) and won in four categories. The PRC may continue to claim Taiwan as an inseparable part of its territory despite the two are represented as discrete entities or even polities on several platforms, but, on this cinematic stage, Taiwan clearly has the upper hand.

Fourth, this incongruity between nation and state, culture and politics, and soft and hard powers can be seemingly papered over by the fluidity of Chineseness as both a national (read ethnic) and transnational marker, indicated by Lee's final sentence in Mandarin and his multiple references to the "home" audience. This fluidity had allowed PRC authorities to simultaneously deny Taiwan's statist existence and co-opt Ang Lee via the cultural discourse of Chineseness: Lee's 2006 success was proclaimed in *China Daily* (a PRC official press outlet) as "the pride of Chinese people all over the world" ("China Praises Lee" 2006). The title of "the glory of the Chinese people" (*huaren zhi guang*) has been bestowed upon Lee on many occasions since Lee's triumph with *CTHD* at the Oscars in 2001. However, the appellation itself, particularly in its Chinese-language renditions, is open to both transnational appropriation and national dispute. In Taiwan, Lee's 2006 award was seized by political parties of both stripes for their own ends, with President Chen Shui-bian of the pro-independence Democratic Progressive Party (DPP) hailing Lee as "the glory of the Taiwanese people" (*Taiwanren zhi guang*), whereas Lien Chan of the pro-unification Nationalist Party (Kuomintang, or KMT) championed Lee instead as "the glory of the Chinese people" (*Zhongguoren zhi guang*) ("Lian Zhan" 2006). Here the fluid but contested qualification of Chineseness is reconfigured as political posturing so that Lien's statement was issued not only to signal an identification with (if not sovereignty over, in political rhetoric at least) a piece of land (*Zhongguo/*China) located across the Taiwan Strait but also as a "corrective" ("Lian Zhan" 2006) to Chen's deliberate absence from the discourse of Chineseness (whether *Zhongguoren* or *huaren*) in order to *not* demarcate the Taiwanese as a separate category in both ethnic and political terms. A soft-power resource mobilized for hard power use, the discourse of Chineseness can equally serve to divide within Taiwan and to unite across the Taiwan Strait depending on one's political color.

Finally, the episode demonstrates that soft power can be extended from its originating realm to other arenas whereby stakeholders in the latter could capitalize on the appeal of the former to forward their own agendas. In fact, it is not just politicians who have been eager to prove that Lee's achievements extend beyond the film world. Lee's meteoric rise from an unknown director from a little-known island to a major player in Hollywood is an embodiment of the American dream—a motivational story with general application as much as a role model of hard work and enterprising spirit worthy of business guides and self-help books. In Taiwan, Lee became the subject of a cover story on "success" in an issue of *Business Weekly* published in March 2013, which featured a photograph of Lee kissing the Oscar statuette for the Best Director award for *Life of Pi*;[2] he also graced the cover of another financial magazine, *CommonWealth*, in September 2016 under the title "Ang Lee Surpassing Ang Lee" to coincide with the promotion of his then new film, *Billy Lynn's Long Halftime Walk* (2016; hereafter *Billy Lynn*). In the United States, Lee was included (see Mills 2013) in a 16-volume book series entitled "Asian Americans of Achievement," featured alongside, among others, the architect I. M. Pei, cellist Yo Yo Ma, novelists Amy Tan and Maxine Hong Kingston, and Yahoo founder Jerry Yang.[3] In China, a television documentary series, *The World Is Not Enough* (*Huaren zongheng tianxia*, meaning "Chinese sweep through the world"), showcases the success stories of 108 luminaries ranging from Nobel laureate Franklin Yang Chen-Ning and business magnate Li Ka-shing to movie tycoon Run Run Shaw—and Ang Lee (see Zhang 2005 for an accompanying book on Lee). Within academia, interest in Lee similarly extends beyond the purely cinematic: an edited book explores both the "Eastern" and "Western" philosophies in his films, encompassing aspects as varied as Daoism and Confucianism to Machiavelli and molecules (see Arp, Barkman, and McRae 2013). From aspirational migrant to model minority citizen, from entrepreneurship to philosophy, it would appear that the soft power appeal of Lee and his cinema knows no bounds.

The Soft Power of Ang Lee's Cinema

This chapter aims to illustrate the soft-power appeal of Lee's cinema by tracing the industrial turns his career has taken at various stages. A director who defies categorization, Lee's flexibility in filmmaking has enabled him to cross geographical, national, linguistic, generic, cultural, and industrial borders. Moreover, his trajectory at the Academy Awards problematizes the three keywords (namely, authorship, transnationality, historiography) in the subtitle of this book, which I shall discuss in this section before moving on to account for Lee's industrial turns. As stated in the Introduction of this book, authorship is the most effective weapon in Taiwan New Cinema's (hereafter TNC) arsenal of soft power. Among the quartet of key TNC directors (Hou Hsiao-hsien, Edward Yang, Tsai Ming-liang, and Lee) that has put Taiwan cinema on the world map by winning awards at international film festivals, Lee distinguishes himself as the only one to have won at both the Oscars and European film festivals (see Table I.1 in the Introduction for a list of awards). If the top-three European festivals (Berlin, Cannes, and Venice) have an art house bent and international scope where the films of Hou, Yang, and Tsai would find a natural home, Lee's frequent participation beyond the Foreign Language Film category at the Oscars, a largely commercial and American affair, has been facilitated by his turn to English-language filmmaking since the mid-1990s.[4] More important, Lee's success in both arenas exemplifies a paradox inherent in classical auteur theory that, on the one hand, advocated that directors should have a free rein to "write their dialogue" and to "invent the stories they direct" (Truffaut 2008, 16) and, on the other hand, admires American cinema, "where the restrictions of production are heavier than anywhere else" (Bazin 2008, 27).[5] In this light, it is noteworthy that Lee had claimed that he did not like writing scripts and that he only contributed to the screenplays of his first three feature-length films because nobody was giving scripts to him (Berry 2005, 339). If Hou, Yang, and Tsai are widely perceived as auteurs with unique cinematic visions, Lee is sometimes regarded as "merely one of the screws in the making of the machine" (Shih S-m. 2007, 57), pointing to the paradox in theories of authorship as much as to his brand of soft-power appeal.

The crucial reason behind Lee's success at the Oscars resides in the second keyword: transnationality. Trained in the American idiom of filmmaking at New York University's (NYU) Graduate Film School, Lee was persuaded, in 1985, by an agent at the William Morris Agency to remain in the United States after the agent saw Lee's graduation short film, "Fine Line" (1984), which had won the Best Director and Best Film awards at the NYU film festival (Zhang 2002, 51). While the agent thought Lee had a bright future making films in the United States, Lee would end up spending six years in "development hell" (Zhang 2002, 52) before he received his first break—in Taiwan. Lee's career, however, has been transnational from the very beginning. His first three feature-length films, namely *Pushing Hands* (*Tuishou*, 1991), *The Wedding Banquet*, and *Eat Drink Man Woman*, were all co-productions by Taiwan's state-sponsored Central Motion Picture Corporation (CMPC), the US-registered company Ang Lee's Productions, and another US company (Good Machine).[6] Remarkably, Lee followed these Chinese-language films (the so-called father-knows-best trilogy) with three English-language films of hugely disparate settings, namely a Regency-era period drama (*Sense and Sensibility*, 1995), a film set in suburban America of the 1970s (*The Ice Storm*, 1997), and an American Civil War film (*Ride with the Devil*, 1999), before returning to Chinese-language filmmaking with *CTHD*. Indeed, *Sense and Sensibility*, his first foray into English-language filmmaking, already earned the film a Golden Bear at Berlin in 1996 and Lee nominations in the Best Director category at the Golden Globes and BAFTA (British Academy of Film and Television Arts) awards. Although Lee did not receive any nomination in the Best Director category at the Oscars prior to the new millennium, the transition from Chinese-language to English-language filmmaking and, more important, the shift from collaborating with Taiwan's cottage film industry to working with major Hollywood studios in the 1990s prepared the ground for his later triumph as a full-fledged Hollywood director.[7] This chapter thus foregrounds Lee's trans-Pacific trajectories that have enabled this industrial turn, which, as the case study of *Life of Pi* will show, also returns to Taiwan to engage with soft-power initiatives on the part of the Taiwanese authorities at both local and national levels.

Lee's industrial turn poses a potential problem for film historiography, that is, which film history do he and his films belong? At the time of this writing (end of 2020), Lee has made 14 feature-length films, 5 in Chinese languages (mainly in Mandarin but also featuring some dialogue in Shanghainese and Cantonese) and the rest in English languages (including British English and American English). Unlike Hou who only made the occasional non-Sinophone films (see Chapter 2) and Tsai who has a couple of films containing some dialogue in French, Lee presents more thorny issues for film historiography because he has based his entire career in the United States while mobilizing resources (cast, crew, location, and finance) from East Asia, Europe, and North America. European émigré directors to the United States from earlier eras have become objects of study (Brook 2009; Smedley 2011) and have been included in historiographical accounts of American cinema (Lewis 2007; Lucia, Grundmann, and Simon 2012). It remains to be seen the extent to which more recent East Asian directors such as John Woo and Ang Lee who had spent a big part or the whole of their careers in the United States would be accounted for within American film historiography.[8]

The Industrial Turn

Lee's trans-Pacific crossings trouble notions of authorship, transnationality, and historiography, and these crossings are reflected in the industrial turns that his career has taken, which can be categorized into four stages with overlapping time frames, as follows:[9]

- Early career as TNC director (national cinema, diasporic cinema), 1991–1994
  Pushing Hands (1991), *The Wedding Banquet* (1993), *Eat Drink Man Woman* (1994)
- Industrial turn (1): Venture into Anglo-American independent filmmaking, since 1995 (production budget under US$40 million)
  Sense and Sensibility (1995), *The Ice Storm* (1997), *Ride with the Devil* (1999), *Brokeback Mountain* (2005), *Taking Woodstock* (2009)

- Industrial turn (2): (Re)turn to transnational Chinese cinemas, since 2000 (trans-Pacific co-production)
  Crouching Tiger, Hidden Dragon (2000), *Lust, Caution (Se, jie, 2007)*
- Industrial turn (3): Big-budget movies with technological breakthroughs, since 2003 (production budget typically over US$100 million)[10]
  Hulk (2003), *Life of Pi* (2012), *Billy Lynn's Long Halftime Walk* (2016), *Gemini Man* (2019)

As Table 4.1 indicates, from his debut film's production budget of New Taiwan dollar NT$13.5 million (approximately US$350,000; see Norman 2016, 42), which Lee claimed was not "low budget" but "no budget" (Chou 1991, 20), to the staggering US$138 million for his most recent film *Gemini Man*, a 394-fold increase; from a gross of US$152,322 for *Pushing Hands* to breaking the box-office record for foreign-language films in the US with *CTHD*, which took in over US$128 million in total and opened in over 2,000 screens, grossing over US$4.6 million in that weekend alone; from films produced solely by one independent studio (*Taking Woodstock*) to trans-Pacific collaboration involving eight companies from three regions (*CTHD*)—Lee has been straddling film industries of various countries, scales, modus operandi, and modes of address and making films with drastically different themes, genres, and languages. Lee even managed to clinch two Golden Lion awards for films in different languages (*Brokeback Mountain* in 2005, *Lust, Caution* in 2007)—and with only a year separating them—surely an astonishing achievement for any director in film history.

Out of the films made in Lee's multiple career trajectories, this chapter will focus on *Life of Pi* because it is not merely a trans-Pacific co-production but a simultaneously turn toward (indeed, a return to) Taiwan. Moreover, with *Life of Pi*, Lee used 3D technology for the first time and raked in the highest worldwide box-office intake of his career to date; winning a second Oscar for Best Director for the adaptation of a novel widely regarded as "unfilmable" (Hiscock 2016, 115) also cemented his status as one of Hollywood's most bankable directors in both critical and commercial terms.[11] More important for my purpose here, the production of *Life of Pi* provides a case study of soft-power efforts by Taiwanese local governments (in this case, Taichung) to promote their cities as filming locations in the hope of generating tourism. Bringing Lee's career full circle to its originating point of Taiwan, *Life of Pi* demonstrates how Lee has transformed himself into a cultural broker between Hollywood and Taiwan as well as how cinema collaborates with other industries (in this case, city branding and location tourism) to spread Taiwan's soft power domestically and globally.

Table 4.1 Stages of Ang Lee's career with production budgets and box-office intakes[a]

Film	Production companies	Budget	Box-office: Taiwan/US/ worldwide
(I) Early career as TNC director			
Pushing Hands (1991)	Ang Lee Productions/ Central Motion Picture Corporation (CMPC)	NT$12 million (Zhang 2002, 69)+US$350,000 (Norman 2016, 42)[b]	NT$8,447,580 (Luo 1993, 155)/ US$152,322/ n/a
The Wedding Banquet (1993)	Ang Lee Productions/ CMPC/Good Machine	US$750,000 (Fuller 2016b, ix; Zhang 2002, 117)	NT$4,964,260 (Chong 1995, 266)/[c] US$6,933,459/ US$32 million (Zhang 2002, 117)
Eat Drink Man Woman (1994)	Ang Lee Productions/ CMPC/Good Machine	US$1.5 million (Wei 2005, 109)	NT$50 million (Zhang 2002, 151)/[d] US$7,294,403/ n/a
(II) Industrial Turn (1): **Venture into Anglo-American independent filmmaking**			
Sense and Sensibility (1995)	Columbia Pictures Corporation/Mirage Production	US$16 million (Zhang 2002, 156)[e]	NT$19,475,100 (Wang 1997b, 47)/ US$43,182,776/ US$134,582,776
The Ice Storm (1997)	Fox Searchlight Pictures/ Good Machine/Canal+ Droits Audiovisuels	US$18 million (Zhang 2002, 208)	NT$7,874,990 (Wang 1998, 114)/ US$8,038,061/ n/a
Ride with the Devil (1999)	Universal Pictures/ Good Machine	US$35 million (Zhang 2002, 256)	NT$1,862,340 (Wang 2001b, 124)/ US$635,096/ n/a
Brokeback Mountain (2005)	Focus Features/River Road Entertainment/ Alberta Film Entertainment/Good Machine	US$14 million	NT$50,612,266 (Wang 2007, 235)/ US$83,043,761/ US$178,062,759

Continued

Table 4.1 *Continued*

Film	Production companies	Budget	Box-office: Taiwan/US/ worldwide
Taking Woodstock (2009)	Focus Features	US$30 million	NT$8,481,504 (Wang 2010, 106)/ US$7,460,204/ US$9,975,737
(III) Industrial Shift (2): **(Re)turn to transnational Chinese cinema**			
Crouching Tiger, Hidden Dragon (2000)	Asia Union Film & Entertainment Ltd./ China Film Co-Production Corp./ Columbia Pictures Film Production Asia/EDKO Films/Good Machine International/Sony Pictures Classics/ United China Vision/ Zoom Hunt International Productions Company Ltd.	US$15 million (Zhang 2002, 480)	NT$101,155,665 (Wang 2001c, 132)/ [f] US$128,078,872/ US$213,525,736
Lust, Caution (2007)	Haishang Films/Focus Features/River Road Entertainment/Sil-Metropole Organisation/ Shanghai Film Group Corporation	US$15 million	NT$137,050,890 (Wang 2008, 131)/ US$4,604,982/ US$67,091,915
(IV) Industrial Shift (3): **Big-budget movies with technological breakthroughs**			
Hulk (2003)	Universal Pictures/ Marvel Enterprises/ A Valhalla Motion Pictures/ Good Machine Production	US$137 million	NT$57,464,145 (Wang 2004, 78)/ US$132,177,234/ US$245,360,480
Life of Pi (2012)	Fox 2000 Pictures/Dune Entertainment/ Ingenious Media/ Haishang Films/Big Screen Productions/ Ingenious Film Partners/Netter Productions	US$120 million	NT$229,813,550 (Wang 2014a, 44)/ US$124,987,023/ US$609,016,565
Billy Lynn's Long Halftime Walk (2016)	Bona Film Group/Dune Films/Film4/Marc Platt Productions/Studio 8/ The Ink Factory/ TriStar Pictures/TriStar Productions	US$40 million (Fleming 2016)	NT$72,906,087 (Liang 2017, 38) [g]/ US$1,738,477/ US$30,930,507

Table 4.1 *Continued*

Film	Production companies	Budget	Box-office: Taiwan/US/ worldwide
Gemini Man (2019)	Skydance Media/Jerry Bruckheimer Films/Fosun Group Forever Pictures/ Alibaba Pictures/Orange Corp[h]	US$138 million	US$4,339,267/ US$48,546,70/ US$173,469,516

[a] Information on production companies is drawn from related pages on the Internet Movie Database; those on box-office intakes and production budgets, unless otherwise stated, is drawn from Box Office Mojo. Box-office figures for Taiwan are, in most cases, for Taipei City or the Greater Taipei region only.

[b] Elsewhere, Zhang Jingbei lists a total figure of NT$13.5 million or US$480,000 (2002, 472).

[c] The box-office intake for the whole of Taiwan was over NT$120 million (Zhang 2002, 117).

[d] This figure is actually for the whole of Taiwan even though the source states that it is for Taipei. The context suggests otherwise as the other figure cited for comparison (the box-office intake for *The Wedding Banquet*) is for the whole of Taiwan.

[e] Elsewhere, Zhang Jingbei lists this figure as US$15.5 million (Zhang 2002, 476).

[f] This figure includes the box-office intake for the film's second run in the following year.

[g] It must be qualified that this figure was boosted by the high ticket price (NT$800, compared with the typical NT$250 for a foreign-language film) for the 3D/4K/120fps format screened at a Taipei cinema, and the number of tickets sold in the Greater Taipei region was only 149,150 (Liang 2017, 38). Also noteworthy is that the electronic-ticketing system and information for the whole of Taiwan was made available for the first time in June 2016, and Lee's film, which was released in November 2016, achieved an island-wide intake of NT$108,483,142 (Chen P-c. 2016, 110), with the Greater Taipei region intake constituting around two-thirds of the total.

[h] I thank Timmy Chen for helping me access this information.

Cinema, City Branding, and Location Tourism

If, in the context of nation branding, the process of branding "not only explains nations to the world but also reinterprets national identity in market terms and provides new narratives for domestic consumption" (Jansen 2008, 122), these functions can similarly be served at the city level, evidenced by the popularity of such branding efforts among European and other cities for more than half a century. The historical trend of city branding can be dated to the 1970s with the promotion of the notion of "entrepreneurial city" as a response to the collapse of traditional industries and the adoption of a more businesslike approach to urban governance (Kavaratzis 2004, 59). More recently, the relationship between cities and a "creative class" (Florida 2005) has gained much traction in academia and beyond, with a vibrant cultural life seen as a prerequisite in branding a city to appeal to this creative class (Dinnie 2011a, 4).

With creativity, innovation, and boldness regarded as a "common denominator" in city-branding efforts (Dinnie 2011b, 97), approaches that have become fashionable among urban planners include "personality branding" (such as surrounding a figure like Gaudí for Barcelona), "flagship construction" (the Pompidou model in Paris), and "events branding" (the Edinburgh festival being a prime example) (Kavaratzis 2004, 70). It is noteworthy, though, that many of these personalities, constructions, or events were not originally planned or intended for the purpose of city branding (Kavaratzis 2004, 71); rather, cities have sometimes simply capitalized on historical and available cultural resources and symbols in their soft-power strategies. In this regard, cinema can become an inadvertent or intentional means toward the end of city branding; its images of particular cityscapes serving as promotional materials to attract potential tourists to visit the destinations portrayed.

Cinema can play a crucial role in such city-branding exercises insofar as "all encounters with the city take place through perceptions and images" (Kavaratzis 2004, 66). From falling in love with cities via characters played by Audrey Hepburn and Gregory Peck in *Roman Holiday* (dir. William Wyler, 1953) as well as Meg Ryan and Tom Hanks in *Sleepless in Seattle* (dir. Nora Ephron, 1993), to getting acquainted with the cityscapes of New York and Hong Kong via the films of, respectively, Woody Allen and Wong Kar-wai (Li 2009, 44), cinema is adept at projecting images of cities that inspire affective attachments as much as it is a medium through which to reflect upon a city's identity, in addition to contributing to a city's cultural and economic influence (Chen and Shih 2019, 507).

Among the many reasons why tourists would visit a city, a wish to pay homage to cinema by including shooting locations of films into one's itinerary results in location tourism, which forms part of a wider spectrum of what Sue Beeton calls "film-induced tourism." On the one hand, for Beeton, while economic gain is typically highlighted by governmental and trade reports as "the first (and only) tourism performance indicator," tourism may also lead to the deterioration of communities and the environment, thus carrying with it "the seeds of its own destruction" (2005, 12). On the other hand, if the cinematic images of the place portrayed are seen as "realistic, evocative and desirable," they could increase a sense of belonging among residents to the extent that residents will view any location tourism brought about by the films in a positive light (Beeton, 2005, 14).

Cinema as a soft-power resource and city branding and location tourism as promotional and marketing strategies can, therefore, coalesce at the nexus of cultural policy. In his book on brand nationalism in Japan, Koichi Iwabuchi suggests that, in the attempt to use media cultures as part of a national foreign policy strategy, "the soft power argument has been replaced by a shallower policy discourse on the enhancement of international images" (2015, 15). For Iwabuchi, nation-branding policy discussion should not be taken at its face value

(16). Rather, drawing on Raymond Williams's distinction between "cultural policies proper" and "cultural policies as display," Iwabuchi highlights the former as being concerned with social democratization and the latter as serving national and economic interests (39–40). Critical of the "Cool Japan" policy promoted by various governmental institutions and nongovernmental agents, Iwabuchi argues that Nye's clear separation of economy and culture is "untenable if we are to understand the power structure of market-driven globalization" (32). In what follows, I heed Iwabuchi's call to understand the complicated process of (in my case, city) branding by providing a discussion of policies and their implementation and effects in Taichung City government's attempt at branding via an engagement with the production of *Life of Pi*.

Taiwan's City-Branding and Cinema-Promotion Efforts

In Taiwan, several city and county governments have initiated, in the twenty-first century, financial and other support schemes to attract filmmakers to use their landscapes as locations in the hope of boosting tourism. In 2003, the government of Kaohsiung City, the second-largest city in Taiwan, designated film and television as an industry for development and established, in 2004, a dedicated film commission to promote and support filmmaking activities there; Tsai Ming-liang's *The Wayward Cloud* (*Tianbian yiduo yun*, 2005) became a high-profile beneficiary of the scheme when it was awarded NT$10 million by the city's government after the film, which was shot in Kaohsiung, won a Silver Bear award at the Berlin film festival (Cheng 2010, 72). In 2007, the filmmaking-sponsorship scheme began subsidizing accommodation costs for cast and crew and raised its scope and amount the following year (Hsiang 2010, 68). In 2008, the Taipei City government also launched a similar scheme, a notable sponsored film being Arvin Chen's *Au revoir Taipei* (*Yiye Taibei*, 2010), which boasts Wim Wenders as one of its executive producers (Wen 2011, 22). The result was immediate: in 2009 Taipei welcomed 126 film crews compared to 38 in Kaohsiung (Hsiang 2010, 68). Efforts to promote Taiwanese cities as filming locations were even featured in a documentary made by TRT World, the international news channel of Turkey's state television.[12]

The implementation of city-branding and location-tourism schemes, however, can often be hampered by the "limited knowledge and limited understanding of marketing among people with the task to administer cities" (Kavaratzis 2004, 59). This was clearly the case with the 2008 film *Cape No. 7* (*Haijiao qihao*, dir. Wei Te-sheng), which was filmed at the popular tourist destination of Kenting National Park in southern Taiwan. Before the film's release, the film company's marketing personnel contacted the local authorities in hopes of collaborating on the film's promotion, but the bureaucrats apparently responded by saying that "Kenting's tourism doesn't need cinema's help" and declined the offer (Li 2009, 42). As it turned out, *Cape No. 7* was the top-grossing film in Taiwan that year, leading to a frenzy of touristic interest in the film's shooting locations. The hotel that served as the main site of the film's scenario was fully booked even during the off-peak season (Li 2009, 41), and the phenomenal sale of merchandise owing to the film's product-placement strategy was credited for having kickstarted a closer cooperation between local governments and the film industry (Hsiang 2010, 65).

As the example of *Cape No. 7* demonstrates, location tourism is the most visible effect that cinema can bring to cities whether or not city-branding efforts have been put in place. It is also difficult to ascertain, beyond the inclusion of prominent landmarks during shooting, if a film's tourism effects have been intentional or accidental. *Hear Me* (*Ting shuo*, dir. Cheng Fen-fen, 2009), a film sponsored by the Taipei City government and the preparatory committee of Taipei's Deaflympics, was the top-grossing domestic film in Taiwan in 2009 and performed well at the box office in Hong Kong; many young Hong Kong tourists were apparently attracted by some locations featured in the film and included them into their itinerary, resulting in the film being awarded an "outstanding contribution to marketing Taipei City" prize from the then city mayor (Hsiang 2010, 67). A film buff in Hong Kong even published a book entitled *Film Pilgrimage: Taiwan* (Wong 2017), which lists shooting locations of various Taiwan films for the convenience of tourists.[13] Indeed, pilgrimage tourism to shooting locations, during which scenes from films might be re-enacted (Beeton 2005, 10), is a key component of film-induced tourism. In late 2011, *You Are the Apple of My Eye* (*Naxie nian, women yiqi zhui de nühai*, dir. Giddens Ko, 2011) became the all-time, top-grossing Chinese-language film at the Hong Kong box office, leading to a surge in tourism to the film's shooting locations in New Taipei City. When I visited the small town of Pingxi over the lunar new year period in 2016, many tourists were releasing sky lanterns along the railway track like the romantic leads in the film, and a lot of the conversations I heard both there and on the train journey to the destination were in Cantonese. More than four years after film's release, this shooting location was still drawing in tourists from Hong Kong who were paying homage to the film.

Ang Lee as Cultural Broker

As Taiwan's third-largest city after Taipei and Kaohsiung, Taichung inaugurated, in 2009, a filmmaking support scheme whose mission statement includes, as its aims, the promotion of Taichung City's image. The then Mayor Jason Hu

Chih-chiang also launched another city regeneration project for the defunct Shuinan Airport, whose jurisdiction had been transferred from the military to the Taichung City government in 2007 (Shih H-c. 2007). Hu, who acted as Taiwan's representative in Washington and minister of foreign affairs before being elected mayor of Taichung City in 2001, is perceived as a politician with "an international outlook" who lobbied so hard to have a Guggenheim museum (designed by Zaha Hadid, no less) built in Taichung City that he suffered a stroke during the campaign ("Li An qishilu" 2013). Notwithstanding the city's failure to seal the Guggenheim museum deal,[14] Taichung was named the Intelligent Community of the Year in 2013 by the US-based Intelligent Community Forum ("Greater Taichung" 2013).

In an article on the PRC filmmaker Feng Xiaogang as a cultural broker, Yomi Braester proposes that commercial filmmaking "opens new possibilities" not because it provides "distinct content or cinematic form" but because "the director's entrepreneurial engagement redefines the social forces with which the cinema interacts and determines anew how films ally themselves with other media" (2005, 550). Here I borrow Braester's notion of cultural broker and expand it to examine Ang Lee's engagement with social forces beyond the realm of the mass media to include a local government and its political leader. As it happened, when Lee embarked on the pre-production of *Life of Pi*, he realized that he needed to create a wave tank but, as he said, "there's no way I can do it in LA" (Billington 2012, 108). Having assessed and confirmed the feasibility of Shuinan Airport, which remained unused at the time, Lee decided to bring the cast and crew to Taichung, and more than 80 percent of the pre-production and production of *Life of Pi* ended up taking place in the city (Lee 2012, 15). At the time of scouting Shuinan Airport as a possible shooting location, Lee had already known Jason Hu for over 20 years (Kou 2012), dating to the time when Lee's *The Wedding Banquet* won the Golden Bear in 1993, whose publicity came under the charge of Hu, then director-general of the Government Information Office (GIO) under the central government's Executive Yuan. The long-lasting relationship between Lee and Hu was, therefore, integral to the success of this cultural brokerage.

As noted in the opening of this chapter, many stakeholders from other realms had capitalized on Lee's soft-power appeal after his Oscar-winning feat. In this instance, Lee's film production need was met enthusiastically by Hu's ambition to put Taichung on the world map. Indeed, Lee's choice of Taichung over competing offers from India and Australia as the shooting location for *Life of Pi* (Chung 2013) can be situated against the backdrop of Taichung City government's efforts, as sketched out earlier, to brand the city as a global cultural and tourist destination. Beyond the local city level, the central government's GIO, whose remit covers the overseeing of film production matters, had also reportedly consulted Lee about the best place to build a film studio on the island (Tang

2018). Following the making of *Life of Pi* at Shuinan Airport, there were plans to develop the wave tank facilities into a "Central Taiwan film and television base" in Wufeng (a district in Taichung), whose construction launch received a well-wishing video from Lee ("Zhongshi Wufeng" 2016). It is no surprise, then, that Lee was singled out as the sole representative of the film industry in an article on Taiwan's soft power by a career diplomat published on the website of Taiwan's Ministry of Foreign Affairs (Yeh 2010).

Life of Pi can be regarded as an important episode in Lee's career trajectory and personal journey as it marks his long-awaited return to his birthplace, this being only his second film to be shot on location in Taiwan. On the one hand, while Lee is "anxious" about expressions such as "Ang Lee loves Taiwan" or "Taiwan loves Ang Lee" used by the media (Chen W-c. 2015), his wish to share his Hollywood experience with a younger generation of filmmakers in Taiwan is evident (Tang 2018). On the other hand, Lee is conscious that his role as cultural broker in dealing with stakeholders in Taiwan, particularly government officials, is mainly advisory. Asked about the development of a local filmmaking base during a television interview on episode 236 of News Cloud World in November 2016, Lee said he would share his opinions frankly with government officials who came to him for advice and that he had been doing so for over 20 years, but it was ultimately up to them to pursue the project or otherwise. For Lee, film is an industry that demands governmental support because Taiwan's film market is small compared with the one in China, but he also understands that local and central governments are circumscribed in their efforts to promote the film industry as they are accountable to legislative bodies and to the citizenry (Tang 2018). Cultural brokerage, as a dimension of Lee's soft power, does not exist in a vacuum but negotiates with stakeholders and forces at multiple levels.

Life of Pi: Turn as Return

City-branding efforts are typically geared toward increasing inward investment and tourism (Kavaratzis 2004, 70; Dinnie 2011a, 7), and two hurdles faced by many such attempts are inadequate facilities and limited financial resources (Dinnie 2011b, 93). To bring *Life of Pi*'s scouting team from the US production company, Fox 2000 Pictures, to Taichung, Mayor Hu had to secure a donation of NT$1 million from a media personality because the city government had not budgeted for such an item (Tseng, Huang, and Tsai 2013). After it was confirmed that the film would be made in Taiwan, the rulebooks were broken by the exceptional amounts granted by both local and national authorities. At the time of Lee's turn as return, Taichung's filmmaking-support scheme encompassed financial sponsorship as well as subsidies for accommodation and promotional activities, capped at an amount of NT$10 million per film. *Life of Pi*, nonetheless, was granted NT$59 million, compared to the meager NT$1.6 million each received by four films and NT$8.6 million by one other film in the same first of two rounds of sponsorship in 2011. The disproportionately huge amount awarded to Lee's film was unprecedented and has not been repeated since. In fact, most films in the scheme's history (up until and including the year 2020) were granted no more than NT$4 million each.[15] Furthermore, *Life of Pi* received an additional funding of NT$250 million from the central government's film-sponsorship scheme, bringing the total amount invested in the film by Taiwanese governmental bodies to NT$309 million (Wu and Hsiao 2013).

In his edited book *City Branding: Theory and Cases*, Keith Dinnie points out that city branding "needs to be rooted in reality, rather than a delusion peddled by mendacious marketers," and he calls for cities "to ensure that they have got the tangible evidence to back up their proclaimed strengths" (2011b, 95). However, evidence—and what forms it would take—for the effects of city-branding efforts is not easy to ascertain or gather. Indeed, an official report in 2016 on the effects of Taichung City government's subsidy of film and television activities did not provide any figures on the economic benefits of the subsidy schemes or their contribution to location tourism.[16] According to one news report, the international and local crew of *Life of Pi*, which amounted to some 300 personnel, spent a total of NT$100 million on accommodations alone during the shooting period, increasing the hotel occupancy rate in Taichung City by 10 percent that year (Hong 2012). To put this figure in perspective, a lantern festival held in the city attracted 6.4 million visitors over 12 days, with an estimated income, according to Mayor Hu, of NT$5 billion (Liu 2004), making the amount spent on accommodations by the crew of *Life of Pi* pale in comparison.

Moreover, because Shuinan Airport was merely used as a site for shooting the ocean scenes, Taichung's cityscapes do not actually appear in *Life of Pi*. Unlike, for example, the stunning landscapes in New Zealand that stood in for "Middle-earth" in *The Lord of the Rings* trilogy (Peter Jackson 2001, 2002, 2003), there is not much potential in a disused wave tank in a derelict airport for the purpose of location tourism. Although, one reported benefit of the production of *Life of Pi* in Taichung was the opportunity for Taiwan's film industry personnel to gain experience working with an international crew. A local crew member working on prop and set expressed his appreciation for the international "know-how" brought to Taiwan and said he learned a lesson about "quality" from the British crew who would slightly increase the budget to achieve a better result (Tang 2018). The Taiwanese wave-making expert also noted the tight organization and precise planning of his international counterparts (Tang 2018).

Another result from this episode came when Martin Scorsese decided to make his film, *Silence* (2016), in Taiwan upon Ang Lee's recommendation; the film also received from the Taichung City government NT$6 million for production and NT$2 million in accommodations subsidy. An assistant who worked on *Life of Pi* became a producer on Scorsese's film, and he chose to use the wave pool in Shuinan Airport for its ability to create more than 1,000 kinds of wave and for its safety for shooting (Wang B-j. 2017). Scorsese's 1996 film about the life of the Dalai Lama (*Kundun*) had previously made him an object of criticism of the PRC government (Weinraub 1996); his choice of Taiwan as the shooting location for *Silence* was played up in a report in *Time* magazine, which bore the headline "Martin Scorsese's *Silence* Is a Win for Taiwan but Producers Are Worried About a China Backlash" (Smith 2017). This focus on the international relations dimension of Scorsese's film echoes my broader argument that the operation of cultural soft power cannot be divorced from the realities of political hard power.

It should perhaps be acknowledged that not everything is measurable, a qualification that can serve as a caution if not corrective to the soft-power thesis that tends to be overly instrumental in its conception and appraisal (see the Introduction for a fuller discussion of this issue). To be sure, some of the benefits of soft power would be intangible values such as the promotion of cultural understanding beyond national borders. For the production of *Life of Pi*, an international crew of some 400 filmmakers were brought to Taichung, many of whom with families whose children attended schools there for a semester or two ("World Popular" 2013). The experience of living in another place and interacting with the locals over a substantial period of time can sow seeds of friendship and goodwill that might bear fruits in myriad ways and at unexpected times. While concrete schemes can be established and efforts made by governmental and non-state actors to extend a nation's soft power, these can only be successful if the actual process of cultural exchange is premised upon attraction and affect, which may or may not translate into any tangible outcome within a prescribed time frame. The intangible and affective aspects of cross-cultural encounters, therefore, offer an opportunity to rework the soft-power concept (see Chapter 5 for an elaboration).

Hou Hsiao-hsien, whose film *A City of Sadness* (*Beiqing chengshi*, 1989) unwittingly led to the small mountain town of Jiufen becoming a tourist attraction, had commented that promoting location tourism requires a whole package beyond film sponsorship schemes in order to keep the tourists coming (Hsiang 2010, 71). City-branding efforts also demand many years of sustained commitment (Dinnie 2011b, 95) that, given the vagaries of politics in Taiwan, cannot always be ensured. After Jason Hu, who represented KMT, lost the mayoral re-election in 2014, his 13-year legacy was criticized by a Taichung City councilor from the rival DPP for a tendency to go over budget in public construction projects (Chen S-c. 2015). The slated Central Taiwan Film Studios was nonetheless completed and opened in July 2019, 10 years after the idea was first mooted by Hu and at a time when the mayoral position had been returned to the KMT in the 2018 election. The headline of a report on the opening of the studios begins with "Three Terms of Mayors Listened to Ang Lee's Words," highlighting the power that Lee is perceived to have wielded in bringing the "dream" of constructing this filmmaking facility to fruition (Hsiang 2020). It remains to be seen the extent to which this film studio, while obviously not a tourist destination in itself, might draw in more local and international businesses and visitors to Taichung City.

Technological Turn as Utopia

It is worth noting that the industrial turn occasioned by the making of *Life of Pi* was also a technological turn for Ang Lee as it was the first time he had engaged with 3D technology. Lee confessed he only had "the vaguest idea" about the implications of using 3D because *Avatar* (James Cameron, 2009) had yet to be released at the time of making *Life of Pi* (Lee 2012, 14).[17] Lee was apparently drawn to this new technology for its realistic rather than spectacular effects:

> "You don't have to do unrealistic, big waves to impress anybody," says Lee. "Normal-size waves can really impress you. And because they're realistic and smaller, you feel so hopelessly there, drifting up and down. With a huge, two-hundred-foot wave, you don't feel you're there. You're watching a movie." (Castelli 2012, 37)

Lee's discovery about the properties of 3D technology extended to the aspect of performance when he realized that "the acting should be more subtle most of the time, because you see more" (Castelli 2012, 37).[18] However, the balance between the dramatic and technological aspects of filmmaking is not easily struck. Lee and his cinematographer Claudio Miranda were attacked by members of the visual effects (VFX) industry for failing to recognize the team's contribution in their Oscar acceptance speeches for *Life of Pi*. Lee was also criticized for his complaint about the cost of VFX at a time when resentment had been building in the VFX sector, triggered in part by the bankruptcy of *Life of Pi*'s effects house Rhythm & Hues (Pulver 2013). As I have argued elsewhere on the use of digital technology in contemporary Chinese cinemas, the hierarchy between director and visual effects personnel, and the corresponding values of poetics versus spectacle, have survived from the time of Aristotle to the present day (Lim 2016a, 152). As a way of challenging the notion of authorship, the sacrificial labor force of visual effects personnel should no longer be subsumed under the pedestal of the director-poet but be recognized as integral to the creation of a digital aesthetics as much as new sensual pleasures (Lim 2016a, 163). The backlash by the

VFX sector toward Lee and his cinematographer can thus be seen as a demand for acknowledgment by an un(der)appreciated labor force.

Lee's desire to "see more" was subsequently amplified in his 2016 film *Billy Lynn*, shot not only in 3D but also in 4K clarity and at 120 frames per second (fps; five times faster than traditional movies and nearly three times the 48 fps that Peter Jackson used for *The Hobbit* trilogy) (Fleming 2016). In the words of the film's technical advisor, Ben Gervais, this groundbreaking technology—used for the first time by a major studio to shoot a feature film—has such a "sense of immediacy and intimacy that we haven't been able to experience before" that it shocked the cast and crew into "dead silence" when its effect was shown two weeks before shooting (Fleming 2016). Reviews of the film, however, are less flattering and call it "unwatchable" (Engber 2016) and the "greatest disappointment" of the year (Hammond 2016). Given that there were, at the time of the film's release, only five cinemas in the world equipped to screen the film in its 3D/4K/120fps format and the infancy of this technology, the jury is perhaps still out on the achievement of Lee's technological turn.[19] Taipei was proud to boast one of such cinemas, and, as Figure 4.1 shows, the cinema hailed the technology as "futuristic 3D" on a display board in its lobby when I went to watch the film in December 2016.

I will conclude this chapter by recasting Lee's industrial turns in relation to the three keywords of this book's subtitle. To begin with historiography, it can be argued that, with his use of the 3D/4K/120fps format, Lee's position within film history might go beyond his award-winning achievements to include his experimentation with new filming technologies. His latest film at the time of this writing was *Gemini Man*, in which "something never attempted before (a fully CGI human performance)" in the shape of the protagonist's young clone (played by Will Smith and generated through digital effects) was created (Chow 2019). Embracing digital cinema and 3D technology, Lee claims that, since making *Life of Pi*, cinema keeps telling him it is about to change; he also believes that the "advanced format" he used in *Billy Lynn* "will one day be the minimum standard" (Ma 2016). Lee even sounds rather evangelical when talking about his wish to continue making films in 3D, proclaiming that "we're not doing jobs. We're trying to figure something out that makes you feel alive" (Fleming 2016). Lee appears determined to pursue this path as he is waiting on a "financial green light" for his next dream project—a 3D dramatization of the 1975 boxing match between Muhammad Ali and Joe Frazier (Chow 2019).

To move on to authorship, notwithstanding his seemingly avant-garde stance on the use of new technology for shooting films, Lee also comes across as an old-school auteur devoted to the experience of watching films in the movie theater rather than viewing them on the multiple mobile platforms available today. He likens going to the movies to going to the temple, and, for him, it is precisely

Figure 4.1 *Life of Pi*'s technological breakthrough superimposed on a map of Taiwan on a display board in a Taipei cinema
Photo courtesy of Violet Cheong

the new technological format that would engender "a new kind of cinema where your engagement is different" (Fleming 2016). Lee's analogy of the movie theater as temple and his suggestion that 3D's biggest potential lies in the reading of faces (Fleming 2016) recall Susan Sontag's famous essay, "The Decay of Cinema" (1996), in which she uses the same metaphor of the temple for "cinematheques and clubs"; argues that the wish to submerge oneself in the gigantic image is a "desire to lose yourself in other people's lives . . . faces"; and proposes that, for cinephiles, films are "unique, unrepeatable, magic experiences."[20] However, whereas Sontag is scathing about films "made purely for entertainment (that is, commercial) purposes," describing them as "astonishingly witless" (Sontag 1996), Lee treads a much finer line between auteurism and commercialism. Lee's success on both the commercial and critical fronts exemplifies Timothy Corrigan's notion of the auteur as star in his thesis about "the commerce of auteurism," within which the "wider material strategies of social agency" of the auteur include the very performance of "*the business of being an auteur*" (Corrigan 1990, 47, emphasis in original). Indeed, Lee's technological experimentations had been made possible thanks to the currency of his brand name on which, he admits, he relies to "assuage the fears and misgivings" of film crews and investors (Ma 2016).

Finally, to end with transnationality, Lee's industrial turn as return in the case of *Life of Pi* underscores how "the national continues to exert the force of its presence even within transnational film-making practices" (Higbee and Lim 2010, 10). Lee's Taiwan background had been instrumental in bringing this big-budget Hollywood production to an island that last hosted a US major studio picture in 1966 for the Steve McQueen vehicle, *The Sand Pebbles* (dir. Robert Wise; Castelli 2012, 52).[21] More important, the national manifests here in the form of soft-power strategies that capitalized on cinema as a resource and were aimed at expanding the otherwise constrained local scope to a broader transnational sphere. While no Taiwanese landscape makes any appearance in the film, the computer-generated images of tiger and waves and the use of 3D point toward technology itself as an entity that, like cinema, respects no national boundary and travels transnationally. This, perhaps, is the ultimate lesson to be drawn from Lee's industrial-cum-technological turn: the ability of cinema and technology to create a make-believe world that eschews restrictive conceptions of authorship and (national) historiography whilst demonstrating the soft power of transnational storytelling—both *Life of Pi*'s and Lee's life story—that can only be described as dream-like and utopian.

5

The Affective Turn

Little Freshness as Regional Soft Power

In 2008 Wei Te-sheng's *Cape No. 7* (*Haijiao qihao*, 2008) raked in over New
Taiwan dollar NT$530 million (US$18 million) in Taiwan,[1] making it not only
the island's top-grossing film that year but also, at the time, the second-highest
grossing film (after James Cameron's 1997 *Titanic*) in Taiwan's box office history (Ho 2009, 100).[2] Its intake of NT$250 million in the Greater Taipei region
was more than double those obtained by the Hollywood blockbusters it had
beaten to second place (Rob Cohen's *The Mummy: Tomb of the Dragon Emperor*,
110 million) and third place (Christopher Nolan's *The Dark Knight*, 109 million)
in the same year (Ho 2009, 105). Moreover, in terms of all-time box-office record for domestic films, this figure was almost twice as much as that of its then
closest rival, Ang Lee's *Lust, Caution* (*Se, Jie*, 2007), which took in 136 million
the previous year (Ho 2009, 100), and way above the 101 million intake of Lee's
Crouching Tiger, Hidden Dragon (*Wohu canglong*) in the year 2000 (Wang 2001a,
117). This phenomenal box-office result established Wei as a bankable filmmaker in and beyond Taiwan, and the film attracted interest from a Tony-award-
nominated Broadway director to turn it into a musical, though the project did
not come to fruition owing to a lack of funding ("Zijin" 2017). Building on the
success of *Cape No. 7*, Wei's next project, a two-part film, achieved a box-office
result of over 198 million for its first installment *Warriors of the Rainbow: Seediq
Bale Part 1* (*Saideke Balai [shang]: Taiyang qi*, 2011), making it then the second-
highest grossing domestic film of all time, and an equally impressive figure of
over 135 million for its second installment *Warriors of the Rainbow: Seediq Bale
Part 2* (*Saideke Balai [xia]: Caihong qiao*) (Wang 2012, 50). However, when a
shorter version of Wei's two-part film competed at the Venice film festival in
2011, Taiwan's Government Information Office (GIO) had to file a complaint
with the organizer for listing the originating country of the film as "China and
Taiwan" rather than simply Taiwan (Pulver 2011).[3] This diplomatic gesture by
the government of the Republic of China (ROC, Taiwan's official title) indicates
that soft-power arenas, such as international film festivals, are contested sites
where the hard reality of the island's political standoff with the People's Republic
of China (PRC) is never very far away.

Taiwan Cinema as Soft Power. Song Hwee Lim, Oxford University Press. © Oxford University Press 2022.
DOI: 10.1093/oso/9780197503379.003.0006

The box-office success of *Cape No. 7* opens this chapter because the film has done for Taiwan cinema within a domestic market what *Crouching Tiger, Hidden Dragon* did for transnational Chinese cinemas on a global scale: both films smashed box-office records and injected a new confidence in their products in their respective markets and audiences. More important, the rescaling of the market size and the reorientation of audience from the global to the domestic signal a shift, beyond box-office figures, that I shall call an affective turn. This affective turn demonstrates the operation of soft power in substantive ways (that is, the role of affect in cross-cultural flows) and complicates the three keywords in this book's subtitle. That is to say, whereas notions of authorship and transnationality have been central to the previous three chapters on Hou Hsiao-hsien, Tsai Ming-liang, and Ang Lee, the historiographical account of Taiwan cinema based on global critical acclaim will be reoriented in this chapter toward domestic box-office success. This new account points to, as well as is premised on, a bifurcation between domestic reception and international prestige, a split that finds its roots in the Taiwan New Cinema (TNC) period of the 1980s and that continues to deepen into the twenty-first century. As I shall delineate, this bifurcation can also be expressed in affective terms that correspond to the rescaling of Taiwan cinema's soft-power appeal from the global to the domestic/ regional, operating as it does through a cultural imaginary known as "little freshness" (*xiao qingxin*).

Cape No. 7 as Box-Office Miracle

Hailed by local critics as the most astonishing film phenomenon of the past 20 years (Wen 2009, 18) and widely acclaimed for its landmark status in the "revival" and "renaissance" of audience confidence in popular cinema made in Taiwan (Gao 2011; Ma 2011), *Cape No. 7*'s miracle at the domestic box office has had the greatest implication, among the three keywords in this book's subtitle, on historiography. One obvious way the bifurcation between high international prestige and low domestic consumption of Taiwan cinema has manifested since the 1980s is to routinely cast TNC as a scapegoat responsible for the demise of the film industry.[4] *Cape No. 7*'s success occasioned a new iteration of such scapegoating in the form of a conference jointly organized by the highest-level research institution (Academia Sinica) and the only national film archive of the island. Entitled "Auteurism and Popularity: Post-Taiwan New Cinema in 2008," the conference theme affixed the prefix "post" to the label of TNC not so much to demarcate periodization within a nation's cinema as to attempt to put the final nail into TNC's coffin. This new label represents what Kwame Anthony Appiah calls a "space-clearing gesture" (1997, 61), here aimed at staking a claim in film historiography. Rather than signifying a change in modes of film production, address, consumption, and reception, the prefix "post" functions as a categorical gesture of "moving on" and "moving beyond," in this case from the transnational soft power of auteur-led art cinema to the domestic people power of audience-endorsed popular cinema.

Indeed, *Cape No. 7* can be credited for kick-starting domestic people power as it pushed the market share of domestic films over the 10 percent mark for the first time since 1990. In fact, prior to 2008, the domestic market share of Taiwan films typically hovered around the 1 to 2 percent mark, with percentages in some years plummeting to as low, as we can see in Table 5.1, as 0.17 (2001), 0.30 (2003), 0.44 (1998), and 0.46 (1999). The highest figure before 2008 was in 2007 when the market share was 7.38 percent thanks to Ang Lee's *Lust, Caution*. Thus, the 12.09 percent domestic market share in 2008 was more than 60 percent above its closest counterpart in 2007. Since then, this people power has built a steady momentum. In 2011, the combined success of Wei's aforementioned two-part film and Giddens Ko's *You Are the Apple of My Eye* (*Naxie nian, women yiqi zhui de nühai*, which took in NT$180 million, making it the third-highest grossing domestic film at the time) set a new record of 18.91 percent market share for domestic films. While the market share of domestic films dropped back to its previously dismal low of 2.30 percent in 2009 and a slightly higher 7.31 percent in 2010, it remained above the 10 percent mark every year from 2011 to 2015 but fell below this threshold ever since (until and including 2019). Besides, for a film to achieve an intake of over 100 million (one *yi* in Chinese) is now becoming a realistic ambition rather than an elusive holy grail, and at least one film had crossed that benchmark in the Greater Taipei region (up until 2015) or in the whole of Taiwan (since 2016, but not in 2019) each year.

In a sense, the people have spoken, and the clamor for domestic box-office intake within the film industry and in both critical and popular discourses serves to displace the centrality of transnationality and authorship in my account of Taiwan cinema in all previous chapters of this book. Just as *Crouching Tiger, Hidden Dragon* helped move the *wuxia* genre "from its marginal, subcultural appeal to viewers in American Chinatowns, film festivals and cult followings in the past, to mainstream acceptability today" (Chan 2011, 151), *Cape No. 7* can be said to have led the way in shifting the self-image of Taiwan cinema from the auteur-centered, international-film-festival-participating TNC period of the 1980s and 1990s, to a post-TNC period in the twenty-first century marked by a more popular mode of filmmaking aimed at appealing to a wider domestic audience. The dominance of Wei's filmmaking in this new discursive formation of contemporary Taiwan cinema can be gleaned from a recent edited volume in English (Chiu, Rawnsley, and Rawnsley 2017), which devotes more than half the book to analyses of films directed and produced by Wei.[5]

Table 5.1 Box-office intake and market share of domestic films in Taiwan, 1990–2019[a]

Year	Number of films produced or released[b]	Total box-office intake of Taiwanese films (NT$)	Market share (%)	Films whose intake exceed NT$100 million since the year 2000 in the Greater Taipei region alone
1990	81 (Huang 2003, 160) [c]	104,916,398 (Huang 2003, 161) [d]	5.78	
1991	33	63,777,162	3.56	
1992	40	36,570,610	1.68	
1993	26	103,144,502	4.15	
1994	29	84,534,960	3.77	
1995	28	31,033,280	1.30	
1996	18	39,583,272	1.46	
1997	29	25,401,536	0.89	
1998	23	12,367,760	0.44	
1999	16/ 10[e]	11,676,805/ 11,053,275	0.46/0.44	
2000	19 (Wang 2001c, 130–133)/17	32,268,793[f]/ 32,199,080	4.65/1.28	*Crouching Tiger, Hidden Dragon*: 101,155,665 (ibid., 132)
2001	10 (Wang 2002, 58-59)/13	3,103,651/ 3,696,865	0.17/0.17	

2002	16 (Wang 2003, 63)/16	52,183,102/ 52,662,182	2.21/2.24	
2003	15 (Wang 2004, 82)/ [g]18	6,024,045/ 6,024,055	0.30/0.30	
2004	23 (Wang 2005, 264)/ [h]25	28,586,198/ 29,062,110	1.11/1.13	
2005	24 (Wang 2006, 225)/25	43,279,294/ 42,469,745	1.59/1.59	
2006	17 (Wang 2007, 246)/19	43,392,938/ 43,392,928	1.62/1.62	
2007	21 (Wang 2008, 141)/22	198,820,829/ 198,782,192	7.38/7.38	*Lust, Caution*: 137,050,890 (ibid., 131)
2008	29 (Wang 2010, 108–110)/29	305,426,021/ 305,426,019	12.09/12.09	*Cape No. 7*: 232,326,877 (ibid., 78)
2009	28 (Wang 2010, 110–112)/ [i]31	62,480,190/ 58,008,573	2.30/2.13	
2010	40 (Wang 2011, 43)/38	225,582,594/ 225,582,606	7.31/7.31	*Monga*: 117,007,196 (ibid.)
2011	37 (Wang 2012, 50)/36	714,964,158 (ibid.)/ 712,506,985	18.91[j] 18.65	*Warriors of the Rainbow: Seediq Bale Part 1*: 198,600,035; *You Are the Apple of My Eye*: 181,604,478; *Warriors of the Rainbow: Seediq Bale Part 2*: 135,792,420 (all figures from ibid.)

Continued

Table 5.1 Continued

Year	Number of films produced or released[b]	Total box-office intake of Taiwanese films (NT$)	Market share (%)	Films whose intake exceed NT$100 million since the year 2000 in the Greater Taipei region alone
2012	42 (Wang 2014a, 42)/51	428,765,146 (ibid.)/ 430,433,697	12.06/11.90	*Din Tao: Leader of the Parade*: 106,200,840 (ibid., 44)
2013	51 (Wang 2014b, 57)/56	538,995,025 (ibid.)/ 529,863,483	13.69/13.96	*David Lomen*: 122,455,190; *Zone Pro Site*: 104,092,061 (ibid., 58) [k]
2014	42 (Wang 2015, 70)/54	429,362,092 (ibid.)/ 427,833,400	11.60[l]/ 11.54	*KANO*: 118,070,040 (ibid., 66)
2015	66 (Liang 2016, 39–40)/66	467,938,144 (ibid.)/ 467,938,144	11.13 (ibid.)/ 11.13	*Our Times*: 158,731,830 (ibid., 42) [m]
2016	69 (Liang 2017, 36)/71	n/a/388,228,505	n/a/5.37	*The Tenants Downstairs*: 116,129,865 (ibid., 39); *David Lomen 2*: 170,000,000 (rough figure; Wen 2017, 8n1)
2017	80 (Liang 2018, 72)/63	729 million (Liang 2019, 86)/ 728,849,536	n/a/6.90	*The Tag-Along 2*: 105,729,876 (ibid., 76)
2018	64 (Liang 2019, 86)/64	810 million (ibid.)/ 810,294,432	n/a/7.52	*More than Blue*: 226,022,046; *Gatao 2: Rise of the King*: 127,897,332; *Back to the Good Times*: 102,160,797 (all figures from Liang 2019, 88–89)
2019	n/a/77	n/a/702,765,192	n/a/6.90	

^a All online sources listed were accessed on December 2, 2020, with previously accessed dates indicated where some web links no longer work. Box-office figures are for Taipei City or the Greater Taipei region only, except for the ones since 2016 because figures for the whole of Taiwan are only available after July 2016. The original source for figures dating up to 2011 came from "Collection of Box Office Earnings of First-Run Theaters in Taipei (1999–2011.09)," *Taiwan Cinema*, 12 July 12, 2011, accessed August 16, 2011, http://www.taiwancinema.com/ct.asp?xItem=508968&ctNode=1448&mp=2, but the web link no longer existed when I attempted to access it 23 February 23, 2018. The original webpage contains records dating back to 1996, though the title erroneously lists it as going back only to 1999.

b It is difficult to ascertain from the sources whether the figures are for films produced or released. Some figures (such as Wang 2003, Wang 2004) even include films released only at small local festivals.

c Figures for number of films produced from 1990 to 1999 are all cited from Huang 2003, 160, which have, in turn, been culled from the *Cinema Yearbooks of the Republic of China* of the years concerned.

d Figures for box-office intake and market share of domestic films from 1990 to 1999 are all cited from Huang 2003, 161, which have, in turn, been culled from a webpage whose link no longer works: http://cinema.nccu.edu.tw.

e The second set of figures for number of films produced from 1999 to 2019 comes from a document downloaded from the Bureau of Audiovisual and Music Industry Development, Ministry of Culture website (see "Zhonghuaminguo yingpian," n.d.). I thank Lin Yennan for bringing this source to my attention.

f The second set of figures for total box-office intake and market share of domestic films from the years from 1999 to 2019 also comes from "Zhonghuaminguo yingpian," n.d. Note that the box-office intake for domestic films in 2000 provided by both sources is less than the intake of Ang Lee's *Crouching Tiger, Hidden Dragon* alone because the latter includes intake from the film's second commercial release in 2001 (Wang 2002c, 132). I have retained the market share percentage in the first source (4.65%) as it seems to reflect the surge contributed by Lee's film, though this cannot be verified given that the sources I consulted do not explain how—and which year—the intake of Lee's film fits into the computation.

g This figure is cited as 16 in subsequent yearbooks (e.g., Wang 2005, 264).

h The author's name is missing from both the content's page and the cited source, but I am assuming it is Wang Cheng-hua who has been responsible for this task in almost all the yearbooks that I have cited up until and including the year 2014.

i The year in the heading of the table from which this figure is cited (Wang 2010, 110) should be 2009 rather than 2008.

j This percentage is computed based on figures provided in Wang 2012, 42, 50. Wang provides a different percentage for market share of domestic film as 23.4% (2012, 50).

k Note that the documentary, *Beyond Beauty: Taiwan from Above (Kanjian Taiwan, dir. Chi Po-lin, 2013) just misses this mark with an intake of NT$99,828,660 (Wang 2014b, 58).

l This percentage is computed from figures provided in Wang 2015, 65–66.

m This figure is listed as NT$159,001,165 in Liang 2017, 39.

However, to more fully account for this shift in Taiwan filmmaking, I suggest we look beyond industrial-cum-commercial factors and probe an affective dimension—what Raymond Williams famously calls "structure of feeling" (1977, 128–135)—that underpins the new generation of directors, the kinds of films being made, and the popular reception of these films among both domestic and regional audiences. In particular, I highlight an affective structure called "little freshness," a neologism coined to describe a range of cultural products and phenomena that mostly emanates from Taiwan that has captured the imagination of youths in China and Hong Kong. While the phrase can be used as a label for a subgenre of films (represented by the likes of *Cape No. 7* and *You Are the Apple of My Eye*) made in Taiwan since the dawn of the new millennium, it also points to a broader propensity toward miniaturization (*xiao*) in a myriad of cultural formulations in Taiwan that has exhibited a regional soft-power appeal. The affective expressions for little freshness by youths both within Taiwan and across the Taiwan Strait can be regarded as a manifestation of what Lauren Berlant calls an "intimate public," constituting consumers of a particular cultural form who "*already* share a worldview and emotional knowledge that they have derived from a broadly common historical experience" (2008, viii, emphasis in original). After delineating this affective turn in the next two sections, I will argue, in the sections following, that this turn offers an opportunity to rework Joseph Nye's notion of soft power into a form of citizen-to-citizen soft power that is largely free from the intervention of the state and its agents; furthermore, this affective turn allows us to rescale the operation of soft power from an international to a regional and domestic one. Finally, I conclude the chapter by considering the political effect of the seemingly apolitical affect of little freshness.

The Affective Turn

This chapter aims to recast the historiography of post–World War II Taiwan cinema in affective terms and, in so doing, sets the stage for examining Taiwan filmmaking in the twenty-first century as a form of regional soft power anchored in a specific cultural imaginary that is little freshness. The object of my analysis is not the films themselves but the affective expressions that have been triggered within Taiwan and, more importantly, in China and Hong Kong by some of these little freshness films. It argues that the imaginary of little freshness embodies an affective trait shared across the Taiwan Strait by youths whose engagement with a market of miniaturization as cultural producers and consumers is inflected by a sense of generational injustice in the face of neoliberal capitalism. While this chapter opens with *Cape No. 7*, it will not discuss how, for example, Wei's filmmaking signals nostalgia about the Japanese occupation period of Taiwan from

1895 to 1945, a topic that has already generated a substantial body of scholarship. Rather, it proposes that the affect of little freshness, identifiable in *Cape No. 7* and in a wider body of films made after the year 2000, captures a particular structure of feeling in multifarious manifestations in the cultural sphere.

In historiographical terms, if the shift from pre-TNC to TNC can be described as a change from "a cinema of authority" used for bolstering the ruling Kuomintang (KMT) regime's anti-communist rhetoric in the 1960s to the 1970s, to "a cinema of authorship" epitomized by the films of Hou Hsiao-hsien, Edward Yang, Tsai Ming-liang, and Ang Lee in the 1980s to the 1990s (Yeh and Davis 2005, 6), the new millennium has witnessed an intensification of transnationality in the works of TNC auteurs (as seen in Chapters 2 to 4) *as well as* an emergence of a more popular mode of filmmaking that addresses local interests and concerns (this chapter). Thus, the cinema of authorship represented by TNC can be said to have taken a simultaneous turn, in the so-called post-TNC period, toward both transnationality and a "cinema of markets" (Lin 2013, 28), exacerbating the bifurcation between Taiwan cinema's high international prestige and a newly revived domestic box office.

Yet, this broad historiographical stroke fails to acknowledge the affective dimension underpinning these transitions. Indeed, to recast this account in affective terms, we might regard the shift from a cinema of authority (pre-TNC) to that of authorship (TNC) as one from conformity to resistance, the latter mobilized by nativist movements—and sentiments—that set out to challenge the dominant KMT ideology and its state apparatuses. From the adaptation of literary works by the nativist novelist Huang Chun-ming in one of the first TNC films, *The Sandwich Man* (*Erzi de da wan'ou*, 1983),[6] to the landmark film of Hou's *A City of Sadness* (*Beiqing chengshi*, 1989), the first film to deal with the taboo subject of the February 28 incident, this resistance has given voice to Hoklo and Hakka (regional languages widely spoken on the island before KMT imposed the official language of Mandarin) as much as to protagonists living in the underbelly of Taiwanese society and the defining affect of sadness. Furthermore, the shift *within* TNC from the 1980s to the 1990s, as I have argued before, was marked by a move from a "historical I" to a "private I" to the extent that questions of nationhood and collective memory in films by Hou and Yang were replaced by aspects of personal identity such as gender and sexuality in films by Tsai and Lee (Lim 2006, 127–128); to put it differently, affect was rescaled from the national to the personal and relocated from the public to the private sphere within this shift.

Out of around 770 films released in the years 2000 to 2019 that are invariably varied in their subject matter, I want to focus on films that could be loosely categorized under a subgenre called little freshness, films that tend to have one eye on the market (thus a stronger emphasis on genre and youth) and another on giving birth to a new kind of affect.[7] As is evident in films such as *Cape No. 7*, which interweaves contemporary young love with colonial memory, or *Salute! Sun Yat-sen* (*Xingdong daihao: Sun Zhongshan*, dir. Yee Chih-yen, 2014), which quietly subverts a KMT iconography through a campus-set comedy of sorts, this form of filmmaking can be adept at embracing both "historical I" and "private I." However, the *tone* underlying the treatment of these historical materials (love letters between a Taiwanese woman and a Japanese man in *Cape No. 7*) or artifacts (a statue of Sun Yat-sen, ROC's founding father) is no longer necessarily one of immense sadness but rather that of youthful longing, aspiration, frustration, and love,[8] affective elements whose narratorial and stylistic renditions can be encapsulated by the neologism "little freshness."

Before I elaborate, in a later section, how the notion of soft power can be reworked through the discursive construction and creative appropriation of little freshness, let me qualify my use of the term "affect" and provide a preliminary sketch of the affect of little freshness. Whereas I discuss, in the Introduction, affect primarily as a mediating environment that undergirds processes of cultural flows, here I use the terms "affect," "affective," and "affection" both in their more conventional sense of belonging to an emotional realm as well as in ways informed by the recent affective turn in critical theory.[9] In particular, I find a resonance between Berlant's idea of "intimate public" and Williams's notion of "structure of feeling" insofar as they are both concerned with cultural forms that, like the phenomenon of little freshness at the start of the new millennium, are "emergent" or even "pre-emergent" (Williams 1977, 132).[10] Thus, the affective expressions for these cultural forms, even when shared in public, are imbued with a sense of intimacy not dissimilar to that detected in many forms of youth subcultures. Yet, according to Williams, these feelings, however "personal" or "small," articulate changes in feeling and consciousness that are social and material (Williams 1977, 131–132). In this light, expressions of desire by youths toward something as seemingly small and ephemeral as little freshness are of value (both analytic and sociopolitical) because they embody experiences, in Berlant's words, of "living as a certain kind of being in the world," with a promise "to provide a better experience of social belonging—partly through participation in the relevant commodity culture, and partly because of its revelations about how people can live" (2008, viii).

The Affect of Little Freshness

The little freshness phenomenon offers an illustration of how affective expressions have functioned as a form of intimate public—and soft-power resource—across the Taiwan Strait. The term was initially coined in the PRC media as a descriptor for a new musical genre in Hong Kong and Taiwan that resembles British indie pop of the 1980s. It is difficult to pin down exactly where or when the term was first used, but a 2004 post on the Baidu (arguably PRC's answer to Google) website's bulletin board mentioned the term in a manner that indicated its already wide circulation at the time. Reviewing the Hong Kong female singer Cass Phang's (Peng Ling) 1999 album, *A Stalk of Flower*, the web user, who adopted the pseudonym "Unhappy little, little person," wrote:

> Cass Phang's voice, *to use a now fashionable term*, belongs to the "little fresh-ness" type; coupled with the even sweeter backing voices, it splashes in one's ears circles of ripples like clear water. At times refreshing, at times free-floating, at times beautifully sweet, and with blue sky, white clouds, and green grass extending beyond your horizon, the Indie-Pop in "A Stalk of Flower" refreshes your ears, your heart, and this dust-filled world. Listening to all 13 songs in one breath is like sitting by a window bathed in sunlight at dusk, like bathing in the wind of spring, enjoying the faint smell of mint, a plate of delicious dessert already laid out by the table. ("Dieping" 2004, emphasis mine)

Affect is here invested in and manifested by the ability of Phang's musical style to momentarily transport this unhappy, little person in the PRC to another world, where everything is clean and clear and where the sky is blue, the clouds white, and the fields green—an imagery that, as we shall see later, would emerge as emblematic of the little freshness phenomenon. This web user demonstrates, through her[11] written words, that affects happen in "impulses, sensations, expectations, daydreams, encounters, and habits of relating" (Stewart 2007, 2), and, by sharing her intimate feelings on a public forum, a faith that such affects do not exist alone and that it might be possible to imagine a community of "publics and social worlds" (Stewart 2007, 2) that would break her isolation and unhappiness.

By affective turn, I refer to a selection of cultural products, particularly in music and film (also, in the use of music and songs *in* films), in contemporary Taiwan that embody, exhibit, and elicit the affect of little freshness that is recognizable, like any structure of feeling, by its "characteristic elements of impulse, restraint, and tone" (Williams 1977, 132). These elements, in the example of the post by the unhappy, little person, include aspects of identity that we might presume to be female (gender), young (age), and petite bourgeoisie (class); they display a sensitivity toward and sensibility for an imaginary of cleanness and clearness that encompasses both audio ("splashes in one's ears") and visual ("extending beyond your horizon") registers; they even trigger the sensoria of smell ("faint smell of mint") and taste ("delicious dessert"). Thus, Phang's voice instigates affects that "pick up density and texture as they move through bodies, dreams, dramas, and social worldings of all kinds," whose significance lie in "the intensities they build and in what thoughts and feelings they make possible" (Stewart 2007, 3).

Moreover, little freshness can be considered as partaking in a market of miniaturization whose über term is "small exact happiness" (*xiao quexing*). Coined by and popularized through the works of the Japanese cult author Haruki Murakami,[12] *xiao quexing* has become a catchall phrase for a certain structure of feeling, a transient but concrete moment of little freshness as it were. It has also opened doors to a market in which numerous cultural products and business enterprises have either used the character *xiao* (little or small) in their names or employed imageries similar to those of the little freshness style described before. In Taiwan, this market includes, to take but a few examples, lifestyle magazine *Xiao rizi* (*C'est si bon*, literally little days); café *Xiao ziyou* (little freedom), bed-and-breakfast hotel *Xiao zizai* (little carefree); and social movements and enterprises invested in the ethos of sustainability, such as *xiaonong* (little farming), *xiao geming* (little revolution), and *xiao jingji* (little economy); even a cosmetic surgery clinic calls itself *Xiao quexing*. This market of miniaturization also exists in China, where a series of novels, manga, and films entitled *Xiao shidai* (*Tiny Times*) has been making waves since 2008. In Hong Kong, the most popular indie band is called My Little Airport and singer Silian Wong released the song "Little Freshness" in 2015.[13]

Taken together, this affective turn in three locales across the Taiwan Strait at the dawn of the new millennium bespeaks a "social experience which is still in process, often indeed not yet recognized as social but taken to be private, idiosyncratic, and even isolating, but which in analysis . . . has its emergent, connecting, and dominant characteristics, indeed its specific hierarchies" (Williams 1977, 132). As I elaborate later, as an imaginary that Taiwan cultural products both project to and have been projected upon by youth consumers, little freshness has become an affective manifestation of Taiwan culture's regional soft power. By examining the discursive construction of the term "little freshness" in the PRC media and the appropriation of the film *You Are the Apple of My Eye* for political critique in Hong Kong, I aim to rework Nye's notion of soft power by turning attention away from the role of state agents and to interactions between cultural producers and consumers as a form of what shall be called citizen-to-citizen soft power.[14] To date, studies on soft power have tended to focus on countries with massive hard power such as the United States and China (see this book's Introduction for more discussion). I propose instead that Taiwan, a small island with little international recognition, can similarly have soft power, albeit, in the examples chosen for analysis in this chapter, on a regional scale. Read in the geopolitical context of cross-Strait relations, I argue that little freshness functions like a soft tissue that connects citizens in this region at the same time as the harsh political tensions often threaten to tear them apart.

Little Freshness in the PRC Media

If "affects need objects to come into being" (Flatley 2008, 16), popular music and film from Taiwan were among the first objects to have generated affective expressions of little freshness in the PRC media. As many practices of subcultures have shown, youths often possess the ability to create new meanings and styles from extant objects and formations (Hebdige 1979). As befits the generational demographic of the producers and consumers of the little freshness phenomenon, websites based on user-generated content became the main platform for the coinage of the term as well as for its discursive construction. The term "little freshness" has an entry in major PRC-based websites, including Wikipedia's Chinese-language version and its Chinese counterpart Baidu Baike; it also appears under multiple classifications on Douban, a PRC social-networking service whose launch in 2005 coincided with the release of an album by Taiwan singer-songwriter Cheer Chen (Chen Qizhen).[15] A little freshness group was set up on Douban in 2006, with group members calling themselves "fresh little grass" and membership growing swiftly from several hundred to over 20,000 by 2011; another group, "Cheer Chen," was set up in 2005 and boasted over 60,000 members by 2011 (Li 2011). Meanwhile, an anti-little freshness group was founded in 2007 (Tan 2012), showing that not all netizens were in thrall of the phenomenon and its manifestations.

There is little doubt that Chen is the initial ambassador for Taiwan's soft power in this cross-Strait cultural transaction, as she was crowned the "living Buddha" of the little freshness phenomenon ("Jiegou" 2012) and her song "The Miracle of Travel" ("*Lüxing de yiyi*") was hailed as the "national anthem" of little freshness fans (Li 2011). While insiders of the Beijing pop music scene were skeptical about Chen's market potential when she was scheduled to hold her first solo concert there in 2008, over half of the tickets were snapped up the first day the box office opened, and all tickets were sold out by the end of the week. An additional show was immediately scheduled following inquires and complaints from fans who could not get hold of tickets ("Kaipiao" 2008). Some fans resorted to paying higher prices to ticket touts who wondered "Who is this Cheer Chen?"; many, inspired by Chen's outfit in the music video of her aforementioned song, wore motorcycle helmets to pay homage at their idol's concert (Li 2011).

A study based on news items published on the Baidu website between 2003 and 2007 shows that almost all items that mentioned the term "little freshness" in the PRC news were about music (Zhu 2014, 3); subsequent PRC media reports, however, have begun to trace an alternative source of little freshness to film. Here, Cheer Chen again provides an early link between the two media forms. The 2002 Taiwan film *Blue Gate Crossing* (*Lanse damen*, dir. Yee Chih-yen) has often been retroactively credited in popular discourse as the progenitor of little freshness films. The film inscribes in its text many visual and thematic elements that would later be regarded as belonging to the little freshness genre, from the campus setting and good looking young leads, to summer skies and a light-touch treatment of ambiguous sexuality; its shots were also edited for the music video of a song entitled "Minuet" ("*Xiaobu wuqu*"), written and performed by Chen, which was billed as the film's theme song even though it did not appear in the film at all. In this instance, music video and film joined forces to project an imaginary that, according to a report, was especially appealing to a select group of the PRC audience, namely "literary youths" (*wenqing*) who "yearn for a clear and free life" ("Jiao" 2012).[16]

The affective expressions of yearning for a clear and free life have largely coalesced around the imagery of blue skies, white clouds, and green fields described earlier. An article cited the film *You Are the Apple of My Eye* as the climax of the little freshness phenomenon and went as far to claim that, for the PRC audience, "the *whole* of Taiwan cinema has long been shrouded under a blue sky with sunshine and white clouds" (Xiong et al. 2012, emphasis mine). Another article listed 10 keywords for Taiwan's little freshness films, which include, among others, riding bicycles, same-sex love, little freshness costume (especially school uniform), stunning (natural) landscape, indie music, and summertime setting (Mango 2011). While these features of little freshness might be considered universal, the expressed affection for the specific image of blue skies in these PRC medial and online discourses is arguably more poignant within its local context. After all, the nation's capital is usually so highly polluted that clear blue skies only make an appearance on special occasions—often as a result of political decree to halt factory operation and curtail motorcar traffic—such as during the APEC summit in November 2014 and the big parade in September 2015; hence, the coinage of the terms "APEC blue" (*Yatai lan*) and "parade blue" (*yuebing lan*) (Lu and Chan 2015).[17] Against this background, an affective yearning for blue skies can take on metaphorical meanings and political connotations.

Citizen-to-Citizen Soft Power

The potential for reading different meanings into the appeal of the imagery of blue skies also points to another disjuncture between the Taiwanese producers and the PRC consumers of the little freshness phenomenon. Indeed, the reception of Taiwan cinema in the PRC media not only highlights a distinction between conscious and non-conscious actors but also reverses the conventional direction of soft-power flows. That is to say, while there are always agents involved in the production of cultural forms, not all of these producers consciously package or market their products under a certain label for consumption;

neither are they totally aware of the soft-power appeal of their products beyond their place of production. In 2012, a 13-page special issue entitled "Vive Little Freshness: Incarnation of Youths in Taiwan Cinema" was published in a PRC magazine (Xiong et al. 2012). In its interviews with key Taiwan filmmakers, both Peggy Chiao Hsiung-ping, producer of *Blue Gate Crossing*, and Giddens Ko, director of *You Are the Apple of My Eye*, were bewildered when they were asked what they thought about having their films categorized under the moniker of little freshness because they had never heard of the term. Despite not fully understanding what the term meant, Ko gladly accepted the labeling of his film as such because he said it sounded "cute" (Xiong et al. 2012). Chiao improvised an explanation for the appeal of little freshness, which, according to her, lies in the portrayal, in Taiwan cinema, of life as "an accumulation of everyday details rooted in Taiwan society, full of benevolence, and without any malice" ("Jiao" 2012).

This disjuncture offers an opportunity to rethink the nature of and relations between actors engaged in soft-power transactions. These exchanges between interviewers and interviewees illustrate that little freshness is far from a soft-power weapon wielded by Taiwan's state or nonstate agents but is, instead, an affective discursive construction by PRC youths and journalists in response to Taiwan popular culture, that is, a form of citizen-to-citizen soft power. Given the political stalemate between the PRC and ROC regimes, active promotion of soft power by Taiwanese governmental and nongovernmental agents is understandably circumscribed in China. However, as Nye points out, "the soft power that is becoming more important in the information age is in part a social and economic by-product rather than solely a result of official government action" (2004, 32). As we have seen, the virtual space of the World Wide Web has partly facilitated citizen-to-citizen contacts via the production and consumption of music, film, and other cultural texts, circumventing the political standoff between the two regimes across the Taiwan Strait. The affective expressions by PRC youths toward Taiwan's little freshness phenomenon attest to the materiality of soft-power flows that is at once imaginary and real, imaginative and practical, intimate and public.

Interactions between citizens, therefore, have much to tell us about the potency of imagination, the porosity of national boundaries, and the potentiality of little freshness as a form of cultural connectivity despite political and ideological differences in the region. Moreover, we can move away from a more conventional assumption, in the study of soft power, that agents on the production side of the equation are always active whereas subjects at the receiving end of consumption are necessarily passive.[18] Reversing the direction of cultural flows, the PRC consumers, rather than being passive recipients subject to the influence of foreign cultural products, can claim agency in their active appropriation of Taiwan's soft-power resource to express their affective affiliation with and desire for a cleaner and freer environment (both physical and political). Young fans of popular music—and by extension, of a cultural phenomenon such as little freshness—in China "take their fandom seriously and retrieve from their communities scripts of reality and moments of strong identification" (de Kloet and Fung 2017, 110–111). In the case of little freshness, such "scripts" and "moments" accrue, over time and space, into an intimate public where affective expressions by PRC cultural consumers can be regarded as textual and extra-textual evidence of the citizen-to-citizen soft power of Taiwan's popular film and music. Indeed, as Mark Duffett argues, the practice of screaming by fans may be considered a form of "affective citizenship" that constitutes a "*political* kind of belonging" (2017, 152, emphasis in original), which, in the cases examined here, transcends national boundaries. This notion of affective citizenship is taken to a more literal level in the reception of little freshness in Hong Kong.

Little Freshness in Hong Kong

In contradistinction to the ways a discursive imaginary of little freshness has been constructed in the PRC media as a largely positive identification with Taiwan's clean and clear soft power, Hong Kong citizens' desire for Taiwan's little freshness appears to have been commingled with some negative emotions—namely, fear about the PRC's encroachment on its Special Administrative Region (SAR) and loathing toward Hong Kong's electoral system—to the extent that Taiwan has come to symbolize an ideal destination for emigration. Film and music once again were the chief objects through which these affects had come into being. Giddens Ko's film *You Are the Apple of My Eye* enjoyed phenomenal success in Hong Kong, where it became, in 2011, the all-time top-grossing Chinese-language film at the box office, a record previously held by local star Stephen Chow's 2004 film *Kung Fu Hustle* (*Gongfu*). One reason for this success is the timing of the film's commercial release in October 2011, which coincided with the lead-up to the election of Hong Kong's chief executive in March 2012. The film's poster, which features the young characters sitting in a line on a parapet under blue skies and white clouds and with green fields in the background, was appropriated, in a practice known locally as "secondary creation" (*erci chuangzuo*), by a similarly young generation of Hong Kong netizens to vent their frustrations over the lack of universal suffrage.

Unlike citizens in Taiwan who have witnessed the change of their president from one political color to the other (and back and forth), Hong Kong citizens were (and still are) not entitled to vote in the election of the SAR's chief executive, which is decided by members of a 1,200-strong committee who constitute 0.02 percent of the population. As it turned out, Ko's film became the unwitting champion of antiestablishment sentiments in Hong Kong during the run-up to the 2012 election. One recreated poster of the film replaced the heads of the characters with those of Hong Kong's prominent politicians (including the two candidates in the election) and renamed the film's title, which literally means "the girl we pursued together back in the days," to "the boss's shoes we polished together back in the days" (in Cantonese, to polish someone else's shoes means to curry favor with the person, in this case, the Chinese Communist Party leaders alluded to as "the boss") ("Wangmin" 2011); another poster pointed to a candidate's alleged breaching of building regulations in his own residence. Besides, the film's eponymous theme song, with its lyrics rewritten, was used in a music video whose title became "The Chief Executive We Could Not Elect Together Back in the Days."

Citizen-to-citizen soft power is here manifested in the form of creative appropriation of little freshness imagery for the purpose of political satire. These altered pieces of "secondary creation" went viral on the internet even before the film's official release in Hong Kong, and new versions continued to surface after the election had been held. It should be qualified that Ko's film, based on his eponymous novel first published online, deviates somewhat from the innocent imagery of cleanness and clearness typical of little freshness products, thus allowing it to be appropriated for various purposes in Hong Kong. Instead of images of blue skies, white clouds, and green fields that have made regular appearances in PRC discourses, the focus of media reports on *You Are the Apple of My Eye* in Hong Kong was on how scenes of full rear nudity and masturbation featuring the film's star Kai Ko (Ke Zhendong) incited screams from young female audiences ("*Naxienian*" 2011), signaling, perhaps, a different kind of soft power in action. Moreover, the film's success was also capitalized, beyond the purpose of political satire, for economic gain. Within days of the film's commercial release when it made the news by becoming the top-grossing film for the opening day ("*Naxienian*" 2011), a property developer installed, at one of its sites, a set alluding to the classroom featured in the film, and invited the public to come dressed in school uniforms to pose for a picture, with the best photograph to be picked by Giddens Ko and awarded with prizes. Tour operators, responding to a sudden surge in demand for trips to Taiwan, rescheduled their itineraries to include the film's shooting locations ("Dianying" 2011). Hence, Taiwan's soft-power resources were instantly transformed into business opportunities in Hong Kong, a blatant mercantilism trumping the otherworldliness of the little freshness imaginary.

Taiwan as Desired Other

These examples of political appropriation and commercial exploitation of Ko's film are indicative of a broader social context in which Hong Kong citizens have been simultaneously experiencing the negative push by PRC's hard-power maneuvers and the positive pull from Taiwan's soft-power resources. In the latter case, citizen-to-citizen soft power can be glimpsed from Hong Kong residents' positive perception of Taiwan. The University of Hong Kong's Public Opinion Programme (HKUPOP) has, since 2007, conducted biannual polls on Hong Kong citizens' feelings toward people of various nationalities, including the PRC, Taiwan, Hong Kong, and Macau.[19] Both positive and negative feelings are recorded as percentages of the people polled, with a net value derived by subtracting percentages for negative feeling from positive feeling. The net value recorded for Taiwan was over 50 percent every single year since May 2013, with July 2019 achieving a highest percentage of 74.7.[20] Given recent PRC-Hong Kong relations, it is hardly surprising that net value feeling toward those from the PRC has never exceeded the 10 percent mark since May 2011; in fact, between May 2011 and August 2020, the net value was negative in eight polls, dropping to a lowest percentage of minus 15.1 in the poll conducted in May 2013.[21] However, what made news in the local press was the dismal figure posted for feeling toward Hong Kong people, which dipped to a record low of 28.9 percent in the November 2015 poll, prompting headlines such as "Hongkongers Like Each Other Less Than Ever, Says HKU Survey" (Cheung 2015).[22] It would appear that dissatisfactions with Hong Kong's electoral system and a concomitant fear of PRC's encroachment have transmogrified into a loathing of the Hong Kong self vis-à-vis an affection for the Taiwan other. If affection for the other necessarily indexes positive features embodied by the other, the poll results tell us that it can also register a lack in these positive features or a loathing of negative ones within the self, thus making the other more appealing compared with oneself.

Soft power, therefore, can be as much about desire (for the other) as it is about repulsion (toward the self). Dreams of emigrating to the country of origin of the soft-power resource can be seen as one of the highest forms of flattery since the attraction goes far beyond the consumption and appropriation of cultural products to the possibility of transnational relocation, an operation that demands not just physical, financial, logistical, and legal arrangements but also huge emotional investment. Indeed, affective expressions for the little freshness phenomenon permeate practical considerations for Hong Kong's would-be emigrant to Taiwan. Among recent books published in Hong Kong advising its citizens on how to migrate to Taiwan as well as those about Hong Kong citizens who have made Taiwan their home over the past few years,[23] one emigration manual lists 10 of its "one hundred reasons to embrace Taiwan" under a section entitled *xiao quexing* (Li 2014). This migration wave was even noticed in Japan: in January 2016, NHK World TV aired a documentary *Hong Kong Citizens Flock* to *Taiwan*, which tracks the phenomenon of increasing applications from Hong Kong citizens, particularly by those in their 30s and 40s, to reside in Taiwan. Among reasons given by interviewees for relocating to Taiwan is "human touch" (*renqingwei*), a soft-power value seen to be embodied by Taiwanese citizens. According to the documentary, the number of approved residency applications from Hong Kong and Macau more than tripled between 2011 and 2014, jumping from 2,447 to 7,506 in three years. In fact, this surge in number prompted the Taiwanese government to double, in February 2014, the sum for "invest-ment immigrants" from NT$5 to 10 million, besides tightening regulations for relatives of applicants from Hong Kong and Macau (Chung 2014). It would seem that, from the perspective of the Taiwanese government, the island has become the inadvertent "victim" of the success of the soft power produced by its popular culture in particular and of the affective affiliation shaped by geopolitical forces across the Taiwan Strait in general.[24]

I will end my account of how Nye's notion can be reworked as a form of re-gional citizen-to-citizen soft power on a seeming twist: Hu Xia, the singer of the theme song for *You Are the Apple of My Eye*, hails not from Taiwan but from the PRC.[25] Whereas the choice of Hu for the film's theme song can be read as a clever decision by the film's production team to tap into the emerging PRC market, it also indicates, for my purpose here, that the transnational flows of the little fresh-ness phenomenon might have come full circle to the place (China) where the discourse was first constructed. Taiwan, however, remains the origin of this soft-power resource because Hu first made his name there when he became, in 2010, the first PRC national to have won in the Taiwan TV talent show *One Million Star* (*Chaoji xingguang dadao*) ("Hu Xia" 2010), which began broadcasting in 2007. This was a time when Taiwan's pop music scene was still regarded as the regional leader before the phenomenal success of PRC talent shows such as *The Voice of China* (*Zhongguo hao shengyin*, started in 2012) and *I Am a Singer* (*Woshi geshou*, started in 2013).[26] That is to say, the soft power of Taiwan's pop music scene, in this case a televised talent show, provided the launch pad for a previously un-known PRC national to win in what a PRC media report described as a regional "soft contest" of music talents (note that this was the first time PRC contestants had participated in the show; "Hu Xia" 2010) and to break, a year later, numerous records with the theme song for *You Are the Apple of My Eye*. While soft-power arenas such as music talent shows can become a site of contest(ation) in a geo-political region still fraught with hard political and economic tensions, the little freshness phenomenon has also opened up an alternative space in which youth citizens across the Taiwan Strait can express their affective affiliation with Taiwan popular culture through discursive construction, creative appropriation, and other forms of participation.

Little Freshness as Generational Revolt

To sum up my arguments so far, the transnational flows of little freshness products and discourses across the Taiwan Strait constitute a form of citizen-to-citizen soft power as these transactions have been enacted between cultural producers and consumers with little or no state interference. These flows also reverse the direction of conventional soft-power traffic since it is the youths and the media in PRC and Hong Kong that initiated the affective expressions for Taiwan's cultural products, rather than Taiwanese state and nonstate agents who devised strategies to promote their soft-power resources to the other shore. Via the consumption of the imagery of blue skies, white clouds, and green fields, it is as if the channel of the Taiwan Strait can be momentarily bridged by the soft power of little freshness, through which an intimate public of youth citizens who share a structure of feeling can begin to take shape.

What are the characteristics of this generation of youths, and what are the potential political effects that might be unleashed through their affective investment in the regional soft power of little freshness? The demographic of youths who produce, consume, and embody the little freshness phenomenon is variously called, in the PRC and Hong Kong, the post-80s (balinghou) and post-90s (jiulinghou) generations, or what has been termed in Taiwan as "the collapsed generation" (bengshidai) (Lin et al. 2011).[27] Despite living in different locales within a politically contested region, young people born in the decades of the 1980s and 1990s suffer a structural economic predicament as a legacy of global neoliberal capitalism. In his analysis of Taiwan's Sunflower movement of 2014, Chih-ming Wang argues that youth participants of the movement (whose age would belong to the aforementioned demographic) were driven by fears of becoming "losers" in the era of neoliberal globalization and of being reduced (in the terms of Guy Standing) from the status of citizens to "denizens" (Wang C-m. 2017, 185). As such, Wang reads the Sunflower movement's underlying structure of feeling as generational injustice and the movement itself as an "affective response to the uncertainties of the future released by neoliberalism" (Wang C-m. 2017, 179). While it may be ironic to note the adverse economic conditions that underpin the production of little freshness resources in Taiwan and the detached contexts of their consumption in China and Hong Kong, it is, nonetheless, the same generation of young people who manifested (and continues to manifest) a form of citizen-to-citizen soft power through their desire for little freshness and who also spearheaded Taiwan's Sunflower movement and Hong Kong's Umbrella movement (which also erupted in 2014) as political representations of their rights as citizens of their lands.[28]

Against this background, it can be argued that the production, consumption, and embodiment of the affect of little freshness symbolize a form of generational revolt that, owing to its prominence in the public sphere, has already witnessed a backlash. If notoriety can be understood as an inverse form of praise, the high-profile and widespread critique of this tendency toward miniaturization attests precisely to the perceived reach of the soft-power appeal of *xiao qingxin* and *xiao quexing* both at home and abroad. In Taiwan, the president of the Examination Yuan (in charge of validating the qualification of civil servants) openly criticized the government for formulating its policies on the basis of *xiao quexing*, and a famous tycoon expressed his disbelief that young people's ambition extended only to opening cafés ("Shelun" 2014); a prominent cultural newspaper devoted a special issue to "oppose all things small and light" ("Fandui" 2012); and an academic article in a top-ranking journal aimed to employ Slavoj Žižek's materialist theology "to find salvation for people who have been trapped in the post-capitalist labyrinth" represented by the "abuse" of *xiao quexing* for commercial purposes in Taiwan (Tseng 2015, 109). Furthermore, sociologist Chao Kang lambasted the term as representative of a "cultural unconscious" of a generation who, fearing the economic rise of China, turned inward-looking and championed values such as "courtesy," "tolerance," and "human touch" instead (Chao 2014); the lead singer of the punk rock band Loh Tsui Kweh Commune (*Zhuoshuixi gongshe*) even went as far as to pronounce little freshness as causing harm to the nation (*wuguo*) (Shih 2015).

These critical voices against miniaturization indicate an incomprehension and disapproval of an affective feature permeating youth culture and popular cultural products in Taiwan. They also remind us of the ways affects (and emotions) "work in social and cultural terms as part of the everyday production and reproduction of social identities and unequal power relations" (Harding and Pribram 2009, 4), here manifested by those with political, economic, cultural, and academic powers expressing their opposition to the emergence of a social identity mobilized in affective terms but undermined by its overall lack of power as a generation of youths. By contrast, discourses produced by this generation of youths (and those sympathetic toward it) have repeatedly highlighted the mutually constitutive "social [read economic] structure" and "mental [read affective] structure" that undergird the zeitgeist that is *xiao quexing* (Chen 2014, 35–36), as well as a genuine belief among youths of this generation in values such as freedom, democracy, and diversity, rather than so-called competitiveness in economic terms (Chang 2014). In a recent book that reconfigures the "collapsed generation" as the "misanthropic generation" (*yanshidai*), interviewees acknowledged, somewhat wryly, that embracing *xiao quexing* was one way of making their lives bearable (Wu 2017, 39, 173); after all, according to statistics released by the Taiwanese authorities in May 2016, 40 percent of those aged between 20 and 34 earned an average monthly salary of under NT$25,000, when the average monthly cost of living, in 2015, was NT$27,216 in Taipei City and NT$20,421 island-wide (Wu 2017, 15). The book's subtitle, *Low Salary, Poverty, and an Inability to See the Future*, is, indeed, the flip side of *xiao quexing*.

The Power of Affective Cinema

What, then, is at stake for contemporary Taiwan cinema to have taken an affective turn? What implications does this turn have for the production and consumption of Taiwan films? To return to the bifurcation between high international prestige and low domestic box-office intake that has plagued discourses on Taiwan cinema since the heyday of the TNC period, does the newfound commercial success kick-started by *Cape No. 7* signal a rescaling of vision and reorientation of market in cinematic terms? Above all, what is the import of the central function assumed, in cultural production such as film, by affect—specifically, the structure of feeling known as little freshness, given its youth demographic, gender disposition, and class pretension? In the final analysis, how does this affective cinema impact on our understanding of contemporary Taiwan film historiography?

Indeed, to what extent can the emerging trend that is the subgenre of little freshness films be said to be a form of generational revolt within the film industry? It is noteworthy that the connection between TNC and post-TNC filmmakers is much stronger than the one between TNC filmmakers and their predecessors. Among TNC auteurs, Edward Yang was largely self-taught despite having attended film school at the University of Southern California (Yeh and Davis 2005, 92, 265n1), and Ang Lee graduated from New York University's film school and has based his career in the United States from the very beginning; that is to say, prior to making their debut films, both Yang and Lee had little or no contact with the Taiwan film industry.[29] On the other hand, while Tsai wrote screenplays for some early TNC films (Wen 2002, 244–248), and whereas Hou served an extensive apprenticeship to veteran directors such as Lee Hsing (Hong 2011, 88), their TNC debut films displayed a thematic and stylistic rupture with their predecessors' work in a manner that could hardly be claimed of post-TNC directors.[30] By contrast, many post-TNC filmmakers worked closely with TNC directors before making their own debut films.[31] Wei Te-sheng was an assistant director for Yang's 1996 film *Mahjong* (*Majiang*) and played a key role in the production of Chen Kuo-fu's 2002 film *Double Vision* (*Shuangtong*). Tom Lin, director of *Winds of September* (*Jiujiangfeng*, 2008), worked as first assistant director on Tsai's *The Wayward Cloud* (*Tianbian yiduo yun*, 2005); Hung Chih-yu, director of the historical epic *1895* (2008), assisted on Wu Nien-jen's *A Borrowed Life* (*Duo sang*, 1994) and *Buddha Bless America* (*Taiping tianguo*, 1996) as well as on several films by Hou in the 1990s. Doze Niu Chen-zer, director of the 2010 hit film *Monga* (*Mengjia*), was a lead actor in Hou's debut TNC feature, *The Boys from Fengkuei* (*Fenggui lai de ren*, 1983).

Revolt, of course, can take many forms. Whereas TNC directors vented their frustrations with the filmmaking environment they found themselves mired in via a manifesto (Zhan 1988; see Introduction for a discussion), post-TNC directors have also spoken, albeit in less vehement and coordinated ways, about their attempts to escape from the shadows of their predecessors and, crucially, their decision to make more commercial films. Niu said in an interview that he knew early on that he would not become the kind of filmmaker that Hou is.[32] Rather than turn himself into "box-office poison," Niu declared his wish to make "commercial films with substance" ("Niu" 2012)—a wish fulfilled when *Monga* became the only film whose intake crossed the NT$100-million threshold in the Greater Taipei region in 2010.[33] As for Wei, when asked by the PRC media to define little freshness (films), he suggested that it is a form of low-budget filmmaking aimed at producing crowd-pleasing work, whose creative process does not have as much "baggage" (Xiong et al. 2012)—an allusion, perhaps, to the historical baggage associated with TNC auteurs. Giddens Ko, an outsider of the Taiwan film industry, simply said he wanted to make films that will "collect money" (Xiong et al. 2012).

In historiographical terms, a generational revolt in contemporary Taiwan cinema can be summarized as post-TNC directors' preference for achieving high domestic box-office intake and (however unwittingly) regional soft power through their little freshness films (as mapped out in this chapter), rather than follow the well-trodden path of their TNC predecessors who trade on the currency of authorship and transnationality on the international stage (discussed in Chapters 1 to 4). Yet, post-TNC directors' rescaling of vision from the global to the local and a reorientation of market toward commercial considerations—and, by implication, the taste of the domestic audience—do not adequately explain the prominence of little freshness in cinematic representation nor the success of other kinds of commercial filmmaking. In fact, one name that has yet to make an appearance in this book and that is routinely shunned in almost all accounts of Taiwan cinema is Chuke Liang (1946–2017), a veteran variety show host whose long career and popularity cut across entertainment forms and generations of audiences in Taiwan. Famous for his roles in Lunar New Year films (*hesui pian*), Chuke Liang starred, since 2011, in at least five films whose individual box-office intakes for the whole of Taiwan have all broken the NT$100-million mark (Chen C-c. 2016). In particular, *David Loman* (*Dawei luman*, 2013, dir. Chiu Li-kwan) took in NT$430 million island-wide, a figure that only lagged behind, at the time, Wei's *Cape No. 7* and *Warriors of the Rainbow: Seediq Bale Part 1* (Cheng 2014, 29). If we return to Table 5.1, we will see that, besides films directed or produced by Ang Lee and Wei Te-sheng, as well as those associated with the little freshness phenomenon, films that have also crossed the NT$100-million threshold (in the Greater Taipei region alone) tend to be comedies (*David Loman*), horror films (*The Tenants Downstairs/Louxia de fangke*, dir. Adam Tsuei, 2016), or those with a strong folk flavor (such as *Din Tao: Leader of the Parade/Zhentou*, dir. Fung Kai, 2012), attesting to a different cinematic taste outside Taipei—a revolt of the non-metropolitan audience if you like. Nevertheless, even critics who are fond of accusing TNC of killing the Taiwan film industry in their rhetoric of "authorship versus popularity" do not champion these commercially successful films as showing the path that domestic production should take, and films such as *David Loman* are only mentioned, almost always obligingly, in annual reviews of Taiwan cinema as epitomizing bad taste and crassness (Cheng 2014, 27–29; Wen 2014, 8), condemned as they are to languish in historiographical obscurity.

Little freshness films, therefore, not only represent a cinematic generational revolt but also provide a third term beyond, bridging, or bypassing the bifurcation between the high international prestige of auteur cinema and the low box-office intake of domestic films. It reinvigorates the audience by proving that a reorientation to commercial filmmaking (whilst not descending to the level of Chuke Liang and his ilk) can lead to domestic box-office success and regional soft power without the cachet of art cinema and authorship. However, whereas it is hard to dispute the material outcome (box-office intake) of some little freshness films, the affective dimension (little freshness) that has contributed to this cinematic phenomenon remains contentious. Film scholar Kuo Li-hsin is among the first to spot, in his discussion of *Cape No. 7*, the trend toward miniaturization. In an essay that appraises the scale (*geju*) and future of Taiwan cinema following the "fever" generated by the success of Wei's film, Kuo notes a parallel between a filmmaking tendency privileging small topics about youth and *bildungsroman* and a shrinking of scope in political vision in Taiwan (Kuo 2009, 57). Kuo acknowledges material conditions such as the film industry's structure and the government's cultural policy as possible reasons for the emergence of films that favor small and safe subject matters because they incur a lower cost of production, but he also expresses "regret" if these external conditions were to be internalized as "cultural characters" that would shape the "taste, scale, and vision" of a new generation of filmmakers (56–57). More recently, veteran film critic Wen Tien-hsiang hinted at his reservations about this filmmaking trend by describing little freshness as a "forte (*or indulgence*)" of Taiwan cinema (Wen 2015, 21, emphasis mine), while another critic, Ryan Cheng, suggested that the "fever" of campus-set little freshness films might have "subsided" (Cheng 2015, 52).

Twelve years (2020 at the time of this writing) after the phenomenal success of *Cape No. 7*, this affective cinema has, in fact, shown no sign of waning. In 2015, *Our Times (Wode shaonü shidai*, dir. Frankie Chen Yu-shan), arguably the female version of Ko's *You Are the Apple of My Eye*, surpassed the NT$100-million mark at the box office in the Greater Taipei region, and took in over 400 million across Taiwan and over 2.5 billion worldwide (Wen 2016, 15). Demonstrating the sustaining regional soft-power appeal of little freshness films, it also became, at the time, the most commercially successful Taiwan film in the PRC market, achieving an intake of RMB 360 million (Liang 2017, 39). Besides, the film's lead actor, Darren Wang (Dalu), became an overnight sensation in China; the income he earned in two years from advertising alone was estimated to be in the region of NT$80 million (Chang 2017).

To conclude, even though they only constitute a portion of films released in Taiwan in the twenty-first century, little freshness films have been put under the spotlight here because of their phenomenal domestic box-office success; their prominent regional soft power; and the proliferating cinematic, cultural, and critical discourses they have attracted. This affective cinema (and the wider market of miniaturization of which it is part) may appear, on the surface, to be no more than a passing subcultural fad built upon Taiwan's cultural products; but, given sympathetic examination, the intimate public coalescing around its structure of feeling belies a potential for forms of citizen-to-citizen connectivity that may have an impact on civil society in the region. "Little freshness" and "small exact happiness," therefore, are cultural embodiments of a generation of youths whose desires and despairs in the face of neoliberal globalization are couched in terms that some might perceive as pathetically small. For Berlant, intimate public stands for, among other things, "permission to live small but to feel large" (2008, 3). Youths in Taiwan today may fear that they have become "losers" as an effect of neoliberal capitalism, but Berlant regards any formation of an intimate public as an "achievement":

> Whether linked to women or other nondominant people, [an intimate public] flourishes as a porous, affective scene of identification among strangers that promises a certain experience of belonging and provides a complex of consolation, confirmation, discipline, and discussion about how to live as an *x*. (Berlant 2008, viii)

As we have seen in this chapter, as a basis for social formations, affect (or emotion) can be easily "diminished by [its] long-standing association with women and other purportedly non-rational social groups, leading to the marginalisation of emotion in knowledge production and, too often, to its entrenchment as irrationality, the antithesis of reason" (Harding and Pribram 2009, 1). For youths living in China and Hong Kong, the soft power of Taiwan's little freshness phenomenon provides more than an escapist indulgence through cultural production and consumption. Rather, by appropriating the discursive imaginary of little freshness, these subjects exercise their agency in desiring Taiwan, express their affection for all things small, and generate citizen-to-citizen soft power whose formations may only be emergent and not yet fully institutionalized.[34] Notwithstanding the economic structure that circumscribes Taiwan's collapsed and misanthropic generation, little freshness as a lifestyle option is still deemed possible in Taiwan and desired by many young citizens in the region. This desire is embodied in the imagery of blue skies, white clouds, and green fields in film, music, and other cultural forms from Taiwan and being projected onto by discursive construction in the PRC media and by aspiring emigrants in Hong Kong. If this desire for little freshness signifies the triumph not of "Taiwanese nationalism" but of "neoliberalism's privatizing impulse as the sky of our imagination" (Wang C-m. 2017, 189), it also points to what Berlant calls "cruel optimism" ("when something you desire is actually an obstacle to your flourishing"; 2011, 1), a double-bind from which not only youths across the Taiwan Strait but also most of us living under the logic of neoliberal capitalism have little or no escape. The social, cultural, and political ramifications of the generational revolt by a sizable demographic of youths, as well as the citizen-to-citizen soft power evinced by this affective cinema, may well be long-term and wide-ranging for us all.

Epilogue

Alien Resurrection; or, the Afterlives of Taiwan New Cinema

At the 2013 Golden Horse Awards, Singaporean director Anthony Chen's debut feature film *Ilo Ilo* (*Bama buzai jia*, 2013), already a Camera d'Or winner at Cannes for Best First Feature Film, beat Tsai Ming-liang's *Stray Dogs* (*Jiaoyou*, 2013), Wong Kar-wai's *The Grandmaster* (*Yidai zongshi*, 2013), Jia Zhangke's *A Touch of Sin* (*Tian zhuding*, 2013), and Johnnie To's *Drug War* (*Du zhan*, 2012) to become the surprise winner of the Best Feature Film, making Chen the youngest director to have won in the category (Cheng 2014, 21). The film also won in three other categories, namely, Best New Director and Best Original Screenplay for Anthony Chen, and Best Supporting Actress for Yeo Yann Yann. In a landmark year celebrating the 50th anniversary of Taiwan's answer to the Academy Awards,[1] the conferment of such accolades by the jury headed by Ang Lee to a film by a young director (Chen was 29 years old at the time) was perceived as a symbolic passing of the baton to a new generation of filmmakers in Chinese cinema (*huayu dianying*). The Awards' recognition of young directors of alien nationalities and their debut films would continue in the ensuing years: Bi Gan (b. 1989) from the People's Republic of China (PRC) won the FIPRESCI (International Federation of Film Critics) award for *Kaili Blues* (*Lubian yecan*, 2015) in 2015; another PRC director Zhang Dalei (b. 1982) clinched the Best Feature Film award as well as the FIPRESCI prize for *The Summer Is Gone* (*Bayue*, 2016) in 2016; and, in 2017, yet another PRC director Zhou Ziyang (b. 1983) bagged the FIPRESCI award for *Old Beast* (*Lao shou*, 2017). In 2018, *An Elephant Sitting Still* (*Daxiang xidi er zuo*, 2018) by PRC director Hu Bo (who committed suicide the year before at the age of 29) won the Best Feature Film and Best Adapted Screenplay; another PRC director, Wen Muye (b. 1985) won the Best New Director award for *Dying to Survive* (*Wo bushi yaoshen*, 2018), and the film also won Best Original Screenplay.

I opened this book by discussing a speech by a Taiwan documentary filmmaker at the 2018 Golden Horse Awards ceremony that triggered a PRC boycott of the event from the following year onward. I hereby end this book by noting that this boycott has not stopped the Awards from carrying on its recent tradition, as chronicled in this Epilogue, of recognizing alien filmmakers. In 2019, the

Taiwan Cinema as Soft Power. Song Hwee Lim, Oxford University Press. © Oxford University Press 2022.
DOI: 10.1093/oso/9780197503379.003.0007

year marking the start of the PRC boycott, Yeo Yann Yann returned to win, this time the Best Actress Award, for Anthony Chen's second feature film, *Wet Season* (*Redaiyu*, 2019); another Singaporean film, *A Land Imagined* (*Huantu*, 2018), won Best Original Screenplay for Yeo Siew Hua and Best Original Film Score for Teo Wei Yong. In 2020, the year in which a national security law was imposed in Hong Kong in the aftermath of the Anti-Extradition Law Amendment Bill movement that erupted in the previous year, the mood at the awards ceremony was somber when winning Hong Kong filmmakers made their acceptance speeches;[2] Malaysian filmmaker Chong Keat Aun won Best New Director for *The Story of Southern Islet* (*Nanwu*, 2020), which also bagged the FIPRESCI prize; a Singaporean film, *Number 1* (*Nanerwang*, 2020), took away the Best Makeup and Costume Design award for Raymond Kuek and Azni Samdin; the Best Original Film Song, "Your Name Engraved Herein" (*Kezai wo xindi de mingzi*), was penned by two Malaysians and a Singaporean, albeit for a Taiwan film.

The winning streak by alien filmmakers at the Taiwanese Oscars opens this Epilogue because it attests, first and foremost, to the exercise of soft power by the authorities overseeing the running of the Golden Horse Awards to turn the institution into a transnational event that would embrace Chinese filmmaking from across the world. All the aforementioned films and filmmakers would not have been able to participate in the Golden Horse Awards had the Award's remit not been expanded, in 1997, to allow in foreigners and their works. Second, this inclusive gesture is indicative of the appeal of Taiwan cinema in general and of Taiwan New Cinema (hereafter TNC) in particular to ethnic Chinese filmmakers of other nationalities to the extent that Taiwan has become both a magnet that draws in young directors to learn their craft and a mecca for their pilgrimage to the source of their artistic inspiration and aspiration. As I will detail later, the effects of this broader attraction are wide-ranging, from migrants who only started their filmmaking career in Taiwan and even naturalized as Taiwanese citizens, to young students who have come to study filmmaking in Taiwanese colleges and evidence of homage in the film texts of foreign directors. Third, efforts by the authorities to exercise this soft power have extended to new initiatives such as the Golden Horse Film Academy founded by the veteran TNC auteur Hou Hsiao-hsien and the Golden Horse Film Project Promotion scheme whose Grand Prize of US$30,000 (the largest cash prize within Asia for film production) would help new directors kick-start their planned project.[3]

Taken together, the financial benefits of prizes and the cultural cachet of the opportunity to be trained by established directors make the various initiatives of the Golden Horse institution an appealing soft-power tool that might, in admittedly small and slow ways, contribute to Taiwan's expansion of its influence on the international stage. Indeed, one oft-neglected dimension in the discussion of soft power is that of temporality.[4] To put it differently, it takes time—sometimes,

a very long time—before the effects of soft power unveil themselves; and even
if they do, they often appear in unexpected places and times and, what's more,
are not always recognized as such.[5] For example, whilst TNC had started to win
major international film festival awards within a decade of its birth in 1982 and
its auteurs quickly hailed as cinematic masters, its wider and deeper impact
is only beginning to make its presence felt in the twenty-first century. Olivier
Assayas, whose 1997 documentary on Hou (and TNC) opened the discussion in
Chapter 1, said the following about his 2008 film, *Summer Hours* (*L'heure d'été*):

> I've always felt like a sort of Taiwanese director working in France. When
> I started making movies, the preoccupations of Hou Hsiao-hsien and Edward
> Yang affected me, resonated with my own. Later I became interested in the work
> of Wong Kar Wai and Tsai Ming-liang. They are more my family than French
> cinema of the time, that of directors starting back then, with whom I had little
> in common in the generational sense. . . . As strange as it may seem, with my
> Chinese friends I felt I could have, symbolically, the dialogue I had been de-
> prived of here. (Marques 2008, 6)[6]

As I have discussed elsewhere (Lim 2011b, 21–22), Assayas's statement recalls
the sentiments of the Nouvelle Vague directors who found little in common with
their preceding generation of filmmakers, dismissing their films as "*le cinéma
de papa*" and turning instead to Hollywood for inspiration (Hayward 2006, 33).
Unlike the Nouvelle Vague directors, Assayas's sense of alienation was triggered
by his own generation of French filmmakers (the "*cinéma du look*" of Jean-
Jacques Beineix, Luc Besson, and Leos Carax), but he looked to the East rather
than the West. For these French directors of different generations, Hollywood
and TNC similarly served as a source of affect, affiliation, and attraction, providing alternative models for and different conversations on filmmaking.

Cinematic soft power, therefore, is capable of making the alien (and the alienated) feel more at home on foreign soil than they would have felt in their homeland, a form of transnational imaginary that bridges geographical, linguistic,
ethnic, and other boundaries that can take on a life, in fact, an afterlife, of its
own. In this Epilogue, I intend to advance my thesis laid out in the main body
of this book by demonstrating how a nation's soft power in the form of cinema
can attract aliens to adopt practices and to develop projects—whether within or
without the said nation's territory—that might, in turn, reinvigorate, rejuvenate,
and resurrect that nation's cinema, becoming, as it were, the latter's afterlives.
I contend that, nearly four decades after its inception, TNC continues to exert its
influence across the world, with evidence ranging from open acknowledgment
of affinity (such as Assayas's earlier statement) and specific filmmaking practices
(such as homage and remakes) to other routes and detours (e.g., migration). By

focusing on how TNC attracts aliens to Taiwan—whether to receive awards or training, to make films or even homes—this Epilogue also turns the outward-bound notion of soft power on its head not so much to discount its impact abroad, rather, precisely, to account for the harvesting of its effects as they travel back home like a boomerang. Thus, I end this book by mapping out the implications of this alien resurrection for our understanding of TNC and its afterlives vis-à-vis the three keywords of the book's subtitle and the overarching framework of soft power (here focusing on the role played by Taiwanese institutions).

Soft Power

The Golden Horse Awards has come a long way from its founding mission, in 1962, to award films whose contents were imbued with "righteous or educational meaning." The conferment of prizes, in the new millennium, to PRC and Southeast Asian filmmakers mentioned earlier has been made possible thanks to efforts to gradually loosen regulations to allow foreign nationals and their films to compete at the Awards. Back in 1989, Siqin Gaowai, the PRC-born actress of Swiss citizenship, was ruled ineligible for participation for her role in Stanley Kwan's *Full Moon in New York* (*Ren zai Niuyue*, also known as *Sange nüren de gushi*, 1989). In 1991, the eligibility qualification was relaxed to include all filmmakers of Chinese descent (*huayi*) who were working in the Taiwan and Hong Kong film industries, although this move incurred the wrath of Australian-born cinematographer Christopher Doyle (whose Chinese name is Du Kefeng) who, at the time, had already worked with auteurs such as Edward Yang (on *That Day, on the Beach/Haitan de yitian*, 1983) and Wong Kar-wai (on *Days of Being Wild/Afei zhengzhuan*, 1990). In acknowledgment of increasing co-production of films with China, a new regulation in 1993 permitted films in which PRC nationals did not constitute more than half of the main crew to compete; however, this still ruled out Chen Kaige's *Farewell My Concubine* (*Bawang bieji*, 1993) and Zhang Yimou's *To Live* (*Huozhe*, 1994)—two films bankrolled by Taiwan producers.[7] The biggest expansion of regulations came in 1996 when films made in China were let in under a new qualification in which "all Chinese-language films, including [those spoken in] Hokkien and other dialects, are eligible to submit regardless of production country, funding ratio or nationality of crew."

As a government-sponsored initiative, the Golden Horse Awards' evolution from a propagandistic tool—for both domestic and international consumption, it must be said—of the then-ruling Nationalist Party (Kuomintang, or KMT) to a global platform for Chinese filmmaking evinces the operation of soft power, here deploying the magic of cinema to achieve the goals of all soft-power schemes: to attract alien bodies to consume a nation's product, identify with its values, and, in this instance, even compete on its own shores. In 1997, the Government Information Office (GIO), the official body overseeing the Awards, abolished the legal regulation to award "outstanding Mandarin films" and repositioned the Awards as a global Chinese-language film competition, whose linguistic criterion was further eased in 2007 to allow the participation of films—regardless of the language—whose director and half of the main crew is Chinese. In this sense, the Best Feature Film prize bestowed upon Anthony Chen at the Awards' landmark occasion in 2013 signals a defining moment in Taiwan cinema's recognition of its alien "other"—from the geographic to the linguistic—for *Ilo Ilo* is a film about a Filipino domestic maid working for a Singaporean Chinese family, and its dialogue comprises of a mix of Mandarin, English, and Tagalog. While the continual expansion of the Awards' remit has not always been welcomed by critics at home, especially in years when the performance of Taiwan cinema was dismal, the transformation of the Golden Horse as an institution from a national instrument to a regional and global soft-power tool is a testament to both the Taiwanese government's broadening vision and TNC's appeal among Chinese filmmakers across the world.

Beyond the Awards itself, the expansion of the soft-power reach of the Golden Horse as an institution has been achieved through two specific initiatives. First, the Film Academy, founded in 2009, has played a key role in bringing together aspiring filmmakers from the Chinese-speaking world, engendering an actual rather than imagined community that could, in time, produce acclaimed auteurs in their own right. The list of instructors is filled with luminaries from the world of cinema. In 2020, a master class session featured Palme d'Or winner Ken Loach, Golden Lion winner Roy Andersson, and Golden Lion winner Andrey Zvyagintsev as speakers; and Palme d'Or winner Hirokazu Kore-eda was the leading act in the small workshop called Golden Horse Studio. Second, the Golden Horse Film Project Promotion scheme provides a platform to bring together filmmakers, investors, and distributors, as well as to link regional industry professionals with the international film community. Projects incubated, such as Malaysian Ho Wi-Ding's *Pinoy Sunday* (*Taibei xingqitian*, 2010) and Bi Gan's *Long Day's Journey into Night* (*Diqiu zuihou de yewan*, 2018), would win prizes years later at the Golden Horse Awards.[8] Another standout result of the scheme is the 2011 project by PRC director Yang Chao, whose film *Crosscurrent* (*Changjiang tu*, 2016) went on to win, in 2016, a Silver Bear for Outstanding Artistic Contribution at the Berlin film festival (for Taiwan's Mark Lee Pingbing's cinematography) as well as Best Cinematography and Best Sound Effects at the Golden Horse Awards.

For aspiring filmmakers from outside Taiwan, these initiatives have, no doubt, become launch pads to greater success in their later careers. To put it in a broader context, the indebtedness that some of these alien filmmakers express toward the legacy of TNC owes as much to Taiwan's cinematic soft power as it does to the government's hard political and economic power. One example is Midi Z (Kyawk Dadyin, or Zhao Deyin in pinyin, b. 1982), a fourth-generation Yunnanese Chinese migrant born in Burma (Chang W-c 2016, 43) who had the opportunity to study in Taiwan at the age of 16 thanks to KMT's educational policy for overseas Chinese.[9] Midi Z started making short experimental films as part of his college coursework, and he was selected to attend the very first Golden Horse Film Academy where he learned quite a few tricks from Hou Hsiao-hsien (Zhao 2015, 18–19). After making his first three feature-length film, collectively known as the "homecoming trilogy," from which the third installment, *Ice Poison* (*Bingdu*, 2014), was selected to represent Taiwan in the Foreign Language Film category at the 2015 Academy Awards, Midi was given the Outstanding Taiwanese Filmmaker of the Year award at the 2016 Golden Horse Awards. After the awards ceremony, he posted on social media his acceptance speech, in which he thanked, besides directors Li Hsing, Hou, and Tsai, "Taiwan's freedom, diversity, and democracy" (values amenable to the spread of soft power in Joseph Nye's thesis) for pushing his path toward filmmaking. In fact, Midi Z's Burmese background overlaps, in recent years, with the "New Go South Policy" (*xin nanxiang zhengce*) inaugurated by President Tsai Ing-wen in 2016 to re-establish links with Southeast Asian countries as Taiwan's economy became increasingly squeezed by China's policy and growth. The bureaucrats were clearly aware of cinema's soft power as the policy's official website features an interview with Midi Z entitled "Midi Z: Taiwan, Cradle of My Cinema."[10] By taking up Taiwanese citizenship in 2011 (Chen C. 2016), Midi Z's transformation from an alien to citizenship status demonstrates the complementary roles played by soft-power attraction and hard economic and geopolitical realities.

Authorship

For the alien filmmakers who have won prizes at the Golden Horse Awards or benefited from schemes initiated by its affiliated institutions, the soft power of TNC's authorship is a recurrent theme in their discursive construction in interviews. As the documentary *Flowers of Taipei: Taiwan New Cinema* (*Guangyin de gushi: Taiwan xindianying*, dir. Hsieh Chin-lin, 2014; discussed in Chapter 1) demonstrates, cross-cultural cinephilia—with authorship at its code in the case of TNC—can be understood as an expression of soft power. Hou Hsiao-hsien, in particular, has the broadest appeal and deepest influence among young foreign filmmakers who have been taken under the wings of the Golden Horse. Among Golden Horse Awards winners, Zhang Dalei claimed that he only began to understand what film should be like or what kinds of film he would like to make after watching Hou's *The Boys from Fengkuei* (*Fenggui lai de ren*, 1983) (She and Chen 2017), and Chong Keat Aun credited the long takes in Hou's *A Time to Live, A Time to Die* (*Tongnian wangshi*, 1985) for piquing his curiosity about film as a medium (Wu 2020). When Hou was given the Golden Horse Lifetime Achievement award in 2020, the Japanese director Hirokazu Kore-eda not only flew in from Japan (despite the requirement to serve a 14-day quarantine upon arrival owing to the outbreak of the coronavirus pandemic) to present the award, he was also turned into "a little fan" when he was taken by Hou and Mark Lee Ping-bing (head of the jury for that year) to the small town of Jiufen where Hou's *A City of Sadness* (*Beijing chengshi*, 1989) was shot (Lu 2020). The photographs they took together and made public are evidence of a meeting of cross-cultural cinephilia (discussed in Chapter 1) and location tourism (discussed in Chapter 4), sealed with the aura of authorship.

If TNC auteurs have served as models for filmmaking to budding alien directors, these aliens have, in turn, been hailed as exemplars for an even younger generation of filmmakers in Taiwan, thus perpetuating, in the manner of a loop, TNC's legacy. After the peaks of Hou and Edward Yang in the 1980s and of Ang Lee and Tsai Ming-liang in the 1990s, Taiwan cinema has been plagued by a lack of auteurs. Outside of the quartet of auteurs just mentioned, only Lin Cheng-sheng, as Table I.1 in the Introduction shows, has won a major award at top European film festivals. Anxiety about the lack of auteurs is palpable in discourses on Taiwan cinema since the turn of the twenty-first century, and it is notably heightened when young alien directors have stolen the limelight at the Golden Horse Awards. After Anthony Chen's *Ilo Ilo* won the Best Feature Film in 2013, Wen Tien-hsiang, veteran film critic and CEO of the Golden Horse Film Festival Executive Committee since 2009, heard, on various occasion, people saying that young Taiwan directors should watch Chen's film (presumably to learn about storytelling), reflecting, in Wen's reading, an anxiety (about Taiwan cinema losing on its home turf) behind the excitement of having discovered a fresh talent in Chen (Wen 2014, 7). When Bi Gan won the Best New Director award in 2015, a report commented that Taiwan cinema did not lack campus romance and New Year festive comedies but "fantastical eyes" like Bi's (Chang C-m 2016).[11]

These alien directors, in their expressed affection for the films of TNC auteurs and via their own filmmaking practice, can stake a claim as TNC's true heirs through whom TNC's afterlife has manifested. In other words, TNC has projected a circuitous soft-power flow that has, like a boomerang, traveled beyond the island's shores and, decades later, returned to Taiwan, albeit under the guise of an alien resurrection. I have argued in this book that Taiwan cinema's soft power has been carried by the currency of authorship on the international stage since the 1980s (Chapters 1 to 4), and that "little freshness" films present an alternative form of soft power on a regional scale in the new millennium (Chapter 5). The dominating image of the auteur, however, has never ceased to haunt Taiwan directors over these decades, hence the discernable anxiety about the lack of auteurs. The generation of Taiwan directors caught between these two forms of soft power has perhaps suffered the most in terms of the burden of TNC's authorship and neglect in film discourse and historiography. Emerging alongside or slightly after Ang Lee and Tsai, this group of directors includes Chen Yu-hsun, Yee Chih-yen, Chang Tso-chi, and Lin Cheng-sheng who made their debut feature films in the 1990s, and Yang Ya-che, Tom Lin, Leon Dai, and Chong Mong-hong who started their careers in the 2000s. These directors encountered the darkest period for the domestic film market when they started out (see Table 5.1 in Chapter 5 for Taiwan cinema's box-office share) and failed to exhibit any substantive form of soft power as their films struggled to find a path (or an identity) between the art cinema of TNC auteurs and a more popular appeal manifested by the likes of Wei Te-sheng's *Cape No. 7 (Haijiao qihao*, 2008; see Chapter 5 for more discussion).[12] In *Face Taiwan: Power of Taiwan Cinema (Women zheyang pai dianying*, dir. Hsiao Chu-chen, 2015), a documentary on TNC's legacy, Chen Yu-hsun spoke ruefully about the shadow of the TNC under which his generation of directors had to work and from which it attempted to escape;[13] Doze Niu, whose acting career began in the early years of the TNC (notably in Hou's *The Boys from Fengkuei*) but whose directorial career only took off in the 2000s, was almost at the brink of tears when he talked about how Hou would dismiss his directorial work as substandard. The bar set by the masters was so high that TNC often appeared, for those who came after, an insurmountable mountain to climb.

Seen in this light, authorship, while a beacon of TNC's soft power on the international stage, can also become an unbearable weight of being for domestic filmmakers who have little power even at home. In the twenty-first century, it is, in fact, alien auteurs who have propelled Taiwan's cinematic soft power on the global front. It is easy to forget that Tsai, who has based his entire career in Taiwan, remains a Malaysian citizen, although all his films represent Taiwan at international festivals.[14] Midi Z, whose *The Road to Mandalay (Zaijian Wacheng*, 2016) won the FEDEORA (Federation of Film Critics of Europe and the Mediterranean) award for Best Film at the Venice film festival, looks best poised to succeed Tsai in this capacity.[15] With his latest documentary, *14 Apples (Shisi ke pingguo*, 2018), receiving its world premiere screening at the International Forum of New Cinema, "the most daring section of the Berlinale,"[16] Midi Z's "poor cinema" (Lim 2018) possesses, I believe, the greatest auteurist potential in spreading Taiwan cinema's global soft power today.[17]

Transnationality

The exercise of soft power is invariably transnational, and one lacuna in film scholarship, as I have argued elsewhere, is precisely the relationship between cinematic new waves and transnational cinema. Whether it is TNC or slow cinema (of which TNC auteurs like Hou and Tsai are its chief practitioners), some new waves can be regarded as a form of "transnational cinema without the national" because their concerns with, for example, questions of time and temporality "do not necessarily have national foundations, manifestations, or ramifications" (Lim 2019b, 5). Moreover, the centrality of the figure of the auteur in cinematic new waves constitutes what Mette Hjort calls "auteurist transnationalism" (2010, 22–24), a cross-border imaginary that can travel to lands near and far, trading on the currency of the auteur whose works might be cited at intertextual, paratextual, and extratextual levels by alien filmmakers.

One way TNC's soft power on alien filmmakers has manifested is through intertextual practices adopted by these directors. The transnational intertextuality I am discussing in this Epilogue is significant for its intra-Asian nature and for the centrality of TNC auteurs as sources of inspiration. Since the dawn of the new millennium, rather than declare admiration for past European masters or Hollywood productions, younger directors from China and Southeast Asia have chosen to affiliate themselves with TNC filmmakers who have attained an undisputed auteur status within world cinema. Compared to Tsai's famed indebtedness to François Truffaut (Lim 2014a, Chapter 2) and the example of Hou's *Flight of the Red Balloon* (*Le voyage du ballon rouge*, 2007; discussed in Chapter 2) as a homage to Albert Lamorisse's short film, this reorientation of cinematic soft power can serve as a corrective to a tendency in which "casual references by Asian filmmakers to European cinema are usually taken up as a grand statement of their bowing in the shadow of a greater influence and heritage that unfortunately gives weight to the Eurocentric impulses of many critics and even scholars" (Needham 2006, 372). Thus, my analysis later in the Epilogue not only acknowledges the importance of TNC authorship and region specificity but also departs from a Eurocentric account of transnational influence in filmmaking.

The practice of invoking works of previous auteurs in one's own work "highlights a deliberate attempt at establishing a network of authorial association [that], in the process, serves to enhance the status of the belated filmmaker by such association with former masters. To admire an auteur is to aspire to or even acquire the apogee of the auteur for oneself" (Lim 2007, 230). Tsai, a keen practitioner of such transnational intertextuality, has, over time, attracted younger alien filmmakers to weave elements of his films into their own works. As I have delineated before (Lim 2011b, 22–24), *4:30* (2005) by Singaporean director Royston Tan can be placed alongside Thai filmmaker Pen-Ek Ratanaruang's *Last*

Life in the Universe (2003) as belonging to a cinema of solitude and loneliness, of which *Vive L'amour* (*Aiqing wansui*, 1994) by Tsai, dubbed the "poet of solitude" (Rapfogel 2004), functions as the ur-text. All three films mentioned feature a young male protagonist who attempts to commit suicide, and Xiao Wu in *4:30*, in particular, is seemingly a younger version of Tsai's alter ego of loneliness, Hsiao Kang (Lee Kang-sheng). Those familiar with Tsai's oeuvre will readily pick up allusions in Tan's film: Xiao Wu ironing his shirt in the living room recalls Hsiao-kang's father doing the same in *The River* (*Heliu*, 1997); and the object of Xiao Wu's affection (a Korean man named Jung) turning in his sleep to unknowingly embrace Xiao Wu, who has been hiding in Jung's bed, shares a similar plot component and visual composition as a scene toward the end of *Vive L'amour*. If loneliness is, as Hamid Naficy suggests, an "inevitable outcome of transnationality, and it finds its way into the desolate structures of feeling and lonely diegetic characters" (2001, 55), here it manifests as a trope inscribed at the textual level on screen, a visual homage paid by an emerging filmmaker to an established auteur as an illustration of cinematic soft power.

To shift our focus to a different location and away from the notion of authorship, just as Ang Lee exemplifies a contradiction inherent in classical auteur theory, he also provides a twist to the notion of transnationality given his trans-Pacific career between the United States and the region across the Taiwan Strait (see Chapter 4). An alien in the United States, Lee's 1994 film, *Eat Drink Man Woman* (*Yinshi nannü*; incidentally, his only film set in real-life spaces in Taiwan), became, in 2001, the subject of a transnational remake—from the United States itself, no less. *Tortilla Soup* (dir. Maria Ripoll), an alien take (from TNC's perspective) on an alien film (from a US standpoint), can be put in the context of Hollywood studios' rush to remake East Asian films (from Japanese horror to Korean blockbusters) at the turn of the twenty-first century. However, not only should we *not* assume that East Asian cinemas necessarily stand to benefit from Hollywood's remake as a kind of "Western recognition," thus reinforcing Eurocentrism, the trans-Pacific transplantation of these films can, in fact, be unwelcome, especially if the outcome is a new form of exotic Orientalist appropriation or a flattening of cultural difference. As it happens, *Tortilla Soup* has been read as "reconfigured discourses of homogenizing ethnic politics . . . symptomatic of a historical depthlessness that obfuscates the specificities of Mexican-American diasporic experiences" (Li 2017, 129). Furthermore, it is revealing that Lee did not helm the sequel to his 2000 global success, that is *Crouching Tiger, Hidden Dragon* (*Wohu canglong*), for *Crouching Tiger, Hidden Dragon: Sword of Destiny* (Yuen Woo-ping, 2016), while directed by the original film's legendary choreographer, has the predominantly Chinese cast speak throughout in English, this being, according to a review, only one of many flaws of the sequel (Sims 2016). In both of these examples, transnational alien afterlives seem to have only alienated viewers with fond memories of the much better original films to which the remake and the sequel have now left a bitter aftertaste. The currency of soft power, used in misguided and unproductive ways, can easily turn into bad debt.

Historiography

As we can see in examples discussed in the previous section, transnational borrowing, homage, or remake in filmmaking often entails a switch in the use of language or the deployment of multiple languages, which can problematize the national identity of the films concerned and have implications for the notion of film historiography. In considering the position of the alien in a nation's body politic, I find the concept of "minor literature" especially helpful. For Gilles Deleuze and Félix Guattari, "minor literature" does not come from a minor language but rather "that which a minority constructs within a major language," and its first characteristic is an affectation of the major language "with a high coefficient of deterritorialization" (1986, 16).[18] In the case of Taiwan cinema, this form of deterritorialization has been registered in the "imperfect" Mandarin uttered in Rich Lee's *Detours to Paradise* (*Qilu tiantang*, also known as *Sincerely Yours*, 2008), whose protagonists are two migrant workers from Indonesia and Thailand who can only communicate with each other in Mandarin; or in the "accented" French spoken by the Chinese au pair played by Song Fang in Hou Hsiao-hsien's *Flight of the Red Balloon*. By broadcasting alien languages (such as Burmese in Midi Z's films) and alien-accented "national" languages through their films, these descendants of TNC (alien or otherwise) challenge purist notions of language as well as lingua-centric models of film historiography (see Lim 2011a for a critique of such models).

To adopt the notion of "minor literature" for a "minor cinema," then, Taiwan film historiography would embrace such films (whether made in Taiwan or beyond) not simply because they are not spoken purely (in both senses of the term) in any officially recognized national languages in Taiwan, but precisely because their use of any of these languages is "contaminated," resulting in a deterritorialization of the language that brings with it a troubling of the very identity, certainty, and centrality of language. Moreover, films that do not feature any of the national languages should also be acknowledged as a condition of migration, such as Ho Wi-Ding's *Pinoy Sunday*, a film about two Filipino men working at a construction site in Taipei, whose main spoken language is Tagalog and with some dialogue conducted in English and Ilonggo (a regional language in the Philippines; Tolentino 2011, 94). Indeed, lingua-centric models of film historiography will be further challenged by films that choose not to contain any spoken words (voice-over or dialogue) at all, such as Ho's 2011 short film, "100," and Tsai Ming-liang's 2020 film, *Days* (*Rizi*), which, while featuring a few lines of dialogue in its 127-minute duration, announces in its opening credits that subtitles will not be provided to highlight the intentional displacement of spoken languages.

The transnational trajectories of these alien filmmakers' careers and their cinematic practices, however, must be situated in the regional context in which TNC's soft power has manifested. To be more specific, we must scrutinize the relationship between Taiwan and Southeast Asia as much as the perception and reception of Southeast Asian migrants in Taiwan as a corollary of this cinematic import. While this is not the place for a full-blown account of the subject, suffice it to say that economic hierarchies do exist in the region and discourses on migrant labor in Taiwan are highly racialized, with migrant workers specifically contracted from Southeast Asia to do "Three D" (dirty, dangerous, demanding) jobs in Taiwan (Lan 2006, 59). Negative perception and stereotyping of migrant workers can spill over into the realm of cinema, as some theater owners in Taiwan were reportedly reluctant to give *Pinoy Sunday* screening slots out of concern that their cinemas would be "flooded" by migrant workers as a result (Zeng and Chen 2010). To the credit of the Taiwanese authorities, some conscious efforts have been made, over the years, to incorporate aliens in nation-(image)-building cinematic projects. In 2011, Ho, who moved to Taiwan in 2001 and had made only one feature film (*Pinoy Sunday*) after living there for a decade, was involved in an omnibus film project initiated by the Taipei Golden Horse Film Festival to celebrate the 100th anniversary of the founding of the Republic of China (Taiwan's official title).[19] As the sole non-Taiwanese director in this tribute film for the nation's landmark birthday, and with Tsai Ming-liang's absence from the project, Ho seemed, at the time, to have taken over the baton from Tsai as a representative alien filmmaker in Taiwan. More crucially, Ho's inclusion in a nation's image-making project signals an openness of Taiwan's attitude toward film historiography, whether in written or cinematic form.

Now with Midi Z joining this company, the presence of ethnic Chinese filmmakers of Southeast Asian origin in Taiwan bespeaks another facet of geopolitics, that is, the dire straits in which descendants of Chinese migrants have found themselves in some of these countries. As I have pointed out in a slightly different context, "unequal power relation also exists within a nation-state so that, for example, a Chinese Malaysian filmmaker, given the suppressed status of the Chinese population in Malaysia, may align his or her filmmaking with the umbrella label of 'transnational Chinese cinema' rather than with the national cinema of Malaysia" (Lim 2011b, 26)—or, in this instance, to make a career and even a home in Taiwan instead. Even a Singaporean youth, Chiang Wei Liang, had been inspired by Wei Te-sheng's *Cape No. 7* to study film directing at the Taipei National University for the Arts (Wu 2016); Chiang's short film, "Anchorage Prohibited" (*Jinzhi xiamao*,

Figure E.1 The final shot of *Flowers of Taipei*, taken from Hou Hsiao-hsien's *Goodbye South, Goodbye*
Copyright 3H Films and Shochiku, 1996

2015), about a young Vietnamese migrant couple in Taiwan, went on to win an Audi Short Film award in 2016 at Berlin as a "Taiwanese" entry because of its source of finance and production (Hong 2016). Over the twentieth century, Taiwan cinema was penetrated, in various periods, by alien filmmakers from Japan, China, and Hong Kong as the tides of geopolitical circumstances ebbed and flowed. In the twenty-first century, the historiography of Taiwan cinema looks set to be increasingly commingled with foreign elements from Southeast Asia. In the final analysis, it is my contention that TNC's resurrection might take place precisely among these alien bodies on whom Taiwan cinema's soft power has had and will continue to have a lasting impact, generating an afterlife for TNC that lives on both within and beyond the island's shores.

***

The main body of this book opened, in Chapter 1, with a discussion of the documentary *Flowers of Taipei*, whose final shot, which accompanies the end credits, is taken from Hou's *Goodbye South, Goodbye* (*Nanguo zaijian, nanguo,* 1996). The shot, as we can see in Figure E.1, is a close to three-minute-long take of three protagonists riding on two motorcycles on a snake-like mountainous road, with Summer Lei's song "Small Town's Sea" (*Xiaozhen de hai*) providing a brooding atmosphere and slowly building up a pulsating rhythm. I want to end this book simply by spotlighting a similar shot in Bi Gan's *Kaili Blues* (shown in Figure E.2),

Figure E.2 A homage shot in Bi Gan's *Kaili Blues*
Copyright China Film (Shanghai) International Media Co, Herui FIlm Culture, China Blackfin (Beijing) Culture & Media Co., Heaven Pictures (Beijing) The Movies Co., 2015

which lasts just over a minute in duration and features a more subdued score by Lim Giong, the protagonist in the foreground in Figure E.1 and an actor and composer on a number of other films by Hou. For me, Bi Gan's homage shot epitomizes TNC's afterlife: a textual haunting that acts like a palimpsest that would allow a knowing viewer to see Hou's shot beneath it, an audio-visual resurrection brought back by alien filmmakers through cinephilic obsession. It also exemplifies TNC's soft power, engineered by authorship, transported through transnational intertextuality, with film historiography reconstructed as a result. Long, winding, mesmerizing, the journey of TNC's soft power, like the two long takes illustrated here, has only just begun.

Filmography

Citation style: English title (original title), director, company credits, year.

Only feature-length films, including documentaries, are listed.

4:30, Royston Tan, NHK / Singapore Film Commission / Zhao Wei Films, 2005.

10 + 10, Sylvia Chang, Chang Tso-chi, Arvin Chen, Chen Kuo-fu, Chen Yu-Hsun, Cheng Wen-tang, Cheng Yu-chieh, Chu Yen-ping, Chung Mong-hong, Leon Dai, Ho Wi-Ding, Hou Chi-jan, Hou Hsiao-hsien, Hsiao Ya-chuan, Shen Ko-shang, Wang Hsiao-ti, Wang Tung, Wei Te-sheng, Wu Nien-jen, and Yang Ya-che, Taipei Golden Horse, 2011.

14 Apples (*Shisi ke pingguo*), Midi Z, Seashore Image Production, 2018.

The 400 Blows (*Les quatre cents coups*), François Truffaut, Les Films du Carrosse / Sédif Productions, 1959.

1895, Hung Chih-yu, Green Film Production.

Afternoon (*Nari xiawu*), Tsai Ming-liang, Homegreen Films, 2015.

Apart Together (*Tuanyuan*), Wang Quan'an, Lightshades Film Productions / Xi'an Movie and Television Production Co. / Jiu Zhou Video and Audio Publishing House / Western Movie Group / Beijing Zhongtian Peak Television Culture Communication, 2010.

The Assassin (*Cike Nie Yinniang*), Hou Hsiao-Hsien, Central Motion Picture Corporation / China Dream Film Culture Industry / Media Asia Films / Sil-Metropole Organisation / SpotFilms / Zhejiang Huace Film & TV, 2015.

Au revoir Taipei (*Yiye Taibei*), Arvin Chen, Beta Cinema Cathay Asia Films / Atom Cinema / greenskyFILMS / Government Information Office of the Republic of China, 2010.

Avatar, James Cameron, Twentieth Century Fox / Dune Entertainment / Lightstorm Entertainment, 2009.

Back to the Good Times (*Huajia daren zhuan nanhai*), Chu Yu-ning, Ambassador Theatres / CMC Entertainment Holding Corporation / Ethos Original / Lots Home Entertainment / Oxygen Film Studio / Shin Kong Cinemas / Showtime International / Skyfilms Entertainment, 2018.

The Banquet (*Yeyan*), Feng Xiaogang, Huayi Brothers Media / Media Asia Films, 2006.

Beijing Bicycle (*Shiqi sui de danche*), Wang Xiaoshuai, Pyramide Productions / Arc Light Films / Public Television Service Foundation / Eastern Television / Asiatic Films / Beijing Film Studio, 2001.

Betelnut Beauty (*Ai ni ai wo*), Lin Cheng-sheng, Arc Light Films / Asiatic Films / Eastern Television / Public Television Service Foundation / Pyramide Productions, 2001.

Beyond Beauty: Taiwan from Above (*Kanjian Taiwan*), Chi Po-lin, Taiwan Aerial Imaging, 2013.

Beyond the Dream (*Huan'ai*), Kiwi Chow, Golden Scene / Iner / Photon Films, 2019.

Billy Lynn's Long Halftime Walk, Ang Lee, Bona Film Group / Dune Films / Film4 / Marc Platt Productions / Studio 8 / The Ink Factory / TriStar Pictures / TriStar Productions, 2016.

Black Coal, Thin Ice (*Bairi yanhuo*), Diao Yi'nan, Omnijoi Media / Boneyard Entertainment China / China Film Group Corporation, 2014.

Black Snow (*Benmingnian*), Xie Fei, Ningxia Film Group / Youth Film Studio of Beijing Film Academy, 1990.

Blind Massage (*Tuina*), Lou Ye, Dream Factory / Les Films du Lendemain, 2014.

Blind Shaft (*Mang jing*), Li Yang, Bronze Age Films / Tag Spledour and Films, 2003.

Blue Gate Crossing (*Lanse damen*), Yee Chih-yen, Arc Light Films / Pyramide Productions, 2002.

Blush (*Hongfen*), Li Shaohong, Beijing Film Studio / Ocean Film, 1995.

A Borrowed Life (*Duo sang*), Wu Nien-Jen, Chang Shu A & V Production / Long Shong Pictures, 1994.

The Boys from Fengkuei (*Fenggui lai de ren*), Hou Hsiao-hsien, Evergreen Film Company, 1983.

A Brighter Summer Day (*Gulingjie shaonian sharen shijian*), Edward Yang, Yang & His Gang Filmmakers, 1991.

Brokeback Mountain, Ang Lee, Focus Features / River Road Entertainment / Alberta Film Entertainment / Good Machine, 2005.

Buddha Bless America (*Taiping tianguo*), Wu Nien-Jen, Taiwan Film Center, 1996.

Café Lumière (*Kôhî jikô*), Hou Hsiao-hsien, Shochiku / Asahi Shimbun / Sumitomo Corporation / Eisei Gekijo / Imagica Corp., 2003.

Cape No. 7 (*Haijiao qihao*), Wei Te-Sheng, ARS Film Production, 2008.

Center Stage (*Ruan Lingyu*), Stanley Kwan, Golden Harvest Company / Golden Way Films Ltd. / Paragon Films Ltd., 1991.

Cheerful Wind (*Feng'er titacai*), Hou Hsiao-Hsien, Galaxy Film Company Ltd., 1981.

A City of Sadness (*Beiqing chengshi*), Hou Hsiao-hsien, 3-H Films / ERA International, 1989.

Clean, Olivier Assayas, Rectangle Productions / Haystack Productions / Rhombus Media / Arte France Cinéma / Film Council / Centre National du Cinéma et de l'Image Animée / Canal+ / Matrix Film Finance / The Film Consortium / Forensic Films / Journeyman Films Ltd., 2004.

Crosscurrent (*Changjiang tu*), Yang Chao, Beijing New Century Media Co. / Central Studio of New Reels / Eracme Cultural & Media Co. / Hua Wen Movie Group / Just Show Production Beijing / Les Petites Lumieres / Ray Productions Co. / Trend Cultural Investment Co. / Zhong Guang Pictures, 2016.

Crouching Tiger, Hidden Dragon (*Wohu canglong*), Ang Lee, Asia Union Film & Entertainment Ltd. / China Film Co-Production Corp. / Columbia Pictures Film Production Asia / EDKO Films / Good Machine International / Sony Pictures Classics / United China Vision / Zoom Hunt International Productions Company Ltd., 2000.

Crouching Tiger, Hidden Dragon: Sword of Destiny, Yuen Woo-Ping, Netflix / The Weinstein Company / China Film Group Corporation / Dongyang Paige Huachuang Film & Media Company / Film 44 / Yucaipa Films / Pegasus Taihe Entertainment, 2016.

Cute Girl (*Jiushi liuliude ta*), Hou Hsiao-Hsien, Superstar (H.K.) Motion Picture Company, 1980.

The Dark Knight, Christopher Nolan, Warner Bros. / Legendary Entertainment / Syncopy / DC Comics, 2008.

David Loman (*Dawei luman*), Chiu Li-Kwan, Polyface Films / Vision Film Production, 2013.

David Loman 2 (*Dawei luman 2*), Chiu Li-Kwan, Central Motion Picture Corporation, 2016.

Days (*Rizi*), Tsai Ming-liang, Homegreen Films / ARTE / La Lucarne, 2020.

Days of Being Wild (*Afei zhengzhuan*), Wong Kar-wai, In-Gear Film, 1990.

The Departed, Martin Scorsese, Warner Bros. / Plan B Entertainment / Initial Entertainment Group (IEG) / Vertigo Entertainment / Media Asia Films, 2006.

The Deserted (*Jia zai Lanruosi*), Tsai Ming-liang, Homegreen Films, 2017.

Detours to Paradise (also known as *Sincerely Yours*; *Qilu tiantang*), Rich Lee, Zoom Hunt International Productions, 2009.

Devils at the Doorstep (*Guizi lai le*), Jiang Wen, Asian Union Film & Entertainment / Beijing Zhongbo-Times Film Planning / CMC Xiandai Trade Co. / China Film Co-Production Corporation / Huayi Brothers Advertising, 2000.

Din Tao: Leader of the Parade (*Zhentou*), Fung Kai, Magnificent Film Entertainment, 2012.

A Dog Barking at the Moon (*Zaijian, Nanping wanzhong*), Xiang Zi, Acorn Studio / Granadian, 2019.

Double Vision (*Shuangtong*), Chen Kuo-Fu, Columbia Pictures Film Production Asia / Nan Fang Film Productions, 2002.

Drug War (*Du zhan*), Johnnie To, Beijing Hairun Pictures Company / Huaxia Film Distribution / CCTV Movie Channel / Milky Way Image Company / Hairun Movies & TV Group, 2012.

Dust in the Wind (*Lianlian fengchen*), Hou Hsiao-hsien, Central Motion Picture Corporation, 1986.

Dying to Survive (*Wo bushi yaoshen*), Wen Muye, Beijing Culture / Beijing Joy Leader Culture Communication / Beijing Talent International Film / Beijing Universe Cultural Development / Dirty Monkey Films Group / Huanhuanxixi (Tianjin) Cultural Investments / Khorgos Dirty Monkeys Studios / Shanghai Mountain of Flowers Films, 2018.

Eat Drink Man Woman (*Yinshi nannü*), Ang Lee, Ang Lee Productions / Central Motion Picture Corporation / Good Machine, 1994.

An Elephant Sitting Still (*Daxiang xidi'erzuo*), Hu Bo, Dongchun Films, 2018.

Evening Bell (*Wanzhong*), Wu Ziniu, August 1st Film Studio / Beijing Film Studio, 1989.

The Eye (*Jiangui*), Danny Pang and Oxide Pang, Film Workshop / Applause Pictures / Mediacorp Raintree Pictures, 2002.

The Eye, David Moreay and Xavier Palud, Lionsgate / Paramount Vantage / Cruise / Wagner Productions / Vertigo Entertainment / VN Productions, 2008.

Face Taiwan: Power of Taiwan Cinema (*Women zheyang pai dianying*), Hsiao Chu-chen, Viewfinder Ltd., 2016.

Farewell My Concubine (*Bawang bie ji*), Chen Kaige, Tomson Films / Beijing Film Studio / China Film Co-Production Corporation, 1993.

Five: Five Long Takes Dedicated to Yasujiro Ozu, Abbas Kiarostami, Behnegar / NHK / MK2 Productions, 2003.

Flight of the Red Balloon (*Le voyage du ballon rouge*), Hou Hsiao-hsien, Margo Films / Les Films du Lendemain / 3H Productions, 2007.

A Flower in the Rainy Night (*Kanhai de rizi*), Wang Tung, Montage Film, 1983.

Flowers of Taipei: Taiwan New Cinema (*Guangyin de gushi: Taiwan xindianying*), Hsieh Chin-lin, Rice Flower Films, 2014.

Full Moon in New York (*Ren zai Niuyue*, also known as *Sange nüren de gushi*), Stanley Kwan, Golden Glory Production / Shiobu, 1989.

Gatao 2: Rise of the King (*Jiaotou 2: Wangzhe zaiqi*), Yen Cheng-kuo, Energy Moana Technology / Hua Ren Entertainment / Jye Tai Precision Industrial / Kingshine Entertainment / Leday Multimedia / Polyface Entertainment / Roadpro / Shenghua Entertainment Communication / T-Lang Cultural and Creative Entertainment, 2018.

Gemini Man, Ang Lee, Skydance Media / Jerry Bruckheimer Films / Fosun Group Forever Pictures / Alibaba Pictures / Orange Corp, 2019.

Good Men, Good Women (*Hao nan hao nü*), Hou Hsiao-Hsien, 3H Films / Chang Su Productions / Fujian Film Studio / Painted Face Communication / Shochiku Team Okuyama, 1995.

Goodbye, Dragon Inn (*Busan*), Tsai Ming-liang, Homegreen Films, 2003.

Goodbye South, Goodbye (*Nanguo zaijian, nanguo*), Hou Hsiao-hsien, 3H Films / Shochiku, 1996.

The Grandmaster (*Yidai zongshi*), Wong Kar-wai, Block 2 Pictures / Jet Tone Production / Sil-Metropole Organisation / Bona International Film Group, 2013.

The Great Wall (*Changcheng*), Zhang Yimou, Legendary East / Atlas Entertainment / China Film Group Corporation / Dentsu / Fuji Television Network / Kava Productions / Le Vision Pictures / Legendary Entertainment, 2016.

The Green, Green Grass of Home (*Zai na hepan qing cao qing*), Hou Hsiao-Hsien, Tung Tai FIlm Company, 1983.

Happy Together (*Chunguang zhaxie*), Wong Kar-wai, Block 2 Pictures / Jet Tone Production / Prénom H Co. Ltd. / Seowoo Film Company, 1997.

Hear Me (*Ting shuo*), Cheng Fen-fen, Great Vision Film & TV Production / Trigram Films, 2009.

Hero (*Yingxiong*), Zhang Yimou, Beijing New Picture Film Co. / China Film Co-Production Corporation / Elite Group Enterprises / Sil-Metropole Organisation / Zhang Yimou Studio, 2002.

HHH: Portrait de Hou Hsiao-hsien, Olivier Assayas, Audiovisuel Multimedia International Productions, 1997.

The Hobbit: The Battle of the Five Armies, Peter Jackson, Metro-Goldwyn-Mayer / New Line Cinema / WingNut Films / 3Foot7, 2014.

The Hobbit: The Desolation of Smaug, Peter Jackson, Metro-Goldwyn-Mayer / New Line Cinema / WingNut Films, 2013.

The Hobbit: An Unexpected Journey, Peter Jackson, Metro-Goldwyn-Mayer / New Line Cinema / WingNut Films, 2012.

Holy Motors, Leos Carax, Pierre Grise Productions / Théo Films / Pandora Filmproduktion / Arte France Cinéma / WDR / Arte / Canal+ / Centre National du Cinéma et de l'Image Animée / Soficinéma 8 / Wild Bunch, 2012.

The Hour of the Furnaces (*La hora de los hornos: Notas y testimonios sobre el neocolonialismo, la violencia y la liberación*), Octavio Getino and Fernando E. Solanas, Grupo Cine Liberacion / Solanas Productions, 1968.

Hulk, Ang Lee, Universal Pictures / Marvel Enterprises / A Valhalla Motion Pictures / Good Machine Production, 2003.

I Don't Want to Sleep Alone (*Heiyanquan*), Tsai Ming-liang, Centre National du Cinéma et de l'Image Animée / Dama Orchestra Malaysia / EMI Music Taiwan / Government Information Office of the Republic of China / Homegreen Films / New Crowned Hope / Soudaine Compagnie, 2006.

Ice Poison (*Bingdu*), Midi Z, Seashore Image Productions / Myanmar Montage Films / Flash Forward Entertainment, 2014.

The Ice Storm, Ang Lee, Fox Searchlight Pictures / Good Machine / Canal + Droits Audiovisuels, 1997.

Ilo Ilo (*Bama buzai jia*), Anothny Chen, Singapore Film Commission / Ngee Ann Polytechnic / Fisheye Pictures, 2013.

In Love We Trust (*Zuoyou*), Wang Xiaoshuai, Debo Film Ltd. / WXS production / Stellar Megamedia / DUOJI Production / Dongchun Films, 2008.

In the Mood for Love (*Huayangnianhua*), Wong Kar-wai, Block 2 Pictures / Jet Tone Production / Orly Films / Paradis Films, 2000.

In Our Time (*Guangyin de gushi*), Tao Te-chen, Edward Yang, Ko I-cheng, and Chang Yi, Central Motion Picture Corporation, 1982.

Infernal Affairs (*Wujiandao*), Andrew Lau and Alan Mak, Media Asia Films / Basic Pictures, 2002.

Judou, Zhang Yimou and Yang Fengliang, China Film Co-Production Corporation / China Film Release Import and Export Company / Tokuma Shoten / Xi'an Film Studio, 1990.

Kaili Blues (*Lubian yecan*), Bi Gan, China Film (Shanghai) International Media Co. / Beijing Herui FIlm Culture / Blackfin (Beijing) Culture & Media Co. / Heaven Pictures (Beijing) The Movies Co., 2015.

KANO, Umin Boya (Ma Chih-Hsiang), ARS Film Production, 2014.

Kundun, Martin Scorsese, De Fina-Cappa / Dune Films / Refuge Productions Inc. / Touchstone Pictures, 1997.

Kung Fu Hustle (*Gongfu*), Stephen Chow, Columbia Pictures Film Production Asia / Huayi Brothers Media / Taihe Film Investment Co. Ltd. / Beijing Film Studio / China Film Group Corporation / The Fourth Production Company Film Group / Star Overseas / China Film Co-Production Corporation / Columbia Pictures, 2004.

A Land Imagined (*Huantu*), Yeo Siew Hua, Akanga Film Productions / Films de Force Majeure / MM2 Entertainment / Volya Films, 2018.

Last Life in the Universe (*Ruang rak noi nid mahasan*), Pen-Ek Ratanaruang, Bohemian Films Cathay Asia Films / Cinemasia Five Star Production Co. Ltd. / Fortissimo Film Sales / Pioneer LDC, 2003.

Life of Pi, Ang Lee, Fox 2000 Pictures / Dune Entertainment / Ingenious Media / Haishang Films / Big Screen Productions / Ingenious Film Partners / Netter Productions, 2012.

Long Day's Journey into Night (*Diqiu zuihou de yewan*), Bi Gan, Beijing Herui Film Culture / CG Cinéma Dangmai Films (Shanghai) / Huace Pictures / Zhejiang Huace Film & TV, 2018.

The Lord of the Rings: The Fellowship of the Ring, Peter Jackson, New Line Cinema / WingNut Films / The Saul Zaentz Company, 2001.

The Lord of the Rings: The Return of the King, Peter Jackson, New Line Cinema / WingNut Films / The Saul Zaentz Company, 2003.

The Lord of the Rings: The Two Towers, Peter Jackson, New Line Cinema / WingNut Films / The Saul Zaentz Company, 2002.

Lost Course (*Mihang*), Jill Li, Human Images, 2019.

Lucy, Luc Besson, EuropaCorp / TF1 Films Production / Grive Productions / Canal+ / Ciné+ / TF1 / Filmagic Pictures Co. / Element Film / Canadian Film or Video Production Tax Credit / Centre National du Cinéma et de l'Image Animée Digital Factory, 2014.

Lust, Caution (*Se, jie*), Ang Lee, Haishang Films / Focus Features / River Road Entertainment / Sil-Metropole Organisation / Shanghai Film Group Corporation, 2007.

Mahjong (*Majiang*), Edward Yang, AtomFilms, 1996.

Memories Look at Me (*Jiyi wangzhe wo*), Song Fang, Xstream Pictures, 2012.

Métro Lumière: Hou Hsiao-Hsien à la rencontre de Yasujirô Ozu, Harold Manning, Diaphana Films / Northern Line Films / Shochiku, 2004.

Millennium Mambo (*Qianxi manbo*), Hou Hsiao-hsien, 3H Productions / Orly Films / Paradis Films / Sinomovie, 2001.

The Moment (*Women de nashi cike*), Yang Li-chou, Na Shih Tzu Ke Co. Ltd. / Backstage Studio Co. Ltd. / CNEX Studio Corporation / CTBC Financial Holding Co. Ltd., 2016.

Monga (*Mengjia*), Doze Niu, 1 Production Film / Greenday Films / Honto Production, 2010.

More than Blue (*Bi beishang geng beishang de gushi*), Gavin Lin, MM2 Entertainment / Good Movie / Bossdom Digiinnovation Group / Wish Entertainment / China Music International / Fox Networks Group Asia Pacific / Wilson Management Consultant / Good Movie, 2018.

The Mummy: Tomb of the Dragon Emperor, Rob Cohen, Universal Pictures / Relativity Media / The Sommers Company / Alphaville Films / Beijing Happy Pictures / China Film Co-Production Corporation / Giant Studios Hivemind Internationale Filmproduktion Blackbird Dritte / Nowita Pictures / Shanghai Film Group, 2008.

My Blueberry Nights, Wong Kar-wai, Block 2 Pictures / Jet Tone Production / Lou Yi Ltd. / StudioCanal, 2007.

Nina Wu (*Zhuoren mimi*), Midi Z, Harvest 9 Road Entertainment / Jazzy Pictures / Myanmar Montage Pictures / Seashore Image Production / Star Ritz International Entertainment, 2019.

No. 7 Cherry Lane (*Jiyuantai qihao*), Yonfan, Far Sun Film Co. Ltd., 2019.

Not One Less (*Yige dou buneng shao*), Zhang Yimou, Bejing New Picture Distribution Company / Columbia Pictures / Film Productions Asia / Guangxi Film Studio, 1999.

Number 1 (*Nanerwang*), Ong Kuo-Sin, MM2 Entertainment / Clover Films / Fox Networks Group Asia Pacific / Hoch Ventures / Kantana Post Production / Lima Capital Asia / Medialink Holdings / Shaw Organisation / Byleft Productions, 2020.

Old Beast (*Lao shou*), Zhou Ziyang, Beijing Daqiao Tangren Entertainment Co. / Dongchun Films / FangJin Visual Media Culture Communication (Beijing) Co. / Glowing Peak Entertainment / Having Me Films / Scenefone Film Equipment Rental, 2017.

Our Time, Our Story (*Baige jihua*), Hsiao Chu-chen, The Government Information Office, Executive Yuan / Public Television / Ying Wu Studio, 2002.

Our Times (*Wode shaonü shidai*), Chen Yu-shan, Focus Films / Hualien Media International, 2015.

Our Youth in Taiwan (*Women de qingchun, zai Taiwan*), Fu Yue, 7th Day Film, 2018.

Paradise in Service (*Junzhong leyuan*), Doze Niu, Ablaze Image / CatchPlay / Honto Production / Huayi Brothers Media, 2014.

Peacock (*Kongque*), Gu Changwei, Asian Union Film & Entertainment, 2005.

People Mountain People Sea (*Renshanrenhai*), Cai Shangjun, Sunrise Media, 2011.

Pinoy Sunday (*Taibei xingqitian*), Ho Wi-Ding, Changhe Films / Les Petites Lumieres / NHK / Spark Films, 2009.

Psycho, Alfred Hitchcock, Shamley Productions, 1960.

The Puppetmaster (*Ximeng rensheng*), Hou Hsiao-hsien, ERA International, 1993.

Pushing Hands (*Tuishou*), Ang Lee, Ang Lee Productions / Central Motion Picture Corporation, 1991.

Raise the Red Lantern (*Dahong denglong gaogao gua*), Zhang Yimou, ERA International / China Film Co-Production Corporation / Century Communications / Salon Films, 1991.

Rebels of the Neon God (*Qingshaonian Nezha*), Tsai Ming-liang, Central Motion Picture Corporation, 1992.

The Red Balloon (*Le ballon rouge*), Albert Lamorisse, Films Montsouris, 1956.

Red Sorghum (*Hong gaoliang*), Zhang Yimou, Xi'an Film Studio, 1988.

Ride with the Devil, Ang Lee, Universal Pictures / Good Machine, 1999.

The Ring, Gore Verbinski, Dreamworks Pictures / Parkes / MacDonald Image Nation / BenderSpink / Vertigo Entertainment, 2002.

Ringu, Hideo Nakata, Basara Pictures / Toho / Imagica / Asmik Ace Entertainment / Kadokawa Shoten Publishing Co. / Omega Project / Pony Canyon / Toho Company, 1998.

The River (*Heliu*), Tsai Ming-liang, Central Motion Picture Corporation, 1997.

The Road Home (*Wode fuqin muqin*), Zhang Yimou, Columbia Pictures Film Production Asia / Guangxi Film Studio, 1999.

The Road to Mandalay (*Zaijian Wacheng*), Midi Z, Bombay Berlin Film Productions / CMC Entertainment / Fine Time Entertainment / Flash Forward Entertainment / House on Fire / Myanmar Montage Films / Pop Pictures / Seashore Image Production / Star Ritz Productions Co., 2016.

Roman Holiday, William Wyler, Paramount Pictures, 1953.

Salute! Sun Yat-sen (*Xingdong daihao: Sun Zongshan*), Yee Chih-yen, 1 Production Film / Lan Se Production / Warner Bros. / Yi Tiao Long Hu Bao International Entertainment Company, 2014.

The Sand Pebbles, Robert Wise, Argyle Enterprises / Solar Productions, 1966.

The Sandwich Man (*Erzi de da wan'ou*), Hou Hsiao-hsien, Zeng Zhuangxiang, and Wan Jen, Central Motion Picture Corporation / Sunny Overseas, 1983.

Sense and Sensibility, Ang Lee, Columbia Pictures Corporation / Mirage Production, 1995.

Shadow (*Ying*), Zhang Yimou, Perfect Village Entertainment / Le Vision Pictures / Shanghai Tencent Pictures Culture Media / Bona Film Group / Tencent Pictures / Tianjin Maoyan Weying Media / Bodi Media Company / Endeavor Content, 2018.

Shanghai Dreams (*Qinghong*), Wang Xiaoshuai, Debo Film Ltd. / Stellar Megamedia / Kingwood Ltd., 2005.

Silence, Martin Scorsese, SharpSword Films / AI-Film / CatchPlay / IM Global / Verdi Productions / Emmett / Furla / Oasis Films / Waypoint Entertainment / G&G / Sikelia Productions / Fábrica de Cine / The Fyzz Facility, Cecchi Gori Group Fin.Ma.Vi. / Taipei Film Development Company, 2016.

A Simple Life (*Taojie*), Ann Hui, Bona International Film Group / Focus Films / Sil-Metropole Organisation, 2011.

The Skywalk Is Gone (*Tianqiao bujian le*), Tsai Ming-liang, Homegreen Films / Le Fresnoy Studio National des Arts Contemporains, 2002.

Sleepless in Seattle, Nora Ephron, TriStar Pictures, 1993.

So Long, My Son (*Dijiutianchang*), Wang Xiaoshuai, Dongchun Films, 2019.

Spring Fever (*Chunfeng chenzui de yewan*), Lou Ye, Dream Factory / Rosem Films, 2009.

Still Life (*Sanxia haoren*), Jia Zhangke, Xstream Pictures / Shanghai Film Studios, 2006.

The Story of Qiu Ju (*Qiu Ju da guansi*), Zhang Yimou, Sil-Metropole Organisation / Youth Film Studio of Beijing Film Academy, 1992.

The Story of Southern Islet (*Nanwu*), Chong Keat Aun, Asteri Production / Bened Global, 2020.

Stray Dogs (*Jiaoyou*), Tsai Ming-liang, Agence Nationale de Gestion des Oeuvres Audiovisuelles / Centre National du Cinéma et de l'Image / Homegreen Films / House on Fire / JBA Production / MEDIA Programme of the European Union / Taipei City Government / Taipei Film Commission / The Swiss Agency for Development & Cooperation / Urban Distribution International, 2013.

The Summer Is Gone (*Bayue*), Zhang Dalei, Beijing Mailis Pictures, 2016.

A Summer at Grandpa's (*Dongdong de jiaqi*), Hou Hsiao-hsien, Central Motion Picture Corporation, 1984.

Summer Hours (*L'heure d'été*), Olivier Assayas, MK2 Productions / France 3 Cinéma / Canal+ / TPS Star / Le Musée d'Orsay / La Région Île-de-France / Soficinéma 3 / Centre National du Cinéma et de l'Image Animée / Cofinova 4, 2008.

Summer Snow (*Nüren sishi*), Ann Hui, Class / Golden Harvest Company / Harvest Crown, 1995.

The Sun Has Ears (*Taiyang you er*), Yim Ho, Moonhill International, 1995.

Super Citizen Ko (*Chaoji da guomin*), Wan Jen, Wan Jen Films, 1995.

The Tag-Along 2 (*Hongyi xiaonühai 2*), Cheng Wei-hao, Ambassador Theatres / CMC Entertainment / Damou Entertainment / HIM International Music / Lots Home Entertainment / Once Upon A Story Company / Showtime International / Skyfilms Entertainment / The Tag-Along, 2017.

Taipei Story (*Qingmeizhuma*), Edward Yang, Evergreen Film Company, 1985.

Taking Woodstock, Ang Lee, Focus Features, 2009.

The Tenants Downstairs (*Louxia de fangke*), Adam Tsuei, Amazing Film Studio / Star Ritz Productions Co. / Edko Films / CMC Entertainment / Vie Vision Pictures / MM2 Entertainment, 2016.

The Terrorizer (*Kongbu fenzi*), Edward Yang, Central Motion Picture Corporation, 1986.

That Day, On the Beach (*Haitan de yitian*), Edward Yang, Central Motion Picture Corporation, 1983.

Three Times (*Zuihao de shiguang*), Hou Hsiao-hsien, 3H Films / Orly Films / Paradis Films / Sinomovie, 2005.

A Time to Live, A Time to Die (*Tongnian wangshi*), Hou Hsiao-hsien, Central Motion Picture Corporation / Yi Fu Films, 1985.

Titanic, James Cameron, Twentieth Century Fox / Paramount Pictures / Lightstorm Entertainment / Baja Films, 1997.

To Each His Own Cinema (*Chacun son cinéma ou Ce petit coup au coeur quand la lumière s'éteint et que le film commence*), Theodoros Angelopoulos, Olivier Assayas, Bille August, Jane Campion, Youssef Chahine, Chen Kaige, Michael Cimino, Ethan Coen, Joel Coen, David Cronenberg, Jean-Pierre Dardenne, Luc Dardenne, Manoel de Oliveira, Raymond Depardon, Atom Egoyan, Amos Gitai, Hou Hsiao-hsien, Alejandro G. Iñárritu, Aki Kaurismäki, Abbas Kiarostami, Takeshi Kitano, Andrey Konchalovskiy, Claude Lelouch, Ken Loach, David Lynch, Nanni Moretti, Roman Polanski, Raoul Ruiz, Walter Salles, Elia Suleiman, Tsai Ming-liang, Gus Van Sant, Lars Von Trier, Wim Wenders, Wong Kar-wai and Zhang Yimou, Cannes Film Festival / Elzévir Films, 2007.

To Live (*Huozhe*), Zhang Yimou, ERA International / Shanghai Film Studios, 1994.

Tokyo Story (*Tōkyō Monogatari*), Yasujiro Ozu, Shochiku, 1953.

Tortilla Soup, Maria Ripoll, Samuel Goldwyn Films / Starz! Encore Entertainment, 2001.

A Touch of Sin (*Tian zhuding*), Jia Zhangke, Xstream Pictures / Office Kitano / Shanghai Film Group Shanxi Film & Television Group / Bandai Visual Company / Bitters End / MK2, 2013.

Tropical Fish (*Redaiyu*), Chen Yu-hsun, Central Motion Pictures Corporation, 1995.

Tuya's Marriage (*Tuya de hunshi*), Wang Quan'an, Maxyee Culture Industry / Xi'an Motion Picture Company, 2006.

Visage (*Lian*), Tsai Ming-liang, JBA Production / Homegreen Films / Musée du Louvre, Paris / Tarantula / Circe Films / Arte France Cinéma, 2009.

Vive L'amour (*Aiqing wansui*), Tsai Ming-liang, Central Motion Picture Corporation, 1994.

The Walkers (*Xingzhe*), Singing Chen, The Walkers Films Ltd., 2014.

Warriors of the Rainbow: Seediq Bale Part 1 (*Saideke Balai [shang]: Taiyang qi*), Wei Te-sheng, ARS Film Production / Central Motion Picture Corporation, 2011.

Warriors of the Rainbow: Seediq Bale Part 2 (*Saideke Balai [xia]: Caihong qiao*), Wei Te-sheng, ARS Film Production / Central Motion Picture Corporation, 2011.

The Wayward Cloud (*Tianbian yiduo yun*), Tsai Ming-liang, Arena Films / Arte France Cinéma / Homegreen Films / Wild Bunch, 2005.

The Wedding Banquet (*Xiyan*), Ang Lee, Ang Lee Productions / Central Motion Picture Corporation / Good Machine, 1993.

Wet Season (*Redaiyu*), Anthony Chen, Giraffe Pictures Hooq / Rediance / Singapore Film Commission / Taipei Film Commission, 2019.

What Time Is It There? (*Ni nabian jidian*), Tsai Ming-liang, Arena Films / Homegreen Films, 2001.

What's for Dinner, Mom? (*Mama, gohan mada?*), Mitsuhito Shiraha, Is.Field, 2016.

White Deer Plain (*Bailu yuan*), Wang Quan'an, Bai Lu Yuan Film Company / Lightshades Film Productions / Xi'an Movie and Television Production Co. / Western Film Group Corporation, 2011.

Winds of September (*Jiujiangfeng*), Tom Lin, Film Mall / Ocean Deep Films / BIG Pictures / Mei Ah Entertainment / See Corporation, 2008.

Women from the Lake of Scented Souls (*Xianghunnü*), Xie Fei, Changchun Film Studio / China Film Group Corporation / Tianjin Film Studio, 1993.

Yi Yi: A One and a Two (*Yi yi*), Edward Yanag, 1 + 2 Seisaku Iinkai / AtomFilms / Basara Pictures / Pony Canyon, 2000.

You Are the Apple of My Eye (*Naxie nian, women yiqi zhui de nühai*), Giddens Ko, Star Ritz Productions Co. / Sony Music Entertainment, 2011.

Your Face (*Nide lian*), Tsai Ming-liang, Homegreen Films / Public Television Service Taiwan, 2018.

Zone Pro Site (*Zongpushi*), Chen Yu-Hsun, 1 Production Film / Central Motion Picture Corporation / Encore Film Co. / Lucky Royal Co. / Ocean Deep Films / Warner Bros. / Yi Tiao Long Hu Bao International Entertainment Company, 2013.

Glossary of Chinese Terms

Afei zhengzhuan 阿飛正傳

Ah Zhong 阿忠

Ai ni ai wo 愛你愛我

Ai Weiwei 艾未未

Aiqing wansui 愛情萬歲

Baidu 百度

Baidu baike 百度百科

Baige jihua 白鴿計劃

Bailu yuan 白鹿原

Bairi yanhuo 白日焰火

balinghou 八零後

Bama buzai jia 爸媽不在家

Bawang bie ji 霸王別姬

Bayue 八月

Beiqing chengshi 悲情城市

bengshidai 崩世代

Benmingnian 本命年

*Bi beishang geng beishang de
 gushi* 比悲傷更悲傷的故事

Bi Gan 畢贛

Bingdu 冰毒

Busan 不散

Cai Guo-Qiang 蔡國強

Cai Shangjun 蔡尚君

Chan, Carlos 陳家樂

Chan, Lillian 陳凱彤

Chang Cho-chi 張作驥

Chang Chu-ti 張筑悌

Chang Hwa-kun 張華坤

Chang Yi 張毅

Changcheng 長城

Changjiang tu 長江圖

Chaoji da guomin 超級大國民

Chaoji nüsheng 超級女聲

Chaoji xingguang dadao 超級星光大道

Chen, Anthony 陳哲藝

Chen, Arvin 陳駿霖

Chen, Cheer (Qizhen) 陳綺貞

Chen, Frankie Yu-shan 陳玉珊

Chen Kaige 陳凱歌

Chen Kun-hou 陳坤厚

Chen Kuo-fu 陳國富

Chen Ming-chang 陳明章

Chen Shui-bian 陳水扁

Chen Si-han 陳思函

Chen, Singing 陳芯宜

Chen Yu-hsun 陳玉勳

Cheng Fen-fen 鄭芬芬

Cheng, Ryan 鄭秉泓

Cheng Wei-hao 程偉豪

Cheung, Maggie 張曼玉

Chi Po-lin 齊柏林

Chiang Kai-shek 蔣介石

Chiang Wei Liang 曾威量

Chiao, Peggy Hsiung-ping 焦雄屏

Chiu Fu-sheng 邱復生

Chiu Li-kwan　邱璓寬

Chong Keat Aun　張吉安

Chong Mong-hong　鍾孟宏

Chow, Kiwi　周冠威

Chow, Stephen　周星馳

Chow Yun-fat　周潤發

Chu, Joyce　朱主愛（四葉草）

Chu Tien-wen　朱天文

Chu Yu-ning　瞿友寧

Chuke Liang　豬哥亮

Chunfeng chenzui de yewan　春風沈醉的夜晚

Chung, Robert　鍾庭耀

Chunguang zhaxie　春光乍洩

Cike Nie Yinniang　刺客聶隱娘

Dahong denglong gaogao gua　大紅燈籠高高掛

Dai, Leon　戴立忍

Dawei luman　大尾鱸鰻

Daxiang xidi'erzuo　大象席地而坐

Diao Yinan　刁亦男

Diaoyu (Island)　釣魚（島）

Dijiutianchang　地久天長

Diqiu zuihou de yewan　地球最後的夜晚

Dongdong de jiaqi　冬冬的假期

Douban　豆瓣

Du Kefeng　杜可風

Du Yun-chih　杜雲之

Du zhan　毒戰

Duo sang　多桑

erci chuangzuo　二次創作

Erzi de da wan'ou　兒子的大玩偶

Feng Xiaogang　馮小剛

Feng'er titacai　風兒踢踏踩

Fenggui lai de ren　風櫃來的人

Fu Yue　傅榆

Fujian (province)　福建（省）

Fung Kai　馮凱

Ge You　葛優

geju　格局

Gong Li　鞏俐

Gongfu　功夫

Gu Changwei　顧長衛

Guangyin de gushi　光陰的故事

Guangyin de gushi Taiwan xindianying　光陰的故事：台灣新電影

Guangyin zhi lü Taiwan xindianying zai lushang　光陰之旅：台灣新電影在路上

Guizi laile　鬼子來了

Gulingjie shaonian sharen shijian　牯嶺街少年殺人事件

Haijiao qihao　海角七號

Haitan de yitian　海灘的一天

Hakka　客家

hao jiqi　好機器

Hao nan hao nü　好男好女

He Yunchang　何雲昌

Heiyanquan　黑眼圈

Heliu　河流

hesui pian　賀歲片

Ho, Michiyo　何念茲

Ho Wi-Ding　何蔚庭

Hokkien (language)　福建（話）

Hoklo　福佬／河洛

Hongfen　紅粉

Honggaoliang　紅高粱

Hongyi xiaonühai 2　紅衣小女孩2

Hou Hsiao-hsien　侯孝賢

Hsiao Chu-chen　蕭菊貞

Hsiao Kang　小康

Hsiao Wan Jan　小宛然

Hsiao Yeh　小野

Hsieh Chin-lin　謝慶齡

Hsu Feng　徐楓

Hsu Li-kong　徐立功

Hu Bo　胡波

Hu, Jason Chih-chiang　胡志強

Hu Xia　胡夏

Huajia daren zhuan nanhai　花甲大人轉男孩

Huan'ai　幻愛

Huang Chun-ming　黃春明

Huang Jianxin　黃建新

Huang Sheng-yuan　黃聲遠

Huantu　幻土

huaren　華人

huaren zhi guang　華人之光

Huaren zongheng tianxia　華人縱橫天下

Huayangnianhua　花樣年華

huayi　華裔

huayu dianying　華語電影

Hui, Ann　許鞍華

Hung Chih-yu　洪智育

Huozhe　活著

I Wan Jan　亦宛然

Ip, Deanie　葉德嫻

Jia zai Lanruosi　家在蘭若寺

Jia Zhangke　賈樟柯

Jiang Wen　姜文

Jiang Wenye　江文也

Jiangui　見鬼

Jiaotou 2 Wangzhe zaiqi　角頭2：王者再起

Jiaoyou　郊遊

Jin Na　金娜

Jingangjing　金剛經

Jinma　金馬

Jinmen (also Kinmen)　金門

Jinzhi xiamao　禁止下錨

Jiufen　九份

Jiujiangfeng　九降風

jiulinghou　九零後

Jiushi liuliude ta　就是溜溜的她

Jiyi wangzhe wo　記憶望著我

Jiyuantai qihao　繼園臺七號

Judou　菊豆

Junzhong leyuan　軍中樂園

Kanhai de rizi　看海的日子

Kanjian Taiwan　看見台灣

Kao Jun-honn　高俊宏

Kaohsiung　高雄

Kenting　墾丁

Kezai wo xindi de mingzi　刻在我心底的名字

Kingston, Maxine Hong　湯婷婷

Kinmen (also *Jinmen*)　金門

Ko, Giddens　柯景騰（九把刀）

Ko I-cheng　柯一正

Ko, Kai Zhendong　柯震東

Koh, Sun　許紋鸞

Kongbu fenzi　恐怖份子

Kongque　孔雀

Kuek, Raymond　郭子勝

Kuomintang　國民黨

Kwan, Stanley   關錦鵬

Lanse damen   藍色大門

Lao shou   老獸

Lau, Andrew   劉偉強

Law Wai-ming   羅維明

Lee, Ang   李安

Lee Hsing   李行

Lee, James   李添興

Lee Kang-sheng   李康生

Lee, Mark Ping-bing   李屏賓

Lee, Rich   李奇（李迪才）

Lei, Summer   雷光夏

Leung, Tony Chiu-wai   梁朝偉

Li Chuan-tsan   李傳燦

Li, Jill   李哲昕

Li Ka-shing   李嘉誠

Li Shaohong   李少紅

Li Tien-lu   李天祿

Li Yang   李楊

Lian   臉

Lianlian fengchen   戀戀風塵

Liao Fan   廖凡

Lien Chan   連戰

Lim Giong   林強

Lin Cheng-sheng   林正盛

Lin, Gavin   林孝謙

Lin Hwai-min   林懷民

Lin Li-chen   林麗珍

Lin, Tom   林書宇

Lou Ye   婁燁

Louxia de fangke   樓下的房客

Lu Yi-ching   陸弈靜

Lubian yecan   路邊野餐

Lüxing de yiyi   旅行的意義

Ma Chih-Hsiang   馬志翔

Ma, Yo Yo   馬友友

Majiang   麻將

Mak, Alan   麥兆輝

Mang jing   盲井

Mao Zedong   毛澤東

Maonü   毛女

Matsu (also *Mazu*)   馬祖

Mazu (also Matsu)   馬祖

Meilidao   美麗島

Mengjia   艋舺

Mengyou   夢遊

Mihang   迷航

Ming   明

Midi Z (also Zhao Deyin)   趙德胤

Nanerwang   男兒王

Nanfang laixin   南方來信

Nanguo zaijian, nanguo   南國再見，南國

Nanwu   南巫

Nari xiawu   那日下午

Nashi cike   那時此刻

Naxie nian, women yiqi zhui de nühai   那些年，我們一起追的女孩

Ni nabian jidian   你那邊幾點

Nide lian   你的臉

Niu, Doze Chen-zer   鈕承澤

Nüren sishi   女人四十

Pang, Danny Phat   彭發

Pang, Oxide Chun   彭順

Pei, I. M.   貝聿銘

Phang, Cass   彭羚

Qianxi manbo   千禧曼波

Qilu tiantang   歧路天堂

Qing   清

Qinghong   青紅

Qingmeizhuma   青梅竹馬

Qingshaonian Nezha   青少年哪吒

Qiu Ju da guansi   秋菊打官司

Qiuri   秋日

Redaiyu (Anthony Chen)   熱帶雨

Redaiyu (Chen Yu-hsun)   熱帶魚

Ren zai Niuyue   人在紐約

renqingwei   人情味

Renshanrenhai   人山人海

Rizi   日子

Ruan Lingyu   阮玲玉

Saideke Balai   賽德克巴萊

Saideke Balai (shang) Taiyang qi   賽德克巴萊（上）：太陽旗

Saideke Balai (xia) Caihong qiao   賽德克巴萊（下）：彩虹橋

Sange nüren de gushi   三個女人的故事

Sanxia haoren   三峽好人

Se, jie   色，戒

Sha   沙

Shaw, Run Run   邵逸夫

Shen Congwen   沈從文

Shi meng   是夢

Shi Nansun   施南生

Shiqi sui de danche   十七歲的單車

Shisi ke pingguo   十四顆蘋果

Shu Kei   舒琪

Shu Qi   舒淇

Shuangtong   雙瞳

Shuinan   水湳

Siao, Josephine   蕭芳芳

Siqin Gaowai   斯琴高娃

Song (also su)   俗

Song Fang   宋方

Su (also song)   俗

Sun Yat-sen   孫逸仙（孫中山）

Taibei xingqitian   台北星期天

Taichung   台中

Taiping tianguo   太平天國

Taiwanren zhi guang   台灣人之光

Taiyang you er   太陽有耳

Taiyu pian   台語片

Tan, Amy   譚恩美

Tan Chui Mui   陳翠梅

Tan, Royston   陳子謙

Tao Te-chen   陶德辰

Taojie   桃姐

Teo Wei Yong   張偉勇

Tian zhuding   天注定

Tianbian yiduo yun   天邊一朵雲

Tianqiao bujianle   天橋不見了

Tien, Hebe   田馥甄

Ting shuo   聽說

To, Johnnie   杜琪峰

Tongnian wangshi   童年往事

Tsai Ing-wen   蔡英文

Tsai Ming-liang   蔡明亮

Tsang, Felix   曾俊榮

Tsuei, Adam   崔震東

Tu Duu-chih   杜篤之

Tuanyuan   團圓

Tuina   推拿

Tuishou   推手

Tuya de hunshi   圖雅的婚事

Wan Jen　萬仁

Wanzhong　晚鐘

Wang Bing　王兵

Wang, Darren Dalu　王大陸

Wang Hsiao-ti　王小棣

Wang Jingchun　王景春

Wang Keng-yu　王耿瑜

Wang Quan'an　王全安

Wang Tung　王童

Wang Xiaoshuai　王小帥

Wei Te-sheng　魏德聖

Wen Muye　文牧野

wenqing　文青

Wo bushi yaoshen　我不是藥神

Wode fuqin muqin　我的父親母親

Wode shaonü shidai　我的少女時代

Wohu canglong　臥虎藏龍

Women de nashi cike　我們的那時此刻

Women de qingchun, zai Taiwan　我們的青春，在台灣

Women zheyang pai dianying　我們這樣拍電影

Wong Kar-wai　王家衛

Wong, Silian　王靖喬

Woo, John　吳宇森

Woshi geshou　我是歌手

Wu Cheng'en　吳承恩

Wu Nien-jen　吳念真

Wu se　無色

Wu wumian　無無眠

Wu Ziniu　吳子牛

Wufeng　霧峰

Wugou　無垢

wuguo　誤國

Wujiandao　無間道

wuxia　武俠

Xiamen　廈門

Xiang Zi　相梓

Xianghunnü　香魂女

xiao　小

xiao geming　小革命

xiao jingji　小經濟

xiao qingxin　小清新

xiao quexing　小確幸

Xiao rizi　小日子

Xiao shidai　小時代

Xiao Wu　小武

Xiao xingyun　小幸運

Xiao ziyou　小自由

Xiao zizai　小自在

Xiaobu wuqu　小步舞曲

xiaonong　小農

Xiaozhen de hai　小鎮的海

Xie Fei　謝飛

Xie Jin　謝晉

xiexie dajia de guanxin　謝謝大家的關心

Ximeng rensheng　戲夢人生

xin nanxiang zhengce　新南向政策

Xing zai shui shang　行在水上

Xingdong daihao Sun Zhongshan　行動代號：孫中山

Xingzhe (Singing Chen)　行者

Xingzhe (Tsai Ming-liang)　行者

Xiyan　喜宴

Xiyou　西遊

Xuanzang　玄奘

Xuanzang (Tsai Ming-liang)　玄奘

Yan'an　延安

Yang Chao　楊超

Yang, Edward De-chang　楊德昌

Yang, Franklin Chen-Ning　楊振寧

Yang, Jerry (Chih-yuan)　楊致遠

Yang Kuei-mei　楊貴媚

Yang Li-chou　楊力州

Yang Ya-che　楊雅喆

yanshidai　厭世代

Yatai lan　亞太藍

Yee Chih-yen　易智言

Yen Cheng-kuo　顏正國

Yeo Siew Hua　楊修華

Yeo Yann Yann　楊雁雁

Yeoh, Michelle　楊紫瓊

Yeyan　夜宴

yi　億

Yi yi　一一

Yidai zongshi　一代宗師

Yige dou buneng shao　一個都不能少

Yige yundong de kaishi　一個運動的開始

Yilan　宜蘭

Yim Ho　嚴浩

Ying　影

Yingxiong　英雄

Yinshi nannü　飲食男女

Yiye Taibei　一頁台北

Yonfan　楊凡

Yong Mei　詠梅

youyi　優異

Yu shen duihua　與神對話

Yuan　元

Yuanxiang yu lisan　原鄉與離散

yuebing lan　閱兵藍

Yuen Woo-ping　袁和平

Yung, Danny　榮念曾

Zai na hepan qing cao qing　在那河畔青草青

Zaijian, Nanping wanzhong　再見，南屏晚鐘

Zaijian Wacheng　再見瓦城

Zeng Jian　曾劍

Zeng Zhuangxiang　曾壯祥

Zhan Hongzhi　詹宏志

Zhang Delei　張大磊

Zhang Sheng　張生

Zhang Yimou　張藝謀

Zhang Yu　張羽

Zhao Deyin (also Midi Z)　趙德胤

Zhentou　陣頭

Zhiyou ni　只有你

Zhongguo　中國

Zhongguo hao shengyin　中國好聲音

Zhongguo, yidian dou buneng shao　中國，一點都不能少

Zhongguoren　中國人

Zhongguoren zhi guang　中國人之光

Zhou Ziyang　周子陽

Zhuangwei　壯圍

Zhuoren mimi　灼人秘密

Zhuoshuixi gongshe　濁水溪公社

Zongpushi　總鋪師

Zuihao de shiguang　最好的時光

Zuoyou　左右

Notes

Introduction

1. Here I qualify the Golden Horse Awards as a competition for Chinese-language film-making for the sake of convenience. The regulations, which are discussed in more detail in the Epilogue, are more complex than this, involving criterion based not just on language but also ethnicity.
2. The Sunflower Student movement was triggered by a protest against the hasty passing of a proposed Cross-Strait Services Trade Agreement with the PRC by Taiwan's then Kuomintang government, an indication of resistance by Taiwanese students toward greater integration with China. The PRC and ROC have conflicting claims of sovereignty on each other's lands since 1949.
3. Throughout the book I use "Taiwan" rather than "Taiwanese" when referring to films made in Taiwan because the latter could also imply Taiwanese-language cinema (that is, *Taiyu pian*, films spoken in Hoklo).
4. Note that some domestic discourses have dated the death of the TNC movement to be as early as around 1989 (Mi and Liang 1991). In this book I use TNC to refer to the movement started in the 1980s (with Hou Hsiao-hsien and Edward Yang as representative figures) and to the 1990s when new directors such as Ang Lee and Tsai Ming-liang were regarded as the movement's second-generation filmmakers. This book's focus, however, is on the legacy of the TNC movement and the works of these directors in the twenty-first century; hence I use "Taiwan cinema" throughout and only mention TNC when referring to the movement as it happened in the 1980s and 1990s.
5. Taiwan struggles to gain membership even to UN agencies such as the World Health Organization (WHO), and it can only participate in the Olympics Games under the moniker of "Chinese Taipei." According to Chia-chi Wu, owing to PRC interventions, in the 1980s, international film festival organizers would only give Taiwan the nod if the films were entered under a "sub-national epithet," and Taiwan films "could not completely rid themselves of the 'Taiwan, China' label until 2005" (Wu 2007, 79).
6. For a list of countries with diplomatic relations with Taiwan, see the Ministry of Foreign Affairs website. Accessed August 1, 2020. https://www.mofa.gov.tw/en/AlliesIndex.aspx?n=DF6F8F246049F8D6&sms=A76B7230ADF29736.
7. According to 2019 estimates, the GDP per capita figure (in USD) was 97,341 for Singapore (ranked 5th in the world), 59,848 for Hong Kong (ranked 18th), and 42,765 for South Korea (ranked 41th). Taiwan's 2018 figure of USD 24,502 places it at 80th out of a table of 228 countries on the World Factbook, published on the CIA website. Accessed August 14, 2021. https://www.cia.gov/the-world-factbook/field/real-gdp-per-capita/country-comparison/.

8. See, e.g., Kurlantzick 2007 and Lai and Lu 2012.
9. Indeed, the island's intelligentsia is not oblivious to this fact: the November 2019 issue of *Global Views Monthly*, an international relations magazine, titled its special issue "Two-sided Taiwan: First-rate Soft Power, Third-rate Hard Power."
10. Note that here Nye draws his materials from Pocha 2003, 9.
11. As such, I only make scant reference to documentaries on TNC or Taiwan cinema that are aimed at domestic consumption, such as *Our Time, Our Story* (*Baige jihua*, dir. Hsiao Chu-chen, 2002); *Face Taiwan: Power of Taiwan Cinema* (*Women zheyang pai dianying*, dir. Hsiao Chu-chen, 2016); and *The Moment* (*Women de nashi cike*, dir. Yang Li-chou, 2016). Note that an earlier version of Yang's documentary, entitled *Nashi cike* in Chinese, was commissioned by and screened at the Golden Horse Awards in 2014.
12. For the Dogme manifesto, see "Dogme 95—The Vow of Chastity (1995)" (2002, 83–84). For a full list of Dogme films, see "Dogme 95 Movies—Chronologically" (2008).
13. See Jan 2019 for a full English translation and Chen 2019 for a discussion of the manifesto.
14. The names of a broadly consensual list of core TNC directors working in the 1980s are Hou Hsiao-hsien, Edward Yang, Wang Tung, Chen Kun-hou, Ko I-cheng, Wan Jen, Zeng Zhuangxiang, and Chang Yi. See Chen 1994, 169–179. The only name absent from the manifesto is Wang Tung, already a veteran director at the launch of TNC. Apparently, Zhan Hongzhi regards Wang's entry film to the movement, *A Flower in the Rainy Night* (*Kanhai de rizi*, 1983), as "relatively mediocre" compared to films by Hou and Yang (Yeh and Davis 2005, 75–76).
15. On Truffaut and the French New Wave, see Vincendeau 2009. On Third Cinema, see Willemen 1990.
16. As Chia-chi Wu notes, measured in terms of production quantity or box-office revenues, TNC never constituted a "national cinema," and it was "too insignificant to help restructure or resuscitate the already collapsing industry" (2007, 85).
17. For a fuller discussion of the shift from the national to the transnational in film studies, see Higbee and Lim 2010.
18. While some may quibble about whether awards for these English-language films should count toward the tally for Taiwan cinema, Ang Lee's example, which shall be discussed in detail in Chapter 4, illustrates precisely the untenability of the national cinema model.
19. See, e.g., an account by Hsu Li-kong, one-time vice president of the state-funded CMPC, of his role in promoting Taiwan cinema on the international film festival (Hsu and Lee 2006).
20. Historical records of films sponsored up to the year 2017 can be accessed at the Bureau of Audiovisual and Music Industry Development, Ministry of Culture website. Accessed on January 9, 2021. https://www.bamid.gov.tw/informationlist_202_1.html.
21. While I draw mainly from Nye's 2004 book, *Soft Power: The Means to Success in World Politics*, Nye first mooted the notion in an earlier book *Bound to Lead: The Changing Nature of American Power* (Nye 1990).

22. The international network, on which I was a steering member, was sponsored by the Arts and Humanities Research Council of the United Kingdom.

23. In a recent result of an annual survey on soft power of 30 countries, China came in at 27th in 2017, down two places from the previous year, apparently because of the country's "hard line on foreign policy and human rights" (Liu 2018).

Chapter 1

1. I have kept the grammatical infelicities in Chen's speech, though I have taken out some repetitive expressions such as "I mean" and "you know."

2. The relationship between youth and cinematic new waves can be traced to the etymology of the French term "new wave" (*nouvelle vague*), which was coined to describe a demographic cohort in France whose formative years fell after the end of World War II and was subsequently borrowed to discuss cinematic movements (Tweedie 2013, 13).

3. In the documentary, Hou, who had already directed three feature-length films prior to the launch of the TNC movement, spoke candidly about the impact these young turks had had on him. Wu Nien-jen described the change evident in Hou's first TNC film, *The Boys from Fengkuei* (*Fenggui lai de ren*, 1983), as a leap from the first to the eighth floor.

4. Speaking just before 1997, Chen had a good basis for his claim given that Ang Lee had won a Golden Bear at Berlin for *The Wedding Banquet* (*Xiyan*) in 1993 and Tsai Ming-liang had bagged a Golden Lion at Venice in 1994 for *Vive L'amour* (*Aiqing wansui*). See Table I.1 in the Introduction for a list of awards won at Berlin, Cannes, and Venice by Taiwan cinema.

5. The gap in this historiography has now been partly filled by the works of Hong 2011 and James Wicks 2015, both of which, incidentally, foreground the transnational even in their historicization of the national.

6. See, e.g., Betz 2009 on European art cinema, Graham and Vincendeau 2009 on the French New Wave, Elsaesser 1989 on New German Cinema, and Ruberto and Wilson 2007 on Italian neorealism.

7. In her article "Festivals, Criticism and the International Reputation of Taiwan New Cinema," Chia-chi Wu mentions a list of "renowned festival writers" who became "enthusiastic advocates of Chinese language cinemas" (Wu 2007, 78). It is noteworthy that four out of the seven names listed in Wu's article (namely, Marco Müller, Tony Rayns, Shu Kei, and Sato Tadao) appear in the documentary *Flowers of Taipei*, thus confirming the long-lasting role these programmers and critics play in acting as willing interpreters, in this case, of TNC.

8. Indeed, by 1979, only 21 countries maintained diplomatic ties with Taiwan whereas 117 had official relations with the PRC, with 46 countries changing allegiance in their China policy from Taipei to Beijing between 1971 and 1979 (Hsieh 1996, 68–69).

9. The Diaoyu/Senkaku Island movement refers to a series of political protests among Chinese students on university campuses in Hong Kong, the United States, and Taiwan in the early 1970s following a dispute about sovereignty over a cluster of rock islands claimed by Japan, the PRC, and the Republic of China (Taiwan). The Formosa incident (also known as Kaohsiung or Meilidao incident) refers to the arrest of opposition leaders following a riot triggered by a rally to mark "International Human Rights Day" in December 1979 (Wachman 1994, 134–135, 140).

10. The other three little dragons were Hong Kong, Singapore, and South Korea. See Vogel 1993 for a study of the four little dragons.

11. The February 28 incident refers to a confrontation, begun on that date in 1947, between the Taiwanese people and the Kuomintang regime, that led to a violent crackdown by troops and an estimated death toll ranging from 1,000 to more than a 100,000 (Wachman 1994, 98–99).

12. Some reviews complain about the documentary's excessive focus on Hou and Yang at the expense of other directors whose films did not receive as much international attention. See, e.g., Huang 2014.

13. The topics of the forums are "New Women and New Cinema," "From New Cinema to New Power," "Cross-Generational Dreamers," and "Film and Literature Dancing Together," a record of which is published in Wang 2015a, 302–332.

14. Commissioned by the Government Information Office and the public television channel, the 2002 documentary was the closing film of a retrospective of TNC's 20th anniversary in Taiwan and participated in film festivals in Hong Kong, Pusan, and Singapore. Unlike *Flowers of Taipei*, whose DVD was released with an accompanying book soon after its premiere, the DVD for *Our Time, Our Story* was not in wide circulation, though it was included as a special feature DVD in the Criterion release of Edward Yang's *A Brighter Summer Day* (*Gulingjie shaonian sharen shijian*, 1991) in 2016.

15. The reviewer, Derek Elley, further adds, "the title suggests a documentary study of the whole movement—sorely needed, given the rewriting of history that has been gradually taking place over the past decade or so" (2017), though no indication is given as to where this rewriting has been taking place.

16. The dual tendency is, on the one hand, a configuration of the nation as a struggle among different communities arising from Taiwan's colonial and postcolonial forces and, on the other hand, a "re-visioning of the nation that hopefully could resolve historical injustice and accommodate differences" (Wu 2007, 76).

17. Tsai, a Malaysian citizen, is a "Taiwan" filmmaker insofar as he has based his entire career in Taiwan and his films represent Taiwan at international film festivals.

18. Incidentally, in 1993 Kore-eda made a documentary about Hou and Edward Yang, which I have not had the opportunity to watch. The documentary was screened at the 2020 Golden Horse Festival during which Kore-eda flew in from Japan to present the Lifetime Achievement Award to Hou.

19. The White Terror campaign refers to the period following the Kuomintang government's imposition of martial law in Taiwan in 1949 up till the 1960s, during

which an unknown number of intellectuals and political dissidents were arrested (Chao and Myers 1998, 50–52). Martial law was finally lifted in 1987.

20. See this book's Introduction for a discussion of the "1987 Taiwan Cinema Manifesto."

21. Note that here Rosen is engaging with the implications of Jean Baudrillard's postmodern notion of simulation.

22. Hou's 2003 film is set in Tokyo and pays homage to Ozu Yasujiro's *Tokyo Story* (1953), whereas his 2007 film is set in Paris and pays homage to Albert Lamorisse's *The Red Balloon* (1956). See Chapter 2 for a discussion of these non-Chinese-language films by Hou in what I call an aural turn.

23. I use, both in the cited 2007 article and here, the term "intratextuality" to refer to connections within an auteur's oeuvre and the term "intertextuality" to refer to connections between works of different directors.

Chapter 2

1. See Table I.1 in the Introduction of this book for a list of awards won by TNC at the top-three film festivals (Berlin, Cannes, Venice).

2. The anticipation was heightened alongside news that Hong Kong director Wong Kar-wai was also in pre-production for a martial arts film around the same time. Wong's *The Grandmaster* (*Yidai zongshi*) was released in 2013, six years after his previous film, *My Blueberry Nights* (2007). Here I am using the English phrase "martial arts film" to encompass the typically period-set, sword-fighting *wuxia* film as well as the more contemporary-set, fist-fighting kung fu film. On digital aesthetics of recent *wuxia* films, see Lim 2016a.

3. Some examples from film reviews should suffice to illustrate the reception of *The Assassin*: "elliptical mode of storytelling" and "strikingly beautiful and elegiac visual poetry" ("View from Cannes" 2015); "the story is told in such an enigmatic manner" and "visually ravishing and formally graceful" (Sobczynski 2015); "opaque and difficult plot" and "mesmeric compositional sense and pure balletic poise" (Bradshaw 2015).

4. I refer to the former two films listed as predominantly in Mandarin because they also contain dialogue in Minnan (or Hoklo), a South China regional language widely spoken in Taiwan. The term Sinophone, used to partly describe the latter two films, is a discursive term that has been used increasingly for the study of modern Chinese literary and cultural products from various Chinese-speaking worlds, whether including the People's Republic of China (preferred by David Der-wei Wang 2017) or not (proposed by Shu-mei Shih 2007).

5. I follow Kenneth Chan 2004 and Stephen Teo 2009 in naming *wuxia* films made after Ang Lee's *Crouching Tiger, Hidden Dragon* (such as Zhang Yimou's 2002 *Hero/ Yingxiong*, Feng Xiaogang's 2006 *The Banquet/Yeyan*) as the transnational *wuxia* film. I thank Ni Ziquan for sharing her knowledge on the topic with me.

6. See the opening of Chapter 1 for a discussion of Assayas's documentary, *HHH: Portrait de Hou Hsiao-hsien*.

7. For more information about the Academy, see the Golden Horse Film Festival web-site. Accessed on August 14, 2020. http://www.goldenhorse.org.tw/academy/about/overview/?r=en. In this book's Epilogue, I discuss the Academy in the context of TNC's soft-power appeal to alien filmmakers from a wider Chinese-speaking world.

8. For an analysis of the relationship between Hou and Ozu, see Needham 2006.

9. The interview was originally published in a Taiwanese magazine, then translated and collected in Christopher Lupke's book on Hou. The other directors included in the original Shochiku omnibus film project, according to Hou, were Abbas Kiarostami, Wim Wenders, and Yukisada Isao (Lupke 2016, 255). Under the aegis of NHK and in the same year as Hou's tribute film, Kiarostami released *Five: Five Long Takes Dedicated to Yasujiro Ozu* (2003), which consists of five long takes at the seaside.

10. Assayas's film, released in 2008, is entitled *Summer Hours* (*L'heure d'été*), which I discuss briefly in the Epilogue.

11. Moreover, the postcolonial dynamic of various linguaphone models differs. The Francophone aegis, e.g., has been extended to countries with no (post)colonial relation with France, including Bulgaria and Romania. I thank Jamie Steele for bringing this to my attention.

12. On a different note, Jacques Derrida's warning about phonocentrism (Derrida 1976) can be said to have "heralded a disciplinary turn away from voice and sound as presence toward a focus on textuality and inscription" (Samuels et. al. 2010, 331). In this vein, Martin Jay's classic work on ocularphobic discourse in twentieth-century French intellectual thought (Jay 1994) also deserves attention.

13. The "Me Too" movement was originally founded in 2006 but the use of hash-tag in front of the term became a worldwide phenomenon following allegations of sexual assault in Hollywood in late 2017.

14. Jiang's biographical sketch is culled from various pages in Liu 2016.

15. See Chapter 1 for a discussion on how watching Taiwan cinema could be a bittersweet experience for some Japanese audiences (such as the film director Hirokazu Kore-eda and critic Tadao Sato) precisely because of the audiences' knowledge of the (post)colonial relationship between Taiwan and Japan.

16. The KMT lost in the presidential election for the first time in the year 2000 then won it back in 2008 before losing it again in 2016.

17. It must be qualified that Jiang's complicated relationship with the notion of nationality was noted in the said event, entitled "This is no country music." For more information on the event, see the webpage of Theater Commons Tokyo. Accessed on August 7, 2020. https://theatercommons.tokyo/2019/en/program/hong-kai_wang/.

18. Tae Hitoto, a dentist turned writer and actress, also has a connection to cinema as her autobiographical book was turned into a film, *What's for Dinner, Mom?*, in 2016 (dir. Mitsuhito Shiraha). Incidentally, Kimiko Yo, the veteran actress who plays Yoko's stepmother in *Café Lumière*, also has a Japanese mother and a Taiwanese father. Despite being born in and having lived in Japan her whole life, Yo never took up Japanese citizenship and, in fact, holds a Taiwanese passport.

19. Hou's Taiwan trilogy begins with *A City of Sadness* (1989) and ends with *Good Men, Good Women* (*Hao nan hao nü*, 1995). Li also appeared in some other films by Hou, including *Dust in the Wind* (*Lianlian fengchen*, 1986) and *A City of Sadness*.

20. My synopsis of the film draws partly from a publication by Hou's long-term script-writer, Chu Tien-wen. Even though Chu was not credited as a scriptwriter on this film, her book (Chu 2009) includes a synopsis of and a script for *Flight of the Red Balloon*. While the information contained in Chu's book does not match the film exactly, it is useful for understanding some of the background to the film's diegesis, e.g., the appearance of Ah Zhong in France.

21. Song Fang, then a film school student in Belgium, released her feature-film directorial debut, *Memories Look at Me* (*Jiyi wangzhe wo*), in 2012. The film includes a scene of a conversation between a mother and a daughter (played by Song herself) that clearly alludes to a similar scene in Hou's *A Time to Live, A Time to Die* (*Tongnian wangshi*, 1985).

22. Birtwistle's book has been extremely helpful for my recasting of an earlier reading of *Café Lumière* (Lim 2016b) from a temporal analysis to the present one from aurality. His book also brings to my attention the works of Peter Gidal and Barbara Kennedy, and I cite the former secondhand from Birtwistle and the latter by returning to the original source.

23. Because my focus in this chapter is the gendered female voice, I will not discuss the use of Jiang Wenye's music in the film. My earlier sketch of Jiang's music career serves to highlight Taiwan's historical sonic soft power rather than lead to an analysis of his music as used in Hou's film.

24. I base my discussion on the DVD released in the United Kingdom by ICA Projects (DAP7721). The order of the opening is slightly different in the Japanese DVD released by Shochiku Home Video (DA0603), which shows the film title *after* the first long take of Yôko, which also ends with a fade-out rather than a cut.

25. Yoko's freelance work status can be seen as a determination to forge a different gendered existence from the other women who appear in the film (all from an earlier generation), from her stepmother (always confined to the kitchen making food) and her own mother (who left the family when Yoko was four years old for unexplained reasons) to Jiang Wenye's real-life widow (still holding onto memories of young romantic love with Jiang but effectively abandoned by Jiang when he left for China in 1938). Moreover, her decision not to marry the father of her child demonstrates her reluctance to rely on a conventional male figure, especially one with too many strings attached (Yoko regards the father of her child, a Taiwanese to whom she used to teach Japanese in Taiwan, as too attached to his mother; besides, his family wants her to join their umbrella-making business in Thailand).

26. For the interrelationship among slowness, stillness, and silence in cinema, see Lim 2014a.

27. Note that Michel Chion thinks that timbre is "not a musical value" (2011, 238) and that attempts to develop the notion in theoretical terms "has been a complete failure" (237).

28. By the same token, it is worth remembering that the medium of film also disguises the real source of its aurality—the loudspeaker—by creating the illusion of so-called synchronized sounds (Chion 1999, 3), as if the sounds of characters' voices, e.g., emanate from the visual images.

29. Reviews of the film have noted Binoche's vocal performance. One suggests that Suzanne seems "most at peace only when she's giving grave, gravelly voice to one of her creations" (Dargis 2008). Another sees Hou's film as animated "not only by the hide-and-seek antics of the red balloon but by [Suzanne's] extravagant turn as a frazzled performance artist," describing Suzanne as "a harried composition in frowsy blonditude, filmy scarves, and mad décolletage—the most dynamic female protagonist in the Hou oeuvre" (Hoberman 2008).

30. This information is drawn from the transcript of an interview with Hou and Binoche, translated and compiled by Taipei's Chang Chu-ti from foreign wire news. It is collected in Chu 2009, in which Chang is not otherwise credited.

31. Hou details, in a French documentary entitled *Métro Lumière: Hou Hsiao-Hsien à la rencontre de Yasujirô Ozu* (Harold Manning, 2004), the bureaucratic restrictions he encountered when filming *Café Lumière* in Tokyo, which he and his crew circumvented with guerilla-style filming on locations such as trains and pedestrian walkways just outside buildings. The documentary is contained in the Japanese DVD released by Shochiku Home Video. On another note, while in both the examples discussed here I can visually see the conditions of production and can cite supporting evidence from secondary sources, I can never ascertain if the sonic elements are truly synchronized sounds or have been recorded in post-production—thus undercutting my argument—without behind-the-scene accounts, once again illustrating the challenge of writing about film sound. I thank Timmy Chen for a stimulating conversation that helped me come to this realization.

32. Here I exclude the three feature-length films Hou directed before the launch of the TNC movement, namely, *Cute Girl* (*Jiushi liuliude ta*, 1980), *Cheerful Wind* (*Feng'er titacai*, 1981), and *The Green, Green Grass of Home* (*Zai na hepan qing cao qing*, 1983). I also do not include Hou's contribution (because it is a short film) to the portmanteau film, *The Sandwich Man* (*Erzi de da wan'ou*, 1983), commonly credited as one of the first TNC films. See Lupke 2016, 317–335 for Hou's filmography and Hong 2011 for a reading of Hou's pre-TNC films.

33. Chu's impact on Hou extends far beyond the collaborative nature of filmmaking. Hailing from a literary family, Chu doubles as a kind of intellectual mentor to Hou, urging him to read Shen Congwen's biography, which resulted in an "observational style . . . that eschewed judgments of the main characters and sought to allow the narrative to build on a series of cascading tableau, one after another" in *The Boys from Fenggui* (*Fenggui lai de ren*, 1983), an "epistemological" turn that Christopher Lupke argues begins with the aforementioned film and is fully realized in the 1984 film *Summer at Grandpa's* (*Dongdong de jiaqi*) (2016, 53).

34. Indeed, Cixous cites the work of the male, French writer, Jean Genet, as a prime example of *écriture feminine* (see Hanrahan 1999). For an interview of Chu on her collaboration with Hou, see Chu 2009, 593–605.

35. Whereas Binoche is noted for her vocal performance in reviews of the film, Hou is praised for his visual virtuosity in turning "minute, equivocal sketches into unexpectedly rich compositions of everyday life" (Goldsmith, 2009), "punctuated by passages of pure cinema" (Hoberman, 2008), and "[playing] with light and space on the small canvas that is Simon and Suzanne's apartment, moving the camera around as gracefully as if it were a brush (or a balloon)" (Dargis 2008).
36. On the February 28 incident, see Chapter 1 note 11.
37. See Lim 2014b for a discussion on the implications of a reading of the relationship between voice and ethnicity for the concept of the Sinophone.
38. The use of voice in puppetry theater, like singing, necessarily introduces highly structured "codes and standards of its own" that can be "more elusive than the linguistic ones" (Dolar 2012, 551). Binoche's use of her voice in the first and third puppetry sequences in Hou's film, compared to Li's in the second sequence, is much more "dramatic," for want of a better word. I am, unfortunately, not equipped to provide an explanation whether this contrast is owed to cultural codes and conventions (Taiwanese versus French puppetry) or gender stereotypes (male versus female).

Chapter 3

1. It is difficult to say in what sense Tsai has come out of his announced retirement from feature-length filmmaking as he has not stopped producing cinematic works since his announcement and they tend to be genre defying. These include a conversation with his regular actor Lee Kang Sheng (*Afternoon*/*Nari xiawu*, 2015, 107 mins.); a portrait of a Japanese friend Teruyo Nogami ("Autumn Days"/*Qiuri*, 2015, 24 mins.); a virtual reality film (*The Deserted*/*Jia zai Lanruosi*, 2017, 55 mins.); and a documentation of 13 faces (*Your Face*/*Nide lian*, 2018, 77 mins.), which features a musical score by Ryuichi Sakamoto. At the time of this writing (late 2020), Tsai's latest work, *Days* (*Rizi*; 2020, 127 mins.), comes closest to a "conventional" feature-length dramatic film; although, it hardly contains any dialogue and announces in its opening credits that there will not be any subtitles.
2. Tsai and Tarr are more than kindred spirits in slow cinema who happened to have announced their retirement from filmmaking within a year or so of each other. In late 2016, Tsai was invited to guest lecture at Tarr's film academy for a week (Pan 2016). Note that the site of Tarr's film school is listed erroneously as Split, Croatia, in a report (Rapold 2012), but the academy was shut down in December 2016 because, according to Tarr, it was becoming too expensive for the university (Croll 2016).
3. See Chapter 4 for more discussion on location tourism in relation to Ang Lee's *Life of Pi* (2012).
4. It is worth noting that, in an earlier short film, "The Skywalk Is Gone" (*Tianqiao bujian le*, 2002), a real Buddhist monk is shown walking very slowly amidst busy human traffic in front of the Taipei train station.

5. The other three directors involved in the 2012 project were Ann Hui (Hong Kong), Gu Changwei (China), and Kim Tae-yong (South Korea). The 2015 project also included films by Huang Jianxin (China), Mohsen Makhmalbaf (Iran), and Yim Ho (Hong Kong).

6. Curated by Malaysian filmmaker Tan Chui Mui and originally entitled *Letters from the South* (*Nanfang laixin*) before being renamed *Homeland & Diaspora* (*Yuanxiang yu lisan*), the series included five other shorts, namely Aditya Assarat's "Now Now Now" (Thailand), Singaporeans Sun Koh's "New New Panda" and Royston Tan's "Popiah," Malaysian Tan Chui Mui's "A Night in Malacca," and Midi Z's "Burial Clothes" (Myanmar).

7. An interview with Tsai on the occasion of his VR film's participation at the Venice film festival begins with the statement that Tsai "should have been the last person to make a virtual reality movie" (Frater 2017). The interview also discloses that Tsai's VR film project was initiated by Marco Müller, veteran programmer for the Venice film festival, thus echoing my earlier argument about the importance of foreign agents in promoting Taiwan cinema (see Chapter 1 for more discussion of such a role played by Müller since the heyday of the Taiwan New Cinema movement).

8. While I situate Tsai's intermedial practice in the context of the mid-twentieth-century tradition of expanded cinema, the question of medium specificity and the discourse of the post-medium age can be viewed from a longer historical perspective in which cinema's birth at the turn of the twentieth century had had to distinguish itself, first and foremost, from "its dominant other, theater" (Bao 2015b, 351).

9. Lu Fei-i (1998, 324) and Peggy Chiao Hsiung-ping (2018, 70–75) have also noted this bifurcation in their books on Taiwan cinema. For an extended discussion on this bifurcation and its implications for Taiwan film historiography, see this book's Chapter 5.

10. The first invitation came, in fact, from the theater world when Danny Yung, artistic director of the legendary Hong Kong experimental theater company Zuni Icosahedron, asked Tsai to create an installation piece besides directing a play for Yung's "One Table Two Chairs" series in 1997 (Lin and Tsai 2016b, 10).

11. To the best of my knowledge, the 2010 DVD released by the Louvre and Arte Editions of *Visage* is the only DVD version available to date.

12. The room no longer exists after June 30, 2018, as the hotel continues to reinvent itself.

13. Between 1994 and 1997, the Taiwan government loosened five times the quota for foreign films, increasing the number of copies for each film from 16 before September 1994 to 58 by 1997. It also increased, over the same period, the number of cinemas in Taipei screening each foreign film from 6 to 18 (Wang 1997a, 40; Wang 1999, 62). Between 1999 and 2007, foreign-language films (mainly from Hollywood) constituted more than 90 percent of the box-office intake every single year in Taipei's first-run cinemas, with the remaining market share split among films from Hong Kong, Mainland China, and Taiwan ("Zhonghuaminguo yingpian," n.d.).

14. For an example of Tsai's disavowal of his relationship to the Taiwan New Cinema movement, see his interview in the documentary *Flowers of Taipei: Taiwan New*

Cinema (discussed in Chapter 1). Also see this book's Introduction for a discussion of the "Taiwan Cinema Manifesto."

15. For an example of Tsai's complaint about how cinema's slant toward entertainment killed his interest in filmmaking, see Su 2014.

16. Moreover, Tsai's solution is not collective but individual action; this separates him from his closest counterpart in Taiwan art cinema, Hou Hsiao-hsien, who, in the new millennium, increasingly assumed more official roles in film institutions and initiatives in his bid to promote film culture in Taiwan (see Chapter 2).

17. On my late-night visit to the exhibition on an October weekend in 2014, there was reportedly an audience of close to 1,000 and a long queue outside the already packed museum, attracted, I must add, in part by the scheduled performance of indie musician Summer Lei (who collaborated with Hou on the soundtrack of *Goodbye South, Goodbye/Nanguo zaijian, nanguo*, 1996).

18. On the ontology of the film image in the digital age, see Rodowick 2007; on the convergence of media forms, see Jenkins 2006; on digital technology as remediation, see Bolter and Grusin 2000.

19. The Visitor Center was initially meant to host Tsai's installation of the Walker series for the first two years (that is, ending in April 2020) but this had been extended as Tsai was still holding events there at the time of this writing (late 2020).

20. Jean-Pierre Rehm, who became FID's artistic director in 2002, has a long-standing interest in Tsai's work. He contributed an article (Rehm 1999) to the first English-language book on Tsai and invited Tsai to present his short film, "A Conversation with God" (*Yu shen duihua*, 2001), for competition the year he assumed the FID post (Vagenas 2013).

21. See, e.g., Michel de Certeau's seminal book *The Practice of Everyday Life* (1984), which includes a chapter entitled "Walking in the City" under a section on "spatial practices."

22. Walking through a passageway (like a staircase) is a form of what has been called "purposive walking," typically performed "in a rather anxious mode, in which we long for arrival at a destination" (Wunderlich 2008, 131).

23. In Taiwan, Tsai's ethos is shared by Lin Li-chen's Legend Lin Dance Theater, whose Chinese name, *Wugou* (literally "no dirt or filth," meaning "purity"), has strong Buddhist connotations. For more about Lin and her troupe, see a documentary incidentally also entitled *The Walkers* (*Xingzhe*, dir. Singing Chen, 2014).

24. The phrase "a sign taken for wonder" is, of course, borrowed from the title of Homi Bhabha's seminal essay on postcoloniality. Though I do not engage with Bhabha's arguments here, it is worth stressing that the notion of hybridity, which I mentioned earlier, is not always a cause for celebration because, as Bhabha notes, it is "the sign of the productivity of colonial power, its shifting forces and fixities; it is the name of the strategic reversal of the process of domination through disavowal (that is, the production of discriminatory identities that secure the 'pure' and original identity of authority)" (1985, 154).

25. It is worth noting that Lavant has a chameleon-like appearance, playing 11 characters in Leos Carax's *Holy Motors* (2012) not long before collaborating with Tsai.

26. For a forceful refutation of such kind of reading, see Chow 1995.

27. Prominent examples of long-duration performance art based on the trope of walking include *The Great Wall Walk* (a.k.a. *The Lovers*) by Marina Abramović and her then-partner Ulay, who each walked 2,500 kilometers from opposite ends of the Great Wall of China to meet in the middle, arriving in June 1988 after 90 days of walking; He Yunchang's carrying of a rock counterclockwise around Britain until he returned the rock at the town of Boulmer where he first took it, arriving more than six months later; and Greg Hindy's one-year performance, entitled *Walking, Silence*, which saw him walk 8,700 miles from New Hampshire to California in silence.

28. Douglas Gordon's installation piece, *24 Hour Psycho* (1993), which stretches Alfred Hitchcock's 1960 film *Psycho* to a slow-motion projection lasting twenty-four hours, is a famous example of the use of technology to slow down motion. For a study of the use of slow-motion photography to achieve an aesthetic of slowness, see Koepnick 2014.

29. E.g., the "Slow Art Day" event, started in 2009, aims to change spectatorial behavior by asking its participants to examine objects in museums and galleries for 5 to 10 minutes each (in contradistinction to an average of 17 seconds spent by museumgoers looking at an individual painting according to a study) before convening to discuss their impressions over lunch (Morse 2011).

30. The exhibition catalogue for *Stray Dogs at the Museum* includes a small booklet that contains three pages of selected notes left by audience members, originally presented as post-it notes pasted on a board on a staircase landing in the museum. The booklet does not contain page numbers (see Lin and Tsai 2016a).

Chapter 4

1. PRC director Chen Kaige's *Farewell My Concubine* (*Bawang bie ji*, 1993) was nominated in the Best Foreign Language Film category of the Academy Awards, but it represented Hong Kong because of the film's production background. Gu Changwei from the PRC also earned a nomination at the Oscars in the Best Cinematography category for the film.

2. I thank Kien Ket Lim for bringing this to my attention by giving me a copy of the magazine when I visited Taiwan in March 2013.

3. While Ang Lee has not, to the best of my knowledge, taken up US citizenship, his success story fits easily into narratives of the American dream and of Asian Americans as the model minority. For a study of the discourse of "Asian Americans of Achievement," see Lee and Zhou 2015.

4. It is revealing that Sheng-mei Ma refers to the aforementioned quartet of TNC directors as "the Big Three plus one," Ang Lee being the "plus one" who, according to Ma, made it to the world stage via "Hollywood" as opposed to Hou, Yang, and Tsai who did so via "Art Cinema" (Ma S-m. 2015, 3).

5. For an expanded discussion on the relationship between auteur theory and Chinese cinemas, see Lim 2007.

6. Sources are inconsistent on information about production companies for Ang Lee's early films. The Internet Movie Database does not include Good Machine for *Pushing Hands*, though the company's involvement is acknowledged in an interview with Lee (Wang C-c. 1991, 9) and in an article (Chou 1991, 20) collected in a booklet on Lee produced by the Taipei Golden Horse International Film Festival Executive Committee. The company's name also seems inconsistent in Chinese translation. While it appears literally as "*hao jiqi*" in the booklet and in the credits of *The Wedding Banquet*, a company by the name of "*youyi*" (meaning "excellence") appears in the credits of *Pushing Hands*, for which I presume is an earlier translation for Good Machine. Moreover, the company's name is absent in the film credits of *Eat Drink Man Woman*, even though it is listed in all published sources I have consulted.

7. Working with major Hollywood studios, however, had also come at a cost for Lee as the studios decided not to grant *Ride with the Devil* and *The Ice Storm* full theatrical release or promotional support in the United States (Berry 2005, 338), resulting in a poor box-office intake (a meager US$635,096 for *Ride with the Devil*, less than 2 percent of its production budget) and these being the least well-known of Lee's films.

8. A recent four-volume anthology of American film history includes a chapter on the subject of Hollywood's relationship to Asia, which, according to the author, "testifies to the significance of this cross-cultural phenomenon" (Chan 2012, 406). The chapter surveys trends of this Hollywood-Asia engagement, including the kung fu and *wuxia* genres, stating Lee's *CTHD* was a "watershed title" that "directed critical and mainstream attention to Chinese and Asian cinemas in general" in the United States (408).

9. I first wrote about Lee's industrial turn in Lim 2012, though that discussion, which draws upon and critiques Hamid Naficy's notion of "accented cinema," is not brought into analysis in this chapter.

10. *Billy Lynn*'s budget does not fit this bracket, but I include the film in this category for its technological experimentation.

11. Since Fox acquired the film rights for Yann Martel's novel in 2003, directors who had reportedly considered and then rejected the adaptation include M. Night Shyamalan and Alfonso Cuaron (Hiscock 2016, 115). Jean-Pierre Jeunet also apparently spent a year in pre-production before giving up the project (Lin and Kang 2013, 110).

12. The documentary, entitled *Taiwan Captured on Film* and first broadcast in January 2018, can be viewed at the TRT World website. Accessed on November 3, 2020. https://www.trtworld.com/video/showcase/taiwan-captured-on-film-showcase-special/5a4f2f799418230025b39591.

13. Taipei, however, is not included in an English-language book series on "World Film Locations," which boasts 41 titles to date (late 2020) and features the East and Southeast Asian cities of Hong Kong, Shanghai, Beijing, and Singapore. See the publisher's webpage. Accessed on November 18, 2020. https://www.intellectbooks.com/world-film-locations?page=1.

14. Hu's ambition for a Guggenheim museum to be built in Taichung City was reportedly held back by interparty politics as well as a lack of support from local and central

governments ("NO! Gugenhan" 2004). Hu initiated, this time successfully, another project on the National Taichung Theater (designed by Toyo Ito), the first national-level performing arts venue to be built in 30 years, which opened in September 2016 ("National Taichung Theater" 2016), after Hu had lost his mayoral re-election in November 2014.

15. Amount sponsored for each film since the inauguration of the scheme can be found on the Taichung City government's Information Bureau website. Accessed on November 3, 2020. https://www.news.taichung.gov.tw/14786/14864/14879/14882/14891/278943/post.

16. The report can be downloaded at the website of the Research, Development and Evaluation Committee of Taichung City Government. Accessed on November 16, 2020. https://www.rdec.taichung.gov.tw/12155/Lpsimplelist?Page=1&PageSize=30&type=. the weblink no longer worked when accessed on August 16, 2021

17. Pre-production for *Life of Pi* began in early 2009, whereas Cameron's film opened in the United States in late December 2009.

18. Lee elaborates on the realistic potential of 3D technology in an interview for *Billy Lynn*: "I'm really eager to persuade people that 3D is . . . not [about] the action or the spectacle. They think 3D is either action or spectacle, maybe a space movie, or a cartoon. I beg to differ. I think the most you get out of this, is reading faces. When you have details, the way you pick up information is different. I think the most worthy thing is watching the faces" (Fleming 2016).

19. The five cinemas equipped to screen *Billy Lynn* at this format were located in Taipei, Beijing, Shanghai, New York, and Los Angeles (Ho 2016).

20. For a discussion of Sontag's essay, see Lim 2014a, 58–59.

21. In 2002, the Asian arm of Columbia Pictures collaborated with Taiwan's Nan Fang Film Production to make *Double Vision* (*Shuang tong*, dir. Chen Kuo-fu) in Taiwan, but the film turned out to be a commercial flop (Lin and Kang 2016, 112). Since the making of *Life of Pi* and besides Scorsese's *Silence*, Luc Besson had also chosen to shoot his film, *Lucy* (2014), in Taiwan.

Chapter 5

1. *Cape No. 7*'s box-office figure, which is for the whole of Taiwan, is obtained from the film's official website. Accessed on December 1, 2020. http://cape7.pixnet.net/blog/post/21746004. The exchange rate is based on figures around the time of the film's release. Henceforth in this chapter all box-office figures in Taiwan will be provided only in New Taiwan dollars (NT$) since exchange rates fluctuate.

2. At the time of this writing (end of 2020), James Cameron's *Avatar* (2009) has taken over the number one spot in Taiwan's box-office history, and many other films have also achieved bigger box-office intakes than both *Titanic* and *Cape No. 7*. Before July 2016, box-office figures were available only for the Greater Taipei region and not the

whole of Taiwan; hence, this ranking is based on and all subsequent figures quoted are for the Greater Taipei region unless otherwise stated.

3. According to the film critic Wen Tien-hsiang, Wei is only the fourth director, after Hou Hsiao-hsien, Tsai Ming-liang, and Chang Cho-chi, to have brought Taiwan cinema into official competition at the Venice film festival (Wen 2012, 12). This account, of course, discounts Ang Lee's participation, indeed victory, at the same festival, albeit for films (*Brokeback Mountain* in 2005 and *Lust, Caution* in 2007) that were not classified as Taiwan cinema (see Chapter 4 for a discussion of how Lee's trans-Pacific and translingual career defies categorization).

4. See this book's Introduction for more discussion on such scapegoating of TNC.

5. The book (Chiu, Rawnsley, and Rawnsley 2017) is divided into three parts. Part II, "Taiwan Cinema and Social change," consists of seven chapters, all of which focus on Wei's role as director and producer, whereas Part III is devoted solely to an interview with Wei as well as his short biography and synopses of his films. Wei's films are also discussed, to varying degrees, in the Introduction and all six chapters in Part I, entitled "International Reception and Taiwan Cinema."

6. *The Sandwich Man* is a portmanteau film consisting of three shorts directed by Hou Hsiao-hsien, Zeng Zhuangxiang, and Wan Jen, all adapted from short stories written by Huang. On nativist literature in Taiwan, see Chang 1993.

7. Categorization is always a messy business, and I have shied away from attempting to provide an "exhaustive" list of films that might be classified as little freshness.

8. It must be qualified that there are also films produced in the same period whose treatment of historical material is more somber, particularly epics such as Wei's two-part film, *Warriors of the Rainbow: Seediq Bale*, and Hung Chih-yu's *1895* (2008).

9. This is not the place to provide a full-blown account of affect theory, though I discussed the notion of affect in this book's Introduction. For a summary of affect theory, see Seigworth and Gregg 2010. For a critique of the affective turn in critical theory, see Leys 2011. On a distinction (or its impossibility) between affect and emotion, see the afterword in Ahmed 2014. The *Oxford English Dictionary* defines the later use of the (usually mass) noun form of affect as "the outward display of emotion or mood, as manifested by facial expression, posture, gestures, tone of voice, etc."

10. For a theorization of the relation between Williams's notion of structure of feeling and affect theory, see Sharma and Tygstrup 2015.

11. For the sake of my argument here, I am going to assume that the gender of this web user is female.

12. Chih-ming Wang translates this term as "little assured happiness." For the genesis of the term in Murakami's work, see Wang C-m. 2017, 186 and Lim 2019a, 302.

13. There are also pop songs in Hong Kong and Taiwan with the titles "*Xiao quexing,*" "*Xiao qingxin,*" and "*Xiao xingyun*" (little fortune). To the best of my knowledge, there are two versions of "*Xiao quexing*" (one by Taiwan songstress Chen Si-han and one by Hong Kong songstress Lillian Chan, the latter featuring rap performed by Hong Kong singer Carlos Chan); two versions of "*Xiao qingxin*" (one by Taiwan duo Joyce Chu and Michiyo Ho and one by Hong Kong songstress Silian Wong); and one version of

"*Xiao xingyun*" (by Taiwan songstress Hebe Tien, formerly a member of S.H.E.). It is perhaps no coincidence that all songs are performed by female singers, with the exception of the rap section performed by a male singer.

14. I thank Lisa Rofel for suggesting the notion of "citizen-to-citizen soft power" in her feedback to an earlier version of Lim 2019a.

15. Entries on little freshness appear in these search engines' webpages. All accessed on December 1, 2020. https://zh.wikipedia.org/wiki/小清新, http://baike.baidu.com/item/小清新/7867946, and, as one example on Douban, https://movie.douban.com/tag/#/?sort=T&tags=小清新.

16. For an analysis of "literary youth," see Wong 2016. There are parallels between the contemporary "literary youth" phenomenon across the Taiwan Strait and the global hipster movement, though this is a topic that deserves separate treatment.

17. According to a CNN report (Lu and Chan 2015), during the weeks leading to the military parade to mark the 70th anniversary of Japan's defeat in World War II, the Beijing authorities ordered hundreds of factories shut and half of Beijing's 5 million registered cars banned from the streets, which resulted in the appearance of blue skies.

18. For a review of methodological approaches to the study of soft power, see Ji 2017.

19. According to a message on the original website of HKUPOP, the program was closed on June 30, 2019. Its director, Dr. Robert Chung, set up a new organization, the Hong Kong Public Opinion Research Institute, to carry on POP's mission. The data I access in the text are from the new site. Accessed on December 1, 2020. https://www.pori.hk.

20. Accessed on December 1, 2020. https://www.pori.hk/pop-poll/people/v006. Note that when a record figure was registered for positive feelings toward people from Taiwan, in July 2019, it coincided with the start, a month earlier, of Hong Kong's Anti-Extradition Law Amendment Bill (anti-ELAB) movement, which opposes proposed changes that would have allowed for the Hong Kong government to consider requests from any country for extradition of criminal suspects, even countries with which it does not have an extradition treaty, including mainland China.

21. Accessed on December 1, 2020. https://www.pori.hk/pop-poll/people/v004.

22. Accessed on December 1, 2020. https://www.pori.hk/pop-poll/people/v002. This record was broken in the November 2016 poll, which registered an even lower net value of 27.6 percent.

23. See, e.g., Huang 2016, Li 2015, and Li 2014.

24. Since the anti-ELAB movement took off in June 2019, there has been another surge in migration figures from Hong Kong to Taiwan (see Yu and Ko 2020).

25. I thank Wang Wan-Jui for bringing to my attention Hu Xia's career and his role in performing the theme song for *You Are the Apple of My Eye*.

26. Talent shows for nonprofessional singers have existed for some time in the PRC, a famous example being *Super Girl* (*Chaoji nüsheng*, started in 2004). Note that participants in *I Am a Singer* are all (ex-)professionals. On the Chinese pop music scene, see Moskowitz 2010.

27. Referencing this same source, Chih-ming Wang translates the term as the "collapsing generation." See Wang C-m. 2017, 179, 189n4.

28. For an analysis of the little freshness generation and its involvement in political movements, more recently in the Taiwanese presidential election, see Chang T-c. 2016.

29. It must be qualified that Ang Lee did complete his college education in drama and film in Taiwan before going to study in the United States. Moreover, because Lee's short film had won a prize in Taiwan in 1983, he was considered as a potential candidate to direct a segment of *The Sandwich Man*; Lee, however, missed this early opportunity to work with Hou Hsiao-hsien because he was then studying at New York University and could not be involved in this project (Chen 2020).

30. I emphasize TNC *debut* film here because, between 1980 and 1982, Hou had directed three popular feature films, which are widely seen as his transition from "healthy realism," the dominant genre with which he was working under apprenticeship, to TNC. Calling this period "Hou Hsiao-Hsien before Hou Hsiao-hsien," Guo-Juin Hong (2011, 89) argues that these films challenged the then existing commercial cinema paradigm and that they already displayed aesthetic traits (long shot and long take) for which Hou would later be known.

31. Information on post-TNC directors has been culled from Sing 2010b, 146 and from relevant pages on the Internet Movie Database (IMDB). Accessed on December 1, 2020. http://www.imdb.com/.

32. Despite Niu's reluctance to follow in Hou's footsteps, the close relationship between the two filmmakers endures; Hou even helped Niu edit his 2014 film *Paradise in Service* (*Junzhong leyuan*) (Wen 2015, 16).

33. *Monga* also took in NT$8.31 million across Taiwan on the first day of release, breaking the opening-day record previously held by James Cameron's 2009 film *Avatar* ("Niu" 2012).

34. As Berlant queries: "Can absorption in affective and emotional transactions that take place at home, on the street, and between intimates and strangers be deemed irrelevant to civil society unless they are somehow addressed to institutions?" (2008, 8).

Epilogue

1. The Golden Horse Awards' official website, from where information on its history is culled here and later in the chapter, states that the Awards is now "considered to be the Chinese-language Oscars." Accessed on January 6, 2021. http://www.goldenhorse.org.tw/awards/about/milestones/?r=en.

2. These awards are Jill Li for her documentary *Lost Course* (*Mihang*, 2019) and Felix Tsang and Kiwi Chow for Best Adapted Screenplay for *Beyond the Dream* (*Huan'ai*, 2019).

3. Information about the Golden Horse Film Project Promotion scheme can be obtained on the official webpage. Accessed on January 6, 2021. http://www.goldenhorse.org.tw/fpp/about/.

4. The point about soft power and temporality originated from a comment by Luke Robinson in a three-way talk he was engaged in with Chris Berry and me on the topic of soft power, film festivals, and cinema, held at the Chinese University of Hong Kong in January 2017. See Lim and Cheung 2018, 213.

5. On the other hand, contrast this with another form of soft power that is the speed at which popular East Asian genre films get remade in Hollywood. Examples include The Ring series by Hideo Nakata, whose first instalment Ringu (1998) was remade by Gore Verbinski as The Ring (2002); The Eye (Jiangui, 2002) by the Pang brothers (Oxide and Danny) remade as The Eye (dirs. David Moreau and Xavier Palud, 2008); and Andrew Lau and Alan Mak's Infernal Affairs (Wujiandao) (2002) remade by Martin Scorsese as The Departed (2006).

6. Readers will probably have spotted that Assayas had mentioned the Hong Kong director Wong Kar-wai in his statement about his affinity with Taiwan filmmakers, though I suspect this is less a mistaken identity on his part than a broader reference to "my Chinese friends."

7. Hsu Feng's company (Tomson Films) produced Farewell My Concubine via its Hong Kong subsidiary; Chiu Fu-sheng's Era International produced To Live.

8. Ho's film won him the Best New Director award in 2010, and Bi's film took away three awards in 2018.

9. The name of the country "Burma" was changed to "Myanmar" in 1989 by the ruling military junta (Holliday 2011, 4–10).

10. The interview, originally published in the magazine Taiwan Panorama (another government publication), can be accessed on the New Southbound Policy Portal hosted by the Ministry of Foreign Affairs. Accessed on January 7, 2021. https://nspp.mofa.gov.tw/nsppe/print.php?post=115885&unit=. I thank Luke Robinson for bringing my attention to the link between Midi Z's filmmaking and Taiwan's "New Go South Policy" in a paper he presented at a conference I organized at the Chinese University of Hong Kong in June 2016.

11. The reference to campus romance films includes the little freshness films I discussed in Chapter 5, where I also noted the omission of New Year festive films in Taiwan film historiography.

12. Special mention must be made to two directors, Wu Nien-jen and Chen Kuo-fu, who defy categorization as they are from the same generation as Hou and Yang but only made their directorial debuts in the 1990s.

13. Chen Yu-hsun finally won a Best Director award at the Golden Horse in 2020, 25 years after making his debut film Tropical Fish (Redaiyu, 1995).

14. As I have indicated elsewhere (Lim 2011b, 26), if Malaysian filmmaker Amir Muhammad had referred to his fellow director James Lee as "Malaysia's Tsai Ming-liang" (Raju 2008, 71), it only serves to highlight that Tsai's career in Taiwan can obscure his Malaysian-Chinese status.

15. In the book accompanying the documentary Flowers of Taipei, the French film critic Jean-Michel Frodon reckoned that TNC auteurs have no descendants after Tsai (Wang K-y 2015a, 42), whereas the British critic Tony Rayns named Midi Z exactly as such (Wang K-y 2015a, 48). Note that the award won by Midi Z mentioned here was

at Venice Days, which is part of the Venice film festival but not of the official selection; hence, Midi's award is not listed in Table I.1 in the Introduction. I thank Elena Pollacchi for clarifying this for me.

16. More information about the Forum section can be seen at the official website. Accessed on January 6, 2021. https://www.berlinale.de/en/das_festival/sektionen_sonderveranstaltungen/forum/index.html.

17. It must be noted that Midi Z drew criticism for being absent from the 2019 Golden Horse Awards ceremony (i.e., the first year of the PRC boycott) even though he had promised to attend and his film *Nina Wu* (*Zhuoren mimi*, 2019) was nominated in eight categories (including Best Director) (Yulezu 2019).

18. I first deployed this concept by Deleuze and Guattari in an essay entitled "Six Chinese Cinemas in Search of a Historiography" (Lim 2011a).

19. The omnibus film *10 + 10* is made up of 5-minute short films by each of the 10 veteran directors and 10 up-and-coming directors (i.e., 20 short films in total); Ho's contribution is the film "100" mentioned in the main text.

References

"99 niandu guochan dianying changpian fudaojin banli yaodian." 99 年度國產電影長片輔導金辦理要點 (2010 domestic feature film sponsorship application key points). 2010. *Wenhuabu yingshi ji liuxing yinyue chanyeju* 文化部影視及流行音樂產業局 (Bureau of Audiovisual and Music Industry Development, Ministry of Culture), March 18. https://www.bamid.gov.tw/information_202_64365.html.

"2019 Statistics." n.d. Women and Hollywood. Accessed on January 1, 2021. https://womenandhollywood.com/resources/statistics/2019-statistics/.

"China accused of 'dollar diplomacy' as Taiwan loses second ally in a month." 2018. *The Guardian*, May 24. https://www.theguardian.com/world/2018/may/24/taiwan-criticises-china-after-burkina-faso-ends-diplomatic-relations.

Ahmed, Sara. 2014. *The Cultural Politics of Emotion*, 2nd ed. Edinburgh: Edinburgh University Press.

Althusser, Louis. 2008. *On Ideology*. Translated by Ben Brewster. London and New York: Verso.

Appiah, Kwame Anthony. 1997. "Is the Post-in Postmodernism the Post-in Postcolonial?" In *Contemporary Postcolonial Theory: A Reader*, edited by Padmini Mongia, 55–71. London: Arnold.

Arp, Robert, Adam Barkman, and James McRae, eds. 2013. *The Philosophy of Ang Lee*. Lexington, Kentucky: University Press of Kentucky.

Augé, Marc. 1995. *Non-Places: Introduction to an Anthropology of Supermodernity*. Translated by John Howe. London: Verso.

Bai Ruiwen 白睿文 [Michael Berry]. 2014. *Zhuhai shiguang: Hou Xiaoxian de guangying jiyi*煮海時光：侯孝賢的光影記憶 (Boiling the sea: Hou Hsiao-hsien's memories of shadows and light). Taipei: Ink.

Balsom, Erika. 2013. *Exhibiting Cinema in Contemporary Art*. Amsterdam: Amsterdam University Press.

Bao, Weihong. 2015a. *Fiery Cinema: The Emergence of an Affective Medium in China, 1915–1945*. Minneapolis and London: University of Minnesota Press.

Bao, Weihong. 2015b. "The Trouble with Theater: Cinema and the Geopolitics of Medium Specificity." *Framework* 56, no. 2: 350–367.

Bazin, André. 2008. "De la Politique des Auteurs (1957)." In Grant 2008, 19–28.

Beck, Jay, and Tony Grajeda. 2008. "Introduction: The Future of Film Sound Studies." In *Lowering the Boom: Critical Studies in Film Sound*, edited by Jay Beck and Tony Grajeda, 1–20. Urbana and Chicago: University of Illinois Press.

Beeton, Sue. 2005. *Film-Induced Tourism*. Clevedon: Channel View.

Berlant, Lauren. 2008. *The Female Complaint: The Unfinished Business of Sentimentality in American Culture*. Durham and London: Duke University Press.

Berlant, Lauren. 2011. *Cruel Optimism*. Durham and London: Duke University Press.

Berry, Chris, and Feii Lu, eds. 2005a. *Island on the Edge: Taiwan New Cinema and After*. Hong Kong: Hong Kong University Press.

Berry, Chris, and Feii Lu. 2005b. "Introduction." In Berry and Lu 2005a, 1–12.

Berry, Michael. 2005. *Speaking in Images: Interviews with Contemporary Chinese Filmmakers*. New York: Columbia University Press.

Betz, Mark. 2009. *Beyond the Subtitle: Remapping European Art Cinema*. Minneapolis and London: University of Minnesota Press.

Bhabha, Homi. 1985. "Signs Taken for Wonders: Questions of Ambivalence and Authority under a Tree outside Delhi, May 1817." *Critical Inquiry* 12, no. 1: 144–165.

Biancorosso, Giorgio. 2013. "Songs of Delusion: Popular Music and the Aestheticsof the Self in Wong Kar-Wai's Cinema." In *Popular Music and the New Auteur: Visionary Filmmakers after MTV*, edited by Arved Ashby, 109–125. New York: Oxford University Press.

Billington, Alex. 2016. "Interview: Ang Lee on the Journey of Bringing *Life of Pi* to the Screen." In Fuller 2016a, 108–114.

Birtwistle, Andy. 2010. *Cinesonica: Sounding Film and Video*. Manchester and New York: Manchester University Press.

Blair, Adam. 2000. "Interview: Michelle Yeoh (*Crouching Tiger, Hidden Dragon*)." *Films in Review*, December 24. http://www.filmsinreview.com/2000/12/24/interview-michelle-yeoh-crounching-tiger-hidden-dragon/. The weblink no longer worked when accessed on January 1, 2021.

Bloom, Michelle E. 2016. *Contemporary Sino-French Cinemas: Absent Fathers, Banned Books, and Red Balloons*. Honolulu: University of Hawai'i Press.

Bolter, Jay David, and Richard Grusin. 2000. *Remediation: Understanding New Media*. Cambridge, MA, and London: MIT Press.

"Bombardment of Quemoy." 1988. *Taiwan Review*, August 1. https://taiwantoday.tw/news.php?unit=4&post=4657.

Bordwell, David. 2005. *Figures Traced in Light: On Cinematic Staging*. Berkeley, Los Angeles, and London: University of California Press.

Bradshaw, Peter. 2015. "*The Assassin* review—enigmatically refined martial arts tale baffles beautifully." *The Guardian*, May 20. https://www.theguardian.com/film/2015/may/20/the-assassin-review-enigmatically-refined-martial-arts-tale-baffles-beautifully.

Braester, Yomi. 2005. "Chinese Cinema in the Age of Advertisement: The Filmmaker as a Cultural Broker." *The China Quarterly* 183: 549–564.

Brook, Vincent. 2009. *Driven to Darkness: Jewish Émigré Directors and the Rise of Film Noir*. New Brunswick, NJ: Rutgers University Press.

Brooks, Xan. 2012. "Death by degrees? Bela Tarr to open film academy." *The Guardian*, September 28. https://www.theguardian.com/film/2012/sep/28/bella-tarr-film-academy-sarajevo.

Brunetta, Gian Piero. 1982. *Storia del cinema italiano: Dal 1945 agli anni '80*. Rome: Editori Riuniti. Quoted in Casetti 1999, 311.

Bruyas, Dimitri. 2009. "Loyrette changes Louvre 'Face.'" *The China Post*, September 27. http://www.chinapost.com.tw/taiwan/intl-community/2009/09/27/226352/Loyrette-changes.htm. Quoted in Bloom 2016, 214n29. The URL no longer worked when accessed on January 1, 2021.

"Cai Mingliang shoubu wei dianying *Xingzhe* shouying, kaowen kuai rensheng yin zhengyi" 蔡明亮首部微電影《行者》首映，拷問快人生引爭議 (Tsai Ming-liang's first micro-film *The Walker* premieres, stirs controversy by questioning fast life). 2012. *Xinhuawang* 新華網 (Xinhua net), April 28. Rpt. in *Wangyi yule* 網易娛樂 (NetEase). https://ent.163.com/12/0428/16/806N0TFR00032DGD.html.

Casetti, Francesco. 1999. *Theories of Cinema 1945–1995*. Translated by Francesca Chiostri and Elizabeth Gard Bartolini-Salimbeni with Thomas Kelso. Austin: University of Texas Press.

Castelli, Jean-Christophe. 2012. *The Making of Life of Pi: A Journey*. New York: Harper Design.

Chan, Bernice. 2015. "*Flowers of Taipei*—on Taiwan cinema's global reach." *South China Morning Post*, June 17. http://www.scmp.com/lifestyle/arts-entertainment/article/1822754/film-review-flowers-taipei-taiwan-cinemas-global-reach.

Chan, Kenneth. 2004. "The Global Return of the *Wu Xia Pian* (Chinese Sword-Fighting Movie): Ang Lee's *Crouching Tiger, Hidden Dragon*." *Cinema Journal* 43, no. 4: 3–17.

Chan, Kenneth. 2011. "The Contemporary Wuxia Revival: Genre Remaking and the Hollywood Transnational Factor." In Lim and Ward 2011, 150–157.

Chan, Kenneth. 2012. "'Asia' as Global Hollywood Commodity." In Lucia, Grundmann, and Simon 2012, 406–426.

Chang Che-ming 張哲鳴. 2016. "Bi Gan qipa niaoyanjing, kan Houdao ye kan *Gongfu Xiongmao*" 畢贛奇葩鳥眼睛，看侯導也看功夫熊貓 (Special talent Bi Gan's birdy eyes watch Hou Hsiao-hsien films as well as *Kungfu Panda*). *Pingguo ribao* 蘋果日報 (Apple daily), April 8. https://tw.appledaily.com/entertainment/20160408/465FILKYTV6CH5EV3NS6VGKTSI/.

Chang Che-ming 張哲鳴. 2017. "Wang Dalu 6 zuo gong Zhongguo, zuida chi sifang, yaojin 8 qianwan" 王大陸6 作攻中國，嘴大吃四方，咬進8千萬 (Darren Wang invades China with 6 works, swallowing 80 million with big mouth). *Pingguo ribao* 蘋果日報 (Apple daily), August 31. https://tw.appledaily.com/new/realtime/20170831/1193790/.

Chang Shih-lun 張世倫. 2015. "Chidao de xinchao, weijing de yundong: 'Taiwan xindianying' de xiandai xiangxiang" 遲到的新潮、未竟的運動——「台灣新電影」的現代想像 (A belated new wave, an unfinished movement: Modern imaginations of Taiwan New Cinema). *Fangying zhoubao* 放映週報 (Funscreen) 563 (May 6). http://www.funscreen.com.tw/headline.asp?H_No=563.

Chang, Sung-sheng Yvonne. 1993. *Modernism and the Nativist Resistance: Contemporary Chinese Fiction from Taiwan*. Durham and London: Duke University Press.

Chang Tieh-chih 張鐵志. 2014. "Cong xiao quexing dao fennu de yidai" 從小確幸到憤怒的一代 (From small exact happiness to angry generation). *Duli pinglun@Tianxia* 獨立評論@天下 (Opinion@commonwealth), April 2. https://opinion.cw.com.tw/blog/profile/7/article/1201.

Chang Tieh-chih 張鐵志. 2016. "Xiao qingxin yu Taiwan daxuan" 小清新與台灣大選 (Little freshness and Taiwan election). *FT Zhongwen wang* FT中文網 (FT Chinese web), January 20. http://big5.ftchinese.com/story/001065825.

Chang, Wen-Chin. 2016. "Poverty and Migration from Burma: Within and without Midi Z's Films." *Independent Journal of Burmese Scholarship* 1, no. 1: 43–85.

Chao Kang 趙剛. 2014. "'Xiao quexing': Taiwan taiyanghua yidai de zhengzhi rentong" 「小確幸」：台灣太陽花一代的政治認同 ('Small exact happiness': Political identification of Taiwan's Sunflower generation). *Kulao wang* 苦勞網 (Coolloud net), December 23. http://www.coolloud.org.tw/node/81194.

Chao, Linda, and Ramon H. Myers. 1998. *The First Chinese Democracy: Political Life in the Republic of China on Taiwan*. Baltimore and London: John Hopkins University Press.

Chen Chien-chia 陳建嘉. 2016. "*Dawei luman 2* piaofang poyi, Zhuge Liang xudang hesuipian wang" 《大尾鱸鰻2》票房破億，豬哥亮續當賀歲片王 (*David Loman*

2's box office exceeds 100 million, Chuke Liang continues to be king of lunar new year films). *Ziyou shibao* 自由時報 (Liberty times net), February 12. http://ent.ltn.com.tw/news/breakingnews/1600940.

Chen, Christie. 2016. "Golden Horse Awards: Midi Z receives outstanding filmmaker award." *Focus Taiwan News Channel*, November 26. http://focustaiwan.tw/news/aedu/201611260019.aspx.

Chen Kai-tang 陳凱棠. 2020. "Lengjing de shenqing: Hou Xiaoxian ruhe chengwei Taiwan xinlangchao dianying duoshou" 冷靜的深情——侯孝賢如何成為台灣新浪潮電影舵手 (Cool devoted love: How Hou Hsiao-hsien became helmsman of Taiwan's new wave cinema). *Wenhua+* 文化+ (Culture plus), no. 71,November 9. https://www.cna.com.tw/culture/article/20201106w004.

Chen Long-ting 陳龍廷. 2010. *Faxian budaixi: Wenhua shengtai, biaoyan wenben, fangfalun* 發現布袋戲：文化生態、表演文本、方法論 (Discovering puppetry theater: Cultural ecology, performance text, methodology). Kaohsiung: Chunhui chubanshe.

Chen Pin-chuan 陳斌全, ed. 2016. *2016 Taiwan dianying nianjian* 2016 台灣電影年鑑 (2016 Taiwan cinema yearbook). Taipei: Taiwan Film Institute.

Chen Pin-chuan 陳斌全, ed. 2017. *2017 Taiwan dianying nianjian* 2017 台灣電影年鑑 (2017 Taiwan cinema yearbook). Taipei: Taiwan Film Institute.

Chen Ru-shou 陳儒修. 1994. *Taiwan xindianying de lishi wenhua jingyan* 台灣新電影的歷史文化經驗 (Historical and cultural experience of Taiwan New Cinema). Taipei: Wanxiang.

Chen Ru-shou 陳儒修. 2015. "30 nianqian de Taiwan xindianying yudong, yiwei zhe sheme?" 30 年前的台灣新電影運動，意味著什麼？ (What does the Taiwan New Cinema movement of 30 years ago imply?). In Wang K-y 2015a, 276–279.

Chen Shih-cong 陳世宗. 2015. "Yusuan bianlie caoshuai? Taizhong yiyuan zhiwen Shuinan dianying zhongxin neng xingma" 預算編列草率？台中議員質問水湳電影中心能行嗎 (Hasty budget preparation? Taichung legislator questions feasibility of Shuinan film centre). *Zhongshi dianzibao* 中時電子報 (China times), May 12. http://www.chinatimes.com/realtimenews/20150512002947-260407.

Chen, Steven, and Eric Shih. 2019. "City Branding through Cinema: The Case Study of Postcolonial Hong Kong." *Journal of Brand Management* 26, no. 5: 505–521.

Chen, Timmy Chih-Ting. 2017. "Sonic Secrets as Counter-Surveillance in Wong Kar-wai's *In the Mood for Love*." In *Surveillance in Asian Cinema: Under Eastern Eyes*, edited by Karen Fang, 156–175. New York: Routledge.

Chen, Timmy Chih-Ting. 2019. "The Revolution of Realism in the '1987 Taiwan Cinema Manifesto.'" *Nang* 6 (April): 14–16.

Chen Wen-chien 陳文茜. 2015. "Zuipa tingdao bieren shuo 'Wo ai Taiwan'. . . , Daoyan Li An: Ai buyong yizhishuo, yizhishuo caishi youwenti" 最怕聽到別人說「我愛台灣」．．．，導演李安：愛不用一直說，一直說才是有問題 (Most afraid of hearing people say: "I love Taiwan" . . . , Director Ang Lee: Love doesn't need to be said all the time; saying it all the time is the problem). *Shangye zhoukan* 商業週刊 (Business weekly), October 14. http://www.businessweekly.com.tw/article.aspx?id=14216&type=Blog&p=2.

Chen Ying-si 陳穎思. 2018. "Yiren Weibo kuangfa aiguo tiewen, Hu Ge ji li Tai: Hen yihan" 藝人微博狂發愛國帖文，胡歌急離台：很遺憾 (Artistes rush to post patri-otic messages on Weibo, Hu Ge leaves Taiwan in haste: Expresses regret). *Xianggang*

01 香港01 (HK01), November 18. https://www.hk01.com/電影/260456/金馬台獨言論風波-藝人微博狂發愛國帖文-胡歌急離台-很遺憾.

Chen Zongyan 陳宗延. 2014. "Xiao quexing" 小確幸 (Small exact happiness). In *Daoguo guanjianzi: Guanyu women zhege shidai, zhege shidai de Taiwan shehuili fenxi* 島國關鍵字：關於我們這個世代，這個時代的台灣社會力分析 (Island-nation keywords: An analysis of Taiwan's social forces in our generation and times), edited by Ding Yungong 丁允恭, 35–36. New Taipei City: Rive Gauche.

Cheng Li-ming 鄭立明, ed. 2010. *2010 nian Taiwan dianying nianjian* 2010年台灣電影年鑑 (2010 Taiwan cinema yearbook). Taipei: Chinese Taipei Film Archive.

Cheng, Ryan 鄭秉泓. 2010. "Qiantan Gaoxiong xianshi 'chengshi xingxiao' xiangguan yingshi zhengce" 淺談高雄縣市「城市行銷」相關影視政策 (The marketing of city: Film & TV policy of Kaohsiung City and County). In Cheng L-m 2010, 70–75.

Cheng, Ryan 鄭秉泓. 2014. "2013 nian Taiwan dianying: Cheng ye bentu, bai ye bentu" 2013年台灣電影：成也本土，敗也本土 (2013 Taiwan cinema: Success and failure both down to nativism). In Lin W-c 2014, 21–38.

Cheng, Ryan 鄭秉泓. 2015. "2014 Taiwan dianying: Linjiedian shang de jueze" 2014台灣電影：臨界點上的抉擇 (2014 Taiwan cinema: Choice at the critical point). In Lin 2015, 44–65.

Cheung, Karen. 2015. "Hongkongers like each other less than ever, says HKU survey." *Hong Kong Free Press*, November 25. https://www.hongkongfp.com/2015/11/25/hongkongers-like-each-other-less-than-ever-says-hku-survey/.

Chi Yan-chi 遲延奇. 1991. "Dianying, lishi yu zhengzhi: *Beiqing chengshi* guanhou zhaji" 電影、歷史與政治：《悲情城市》觀後札記 (Film, history, and politics: Notes after watching *A City of Sadness*). In Mi and Liang 1991, 94–99.

Chiao Hsiung-ping 焦雄屏. 2018. *Yingxiang Taiwan* 映像台灣 (Film Taiwan). Taipei: Gaea Books.

"China praises Lee despite *Mountain* ban." 2006. *The Guardian*, March 7. https://www.theguardian.com/film/2006/mar/07/awardsandprizes.china.

Ching, Leo. 2001. *Becoming Japanese: Colonial Taiwan and the Politics of Identity Formation*. Berkeley and Los Angeles: University of California Press.

Chion, Michel. 1994. *Audio-Vision: Sound on Screen*. Ed. and trans. Claudia Gorbman. New York: Columbia University Press.

Chion, Michel. 1999. *The Voice in Cinema*. Edited and translated by Claudia Gorbman. New York: Columbia University Press.

Chion, Michel. 2011. "Dissolution of the Notion of Timbre." Translated by James A. Steintrager. *Differences: A Journal of Feminist Cultural Studies* 22, nos. 2 & 3: 235–239.

Chitty, Naren. 2017. "Introduction." In Chitty et al. 2017, 1–6.

Chitty, Naren, Li Ji, Gary D. Rawnsley, and Craig Hayden, eds. 2017. *The Routledge Handbook of Soft Power*. Abingdon, Oxon, and New York: Routledge.

Chiu, Kuei-fen, Ming-yeh T. Rawnsley, and Gary D. Rawnsley, eds. 2017. *Taiwan Cinema: International Reception and Social Change*. Abingdon, Oxon and New York: Routledge.

Chiu Li-huei 邱利慧, ed. 2010. *Li Tianlu: Guangying chuanshen Yiwanran* 李天祿：光影傳神亦宛然 (Li Tien-lu: I Wan Jan casting life through light and shadow). Taipei: Taipei Cultural Center.

Chiu Li-ling 邱莉玲. 2017. "Xingxiao dianying yishu diancang gainian, Cai Mingliang dazao baiwan huicangxiang" 行銷電影藝術典藏概念，蔡明亮打造百萬蒐藏

箱 (Promoting the concept of collecting film as art, Tsai Ming-liang creates one-million-dollar collectible box). *Zhongshi dianzibao* 中時電子報 (China times), May 8. Rpt. in *Yahu xinwen* 雅虎新聞 (Yahoo! News). https://tw.news.yahoo.com/行銷電影藝術典藏概念-蔡明亮打造百萬蒐藏箱-215005784--finance.html.

Chong Chiao 鍾喬, ed. 1995. *Zhonghuamingguo bashisan nian dianying nianjian* 中華民國八十三年電影年鑑 (Cinema in the Republic of China 1994 yearbook). Taipei: Taiwan Film Archive.

Chou Hsu-wei 周旭微. 1991. "Rensheng daochang de xiulian" 人生道場的修煉 (Training in life's dojo). In Wang K-y 1991, 20–21.

Chow, Andrew R. 2019. "*Gemini Man* Director Ang Lee Wants to Change the Way We See Movies." *Time*, October 10. https://time.com/5696958/director-ang-lee-gemini-man/.

Chow, Rey. 1995. *Primitive Passions: Visuality, Sexuality, Ethnography, and Contemporary Chinese Cinema*. New York: Columbia University Press.

Chow, Rey. 2017. "The Writing Voice in Cinema: A Preliminary Discussion." In Whittaker and Wright 2017a, 17–30.

Chu Tien-wen 朱天文. 2009. *Hong qiqiu de lüxing: Hou Xiaoxian dianying jilu xubian* 紅氣球的旅行：侯孝賢電影記錄續編 (*Flight of the Red Balloon*: Updated edition of documentation of Hou Hsiao-hsien's films). Shandong: Shandong huabao chubanshe.

Chua, Beng Huat. 2012. *Structure, Audience and Soft Power in East Asian Pop Culture*. Hong Kong: Hong Kong University Press.

"Chuan zhongxuanbu xialing dizhi Jinmajiang, Zhongzi dianying jinzhi baoming" 傳中宣部下令抵制金馬獎，中資電影禁止報名 (Central Propaganda Department reportedly ordered boycott of Golden Horse Awards, China-funded films banned from participation). 2018. *Mingbao OL* 明報OL (Mingpao OL), November 19. https://ol.mingpao.com/ldy/showbiz/latest/20181119/1542621152607/【金馬風波】傳中宣部下令抵制金馬獎-中資電影禁止報名.

Chung, Lawrence. 2014. "Taiwan to tighten residency rules for Hongkongers." *South China Morning Post*, February 7. http://www.scmp.com/news/hong-kong/article/1422363/taiwan-tighten-residency-rules-hongkongers.

Chung, Oscar. 2013. "The legacy of Pi." *Taiwan Today*, March 1. https://taiwantoday.tw/news.php?post=26385&unit=20,29,29,35,45.

Coleman, Joyce. 2007. "Aurality." In *Middle English*, edited by Paul Strohm, 68–85. Oxford: Oxford University Press.

Corrigan, Timothy. 1990. "The Commerce of Auteurism: A Voice without Authority." *New German Critique* 49: 43–57.

Croll, Ben. 2016. "Bela Tarr Speaks: The Retired Hungarian Director Explains Why He Shut Down His Film School Project." *IndieWire*, December 23. http://www.indiewire.com/2016/12/bela-tarr-interview-marrakech-film-school-1201762173/.

Dargis, Manohla. 2008. "Another balloon over Paris, with lives adrift below." *New York Times*, April 4. http://movies.nytimes.com/2008/04/04/movies/04ball.html?_r=1&.

de Certeau, Michel. 1984. *The Practice of Everyday Life*. Translated by Steven Rendall. Berkeley, Los Angeles, and London: University of California Press.

de Kloet, Jeroen, and Anthony Y. H. Fung. 2017. *Youth Cultures in China*. Cambridge: Polity.

Debord, Guy. 1995. *The Society of the Spectacle*. Translated by Donald Nicholson-Smith. New York: Zone Books.

Deleuze, Gilles, and Felix Guattari. 1986. *Kafka: Toward a Minor Literature*. Translated by Dana Polan. Minneapolis and London: University of Minnesota Press.

Dercon, Chris. 2002. "Gleaning the Future." *Vertigo* 2 (2). https://www.closeupfilmcentre.com/vertigo_magazine/volume-2-issue-2-spring-2002/gleaning-the-future/.

Derrida, Jacques. 1976. *Of Grammatology*. Translated by Gayatri Chakravorty Spivak. Baltimore and London: John Hopkins University Press.

"Dianying piaofang jing, yuanzhu xiaoshuo 'fansheng,' *Naxienian* lüxingtuan rebao" 電影票房勁，原著小說「翻生」，《那些年》旅行團熱爆 (Strong box office for film, original novel's fortune 'revives,' demand for *You Are the Apple of My Eye* tours explodes). 2011. *Pingguo ribao* 蘋果日報 (Apple daily), October 28. http://hk.apple.nextmedia.com/news/art/20111028/15748569.

"Dianying shiye ji dianying congye renyuan canjia guoji yingzhan jiangli fudao zhixing yaodian." 電影事業及電影從業人員參加國際影展獎勵輔導執行要點 (Main execution points for sponsoring film industry personnel to attend international film festivals). 2018. *Wenhuabu yingshi ji liuxing yinyue chanyeju* 文化部影視及流行音樂產業局 (Bureau of Audiovisual and Music Industry Development, Ministry of Culture), June 7. https://www.bamid.gov.tw/information_211_64486.html.

"Dieping: Peng Ling 'Yizhi hua,' Xianggang yeyou liuxingyue" 碟評：彭羚《一枝花》，香港也有流行樂 (CD review: Cess Phang's "A stalk of flower," Hong Kong also has pop music). 2004. *Baidu tieba* 百度貼吧 (Baidu bulletin board), November 30. http://tieba.baidu.com/p/6622552. The weblink no longer worked when accessed on January 4, 2021.

Dinnie, Keith. 2011a. "Chapter 1: Introduction to the Theory of City Branding." In *City Branding: Theory and Cases*, edited by Keith Dinnie, 3–7. Basingstoke, Hampshire: Palgrave Macmillan.

Dinnie, Keith. 2011b. "Chapter 11: Introduction to the Practice of City Branding." In *City Branding: Theory and Cases*, edited by Keith Dinnie, 93–98. Basingstoke, Hampshire: Palgrave Macmillan.

Doane, Mary Ann. 1980. "The Voice in the Cinema: The Articulation of Body and Space." *Yale French Studies* 60: 33–50.

Doane, Mary Ann. 2002. *The Emergence of Cinematic Time: Modernity, Contingency, The Archive*. Cambridge, MA, and London: Harvard University Press.

"Dogme 95—The Vow of Chastity (1995)." 2002. In *The European Cinema Reader*, edited by Catherine Fowler, 83–102. London and New York: Routledge.

"Dogme 95 Movies—Chronologically." 2008. *Listal*, September 30. http://www.listal.com/list/dogme-95.

Dolar, Mladen. 2012. "The Linguistics of the Voice." In Sterne 2012a, 539–554.

Duara, Prasenjit. 1995. *Rescuing History from the Nation: Questioning Narratives of Modern China*. Chicago and London: University of Chicago Press.

Duffett, Mark. 2017. "I Scream Therefore I Fan? Music Audiences and Affective Citizenship." In *Fandom: Identities and Communities in a Mediated World*, edited by Jonathan Gray, Cornel Sandvoss, and C. Lee Harrington, 2nd ed, 143–156. New York: New York University Press.

Elley, Derek. 2017. "Review: Flowers of Taipei: Taiwan New Cinema (2014)." *Sino-Cinema*, September 4. http://sino-cinema.com/2017/09/04/review-flowers-of-taipei-taiwan-new-cinema-2014/.

Elsaesser, Thomas. 1989. *New German Cinema: A History*. New Brunswick: Rutgers University Press.

Engber, Daniel. 2016. "It Looked Great. It Was Unwatchable." *Slate*, October 20. http://www.slate.com/articles/arts/movies/2016/10/billy_lynn_s_long_halftime_walk_looks_fantastic_it_s_also_unwatchable.html.

Erlmann, Veit. 2010. *Reason and Resonance: A History of Modern Aurality.* New York: Zone Books.

"Europe Celebrates Tsai Ming-liang's Film Legacy." 2014. Republic of China (Taiwan) Ministry of Culture, March 13. https://www.moc.gov.tw/en/information_196_75848.html.

Ezra, Elizabeth, and Terry Rowden, eds. 2006. *Transnational Cinema: The Film Reader.* London: Routledge.

Fan, Chen-hsu. 2014. "Hsu Li-kong & Tsai Ming-liang at 'Master Forum.'" Taipei Film Commission, December 8. http://www.filmcommission.taipei/en/MessageNotice/NewsDet/3770.

"Fandui yiqie xiao er qing de dongxi" 反對一切小而輕的東西 (Opposing all things small and light). 2012. *Pobao* 破報 (Pots weekly), November 22. Rpt. in *Bahamute dianwan zixunzhan* 巴哈姆特電玩資訊站 (Bahamut gamer forum). https://forum.gamer.com.tw/Co.php?bsn=60084&sn=1929851.

Flatley, Jonathan. 2008. *Affective Mapping: Melancholia and the Politics of Modernism.* Cambridge, MA, and London: Harvard University Press.

Fleming, Mike, Jr. 2016. "Ang Lee on His Game-Changing 'Billy Lynn's Long Halftime Walk.'" *Deadline Hollywood*, October 14. http://deadline.com/2016/10/ang-lee-billy-lynns-long-halftime-walk-frame-rate-technology-interview-1201836438/.

Florida, Richard. 2005. *Cities and The Creative Class.* New York and London: Routledge.

Fraleigh, Sondra. 2010. *Butoh: Metamorphic Dance and Global Alchemy.* Urbana, Chicago, and Springfield: University of Illinois Press.

Frater, Patrick. 2017. "Venice Interview: Tsai Ming-liang on the Craft of VR Film Making." *Variety*, September 4. https://variety.com/2017/digital/asia/tsai-ming-liang-craft-of-vr-film-making-1202542689/.

Frater, Patrick. 2019. "Golden Horse Awards Almost Completely Devoid of China and Hong Kong Nominees." *Variety*, October 1. https://variety.com/2019/film/news/golden-horse-awards-deprived-of-china-hong-kong-nominees-1203354478/?fbclid=IwAR1OIy8Gm3b8JGFn3RuJc_Eodv414O3B8jhHRJ2hNoPt9SO9gtVWHKVYJMQ.

Fujishima, Kenji. 2014. Review of *Journey to the West. Slant Magazine*, April 17. http://www.slantmagazine.com/film/review/journey-to-the-west-2014.

Fuller, Karla Rae, ed. 2016a. *Ang Lee: Interviews.* Jackson: University Press of Mississippi.

Fuller, Karla Rae. 2016b. "Introduction." In Fuller 2016a, vii–xx.

Gao, Pat. 2011. "Secret to Revival." *Taiwan Today*, February 1. https://taiwantoday.tw/news.php?post=25997&unit=20,20,29,35,35,45.

Gao, Pat. 2015. "Fresh Perspectives on New Wave." *Taiwan Today*, June 1. http://taiwantoday.tw/ct.asp?xItem=230293&ctNode=2198&mp=9.

Gidal, Peter. 1975. "Theory and Definition of Structural/Materialist Film." *Studio International* 190, no. 978: 189–196. Quoted in Birtwistle 2010, 14.

Gledhill, Christine, ed. 1987. *Home Is Where the Heart Is: Studies in Melodrama and the Woman's Film.* London: British Film Institute.

Goldsmith, Leo. 2009. "World Tourist: Leo Goldsmith on *Flight of the Red Balloon.*" *Reverse Shot*, December 23. http://www.reverseshot.com/article/8_flight_red_balloon.

Graham, Peter, with Ginette Vincendeau, eds. 2009. *The French New Wave: Critical Landmarks*, new ed. London: British Film Institute.

Grant, Barry Keith, ed. 2008. *Auteurs and Authorship: A Film* Reader. Malden, MA: Blackwell Publishing.

"Greater Taichung named Intelligent Community of 2013." *CNA*, June 9. Rrt. in *Taipei Times*. http://www.taipeitimes.com/News/taiwan/archives/2013/06/09/2003564366.

Gunning, Tom. 1986. "The Cinema of Attraction: Early Film, Its Spectator and the Avant-Garde." *Wide Angle* 8, nos. 3 & 4: 63–70.

Haddon, Rosemary. 2005. "Hou Hsiao-hsien's *City of Sadness*: History and the Dialogic Female Voice." In Berry and Lu 2005a, 55–65.

Hammond, Pete. 2016. "'Billy Lynn's Long Halftime Walk' Review: Ang Lee's Groundbreaking Movie Is Year's Biggest Disappointment." *Deadline Hollywood*, November 10. http://deadline.com/2016/11/billy-lynns-long-halftime-walk-review-ang-lee-movie-disappoints-video-1201852326/.

Hanrahan, Mairéad. 1999. "Genet and Cixous: The InterSext." *The French Review* 72, no. 4: 719–729.

Harding, Jennifer, and Deidre E. Pribram. 2009. "Introduction: The Case for a Cultural Emotion Studies." In *Emotions: A Cultural Studies Reader*, edited by Jennifer Harding and Deidre E. Pribram, 1–23. London and New York: Routledge.

Hayward, Susan. 2006. *Cinema Studies: The Key Concepts*, 3rd ed. London and New York: Routledge.

He Chun-mu 何俊穆. 2015. "Zhuanfang *Guangyin de gushi—Taiwan xindianying* jianzhi Wang Gengyu" 專訪《光陰的故事—台灣新電影》監製王耿瑜 (Interview with Wang Keng-yu, executive producer of *Flowers of Taipei —Taiwan New Cinema*), March 1. http://www.taipeifilmcommission.org/tw/MessageNotice/NewsDet/3909.

Hebdige, Dick. 1979. *Subculture: The Meaning of Style*. London: Routledge.

Heurtebise, Jean-Yves, and Chi-Ming Lin. 2015. "Tsai Ming-liang's *Face* and the Art of Movie-making in a Museum." *Journal of Museum & Culture* 10: 3–33.

Higbee, Will, and Song Hwee Lim. 2010. "Concepts of Transnational Cinema: Towards a Critical Transnationalism in Film Studies." *Transnational Cinemas* 1, no. 1: 7–21.

Higson, Andrew. 2000. "The Limiting Imagination of National Cinema." In *Cinema and Nation*, edited by Mette Hjort and Scott MacKenzie, 63–74. London: Routledge.

Hiscock, John. 2016. "Ang Lee Interview: How He Filmed the Unfilmable for *Life of Pi*." In Fuller 2016a, 115–118.

Hjort, Mette. 2003. "Dogma 95: A Small Nation's Response to Globalisation." In *Purity and Provocation: Dogma 95*, edited by Mette Hjort and Scott McKenzie, 31–45. London: British Film Institute.

Hjort, Mette. 2010. "On the Plurality of Cinematic Transnationalism." In *World Cinemas, Transnational Perspectives*, edited by Natasa Durovicová and Kathleen Newman, 12–33. New York and London: Routledge.

Hjort, Mette, and Duncan Petrie, eds. 2007a. *The Cinema of Small Nations*. Edinburgh: Edinburgh University Press.

Hjort, Mette, and Duncan Petrie. 2007b. "Introduction." In Hjort and Petrie 2007a, 1–20.

Ho, Regina 何瑞珠. 2009. "2008 Taiwan dianying piaofang zonglan" 2008 台灣電影票房總覽 (Overview of 2008 box office for Taiwan films). In Tu 2009, 100–108.

Ho Siu-ban 何兆彬. 2016. "Li An *Bili Lin'en de zhongchang zhanshi* tiqian wujianshi: Xianggang 10 jia 60fps+3D+2K fangying xiyuan gongbu, xiang ti meimiao 120 ge yaofei Taibei" 李安《比利．林恩的中場戰事》睇前五件事：香港10家60fps+3D+2K放映戲院公佈，想睇每秒120格要飛台北 (Five things before watching Ang Lee's *Billy Lynn's*

Long Halftime Walk: Ten Hong Kong cinemas with 60fps+3D+2K announced, fly to Taipei if you wish to see it in 120 fps). *Xinbao* 信報 (Economic journal), November 2. http://lj.hkej.com/artculture/article/id/1424511/李安《比利％EF％BC％8E林恩的中場戰事》睇前五件事：香港10家60fps％2B3D％2B2K放映戲院公佈＋想睇每秒120格要飛台北＋.

Hoberman, J. 2008. "Flight of the Red Balloon Soars." *The Village Voice*, April 1. https://www.villagevoice.com/2008/04/01/flight-of-the-red-balloon-soars/.

Holliday, Ian. 2011. *Burma Redux: Global Justice and the Quest for Political Reform in Myanmar*. Hong Kong: Hong Kong University Press.

Hong Chien-lun 洪健倫. 2016. "*Jingzhi xiamao* huo 'Aodi duanpianjiang'"《禁止下錨》獲「奧迪短片獎」(*Anchorage Prohibited* won Audi short film prize). *Fangying zhoubao*放映週報 (Funscreen) 545, February 21. http://www.funscreen.com.tw/feature.asp?FE_No=1535.

Hong, Guo-Juin. 2010. "Historiography of Absence: Taiwan Cinema Before New Cinema 1982." *Journal of Chinese Cinemas* 4, no. 1: 5–14.

Hong, Guo-Juin. 2011. *Taiwan Cinema: A Contested Nation on Screen*. Basingstoke, Hampshire: Palgrave Macmillan.

Hong Tsai-lun 洪彩綸. 2012. "PI chu shangji! Li An juzu Taizhong zhusufei poyi"「PI」出商機！李安劇組台中住宿費破億 (*Life of Pi* brings business opportunity! Ang Lee's crew spent over 100 million on accommodation in Taichung). *TVBS News*, November 22. https://news.tvbs.com.tw/entertainment/37844.

Hsiang Yi-fei 項貽斐. 2010. "Taiwan dianying maixiang chengshi xingxiao guanjian nian" 淺談高雄縣市「城市行銷」相關影視政策 (The Critical Year of Taiwan Cinema Turning to Marketing of City). In *2010 nian Taiwan dianying nianjian* 2010年台灣電影年鑑 (2010 Taiwan cinema yearbook), edited by Cheng Li-ming 鄭立明, 65–69. Taipei: Chinese Taipei Film Archive.

Hsiang Yi-fei 項貽斐. 2020. "Sanren shizhang 'ting Li An de hua'; lanlü jiebang shinian wancheng zaomeng jidi." 3任市長「聽李安的話」，藍綠接棒10年完成造夢基地 (Three terms of mayor 'listened to Ang Lee's words; 10-year relay between blue and green to complete dream of studio building). *Jing zhoukan* 鏡週刊 (Mirror media), February 1. https://www.mirrormedia.mg/story/20200114insight007/.

Hsiao Ye 小野. 1986. *Yige yundong de kaishi* 一個運動的開始 (The beginning of a movement). Taipei: Shibao wenhua.

Hsieh, Chiao Chiao. 1996. "Pragmatic Diplomacy: Foreign Policy and External Relations." In *Take-off for Taiwan?*, edited by Peter Ferdinand, 66–106. London: Royal Institute of International Affairs.

Hsu Li-kong 徐立功 and Lee Ling-yee 李令儀. 2006. *Rang women zai ai yici: Xu Ligong de dianying shijie* 讓我們再愛一次：徐立功的電影世界 (Let us love again: Hsu Li-kong's cinematic world). Taipei: Tianxia wenhua.

Hsu Ming-han 徐明瀚 and Ella Raidel 日德艾蘭. 2014. "Qu juchang *Xiyou*, lai meishuguan *Jiaoyou*: Fang Cai Mingliang" 去劇場「西遊」，來美術館「郊遊」：訪蔡明亮 (Go to the theater for *Journey to the West*, come to the museum for *Stray Dogs*: Interview with Tsai Ming-liang). *Dianying xinshang* 電影欣賞 (Film appreciation) 159: 70–79.

"Hu Xia *Chaoji xingguang dadao* duoguan, kaiqi neidi xuanshou ling tupo" 胡夏《超级星光大道》奪冠，開啟内地選手零突破 (Hu Xia becomes champion in *One Million Star*, making a breakthrough for Mainland participants). 2010. *Wangyi yule*

網易娛樂 (NetEase entertainment), May 15. https://ent.163.com/10/0515/11/66NIS72M00031HOO.html.

Huang Hsiang 黃香. 2014. "Xingshi yu neirong heyi wei xindianyi lizhuan: *Guangyin de gushi—Taiwan xindianying*" 形式與內容合一為新電影立傳：《光陰的故事—台灣新電影》 (Making a biography for new cinema through the merging of form and content: *Flowers of Taipei—Taiwan New Cinema*), *Fangying zhoubao*放映週報 (Funscreen) 482 (October 28). http://www.funscreen.com.tw/review.asp?RV_id=906.

Huang Jingyu 黃璟瑜. 2016. *Lehu Taiwan: Yiju shenghuo ti'an* 樂戶台灣：移居生活提案 (Happy settling in Taiwan: Living proposals for emigration). Kowloon: Enrich.

Huang Shih-kai 黃詩凱. 2003. "Jiuling niandai Taiwan dianying yingyan shichang fenxi: Chanye jizhongdu de guandian" 九零年代台灣電影映演市場分析：產業集中度的觀點 (A study on the concentration ratio of Taiwan's film market in the 1990s). *Chuanbo yu guanli yanjiu* 傳播與管理研究 (Communication and management studies) 2, no. 2: 157–174.

Iwabuchi, Koichi. 2002. *Recentering Globalization: Popular Culture and Japanese Transnationalism*. Durham and London: Duke University Press.

Iwabuchi, Koichi. 2015. *Resilient Borders and Cultural Diversity: Internationalism, Brand Nationalism, and Multiculturalism in Japan*. Lanham: Lexington Books.

Jan, Hung-tze. 2019. "1987 Taiwan Cinema Manifesto (Providing the Space for an Alternative Cinema to Exist)." Translated by Timmy Chih-Ting Chen and Tom Cunliffe. *Nang* 6 (April): 10–13.

Jansen, Sue Curry. 2008. "Designer Nations: Neo-liberal Nation Branding—Brand Estonia." *Social Identities* 14, no. 1: 121–142.

Jay, Martin. 1994. *Downcast Eyes: The Denigration of Vision in Twentieth-Century French Thought*. Berkeley and Los Angeles: University of California Press.

Jenkins, Henry. 2006. *Convergence Culture: Where Old and New Media Collide*. New York and London: New York University Press.

Ji, Li. 2017. "Measuring Soft Power (Section Overview)." In Chitty et. al. 2017, 75–92.

"Jiao Xiongping: Xiao qingxin tuishou" 焦雄屏：小清新推手 (Chiao Hsiung-ping: Promoter of little freshness). 2012. *Minghui* 名匯 (Famous) 1. Rpt. in *Wenmibang* 文秘幫 (Secretary assistance). https://www.wenmi.com/article/pzui8a00pbua.html.

"Jiegou xiao qingxin" 解構小清新 (Deconstructing little freshness). 2012. *Minghui* 名匯 (Famous) 1. Rpt. in *Xinlang boke* 新浪博客 (Sina blog). http://blog.sina.com.cn/s/blog_684f8a97010144da.html.

josephine. 2014. "Li Kangsheng yingdi zhi zuo, Jiaoyou dayinmu xianliang 50 chang fangying, jianzheng daoyan Cai Mingliang lizuo" 李康生影帝之作，郊遊大銀幕限量50場放映，見證導演蔡明亮力作 (Lee Kang-sheng's best actor film, *Stray Dogs* to have 50 limited public screenings, witness to Tsai Ming-liang's tour de force), February 11. *Vogue Taiwan*. https://www.vogue.com.tw/mobile/feature/content-49987.html.

K. S. 2015. "Huoxu women hai xuyao yibu kepuban de *Guangyin de gushi—Taiwan xindianying*" 或許我們還需要一部科普版的《光陰的故事—台灣新電？ (Perhaps we still need a popular version of *Flowers of Taipei— Taiwan New Cinema?*). *Yule zhongji* 娛樂重擊 (Punchline), March 24. http://punchline.asia/archives/9431.

"Kaipiao yizhou jiu shouqing! Chen Qichen Beijing yanchanghui jiayan yichang" 開票一週就售罄！陳綺貞北京演唱會加演一場 (Tickets sold out in a week after the box-office opens! One show added to Cheer Chen's Beijing concert). 2008. *Beijing wanbao* 北京晚報 (Beijing evening newspaper), October 6. Rpt. in *Fenghuang yule* 鳳

鳳娛樂 (Phoenix entertainment). http://ent.ifeng.com/music/hk/200810/1006_1839_ 818361.shtml.

Kavaratzis, Michalis. 2004. "From City Marketing to City Branding: Towards a Theoretical Framework for Developing City Brands." *Place Branding* 1, no. 1: 58–73.

Keller, Sarah. 2020. *Anxious Cinephilia: Pleasure and Peril at the Movies*. New York: Columbia University Press.

Kelly, Richard T. 2000. *The Name of This Book Is Dogme95*. London: Faber & Faber.

Kennedy, Barbara M. 2002. *Deleuze and Cinema: The Aesthetics of Sensation*. Edinburgh: Edinburgh University Press.

Klawans, Stuart. 2008. "'Un Ballon Est un Ballon,' review of *Flight of the Red Balloon*. *The Nation*, April 28. https://www.thenation.com/article/un-ballon-est-un-ballon/.

Koepnick, Lutz. 2014. *On Slowness: Toward an Aesthetic of the Contemporary*. New York: Columbia University Press.

Kou Shi-ching 寇世菁. 2012. "'Shaonian Pi' Taizhong shouying, Daoyan Li An: Yao rang Taizhongshi bei quanshijie zhidao" 「少年Pi」臺中首映，導演李安：要讓臺中市被全世界知道！(Premiere of *Life of Pi* in Taichung, director Ang Lee: Let the whole world know about Taichung city). *Zhongguo guangbo gongsi* 中國廣播公司 (Broadcasting corporation of China), November 8. https://tw.news.yahoo.com/ 少年pi台中首映-李安-要讓台中市被全世界知道-113711444.html.

Kozloff, Sarah. 2000. *Overhearing Film Dialogue*. Berkeley and Los Angeles: University of California Press.

Kuo Li-hsin 郭力昕. 2009. "'Haijiao re' tuishao zhihou: Taiwan dianying de geju yu weilai" 「海角熱」退燒之後：台灣電影的格局與未來 (When "*Cape*'s fever" has subsided: Scale and future of Taiwan cinema). In Tu 2009, 53–57.

Kuo, Lily. 2018. "Taiwan vows to stand up to China after El Salvador cuts ties." *The Guardian*, August 21. https://www.theguardian.com/world/2018/aug/21/ taiwan-further-isolated-as-el-salvador-switches-allegiance-to-china.

Kurlantzick, Joshua. 2007. *Charm Offensive: How China's Soft Power Is Transforming the World*. New Haven and London: Yale University Press.

Lai, Hongyi, and Yiyi Lu, eds. 2012. *China's Soft Power and International Relations*. Abingdon, Oxon: Routledge.

Laing, Heather. 2007. *The Gendered Score: Music in 1940s Melodrama and the Woman's Film*. Aldershot, Hampshire: Ashgate.

Lan, Pei-Chia. 2006. *Global Cinderellas: Migrant Domestics and Newly Rich Employers in Taiwan*. Durham and London: Duke University Press.

Le Grice, Malcolm. 2011. "Time and the Spectator in the Experience of Expanded Cinema." In Rees et. al. 2011, 160–170.

Lee, Ang. 2012. "Introduction: Another Dimension: Some Thoughts on *Life of Pi*." In Castelli 2012, 12–15.

Lee, Jennifer, and Min Zhou. 2015. *The Asian American Achievement Paradox*. New York: Russell Sage Foundation.

Lefebvre, Henri, and Catherine Régulier. 2004. "The Rhythmanalytical Project." In Henri Lefebvre, *Rhythmanalysis: Space, Time and Everyday Life*, 71–84. Translated by Stuart Elden and Gerald Moore. London and New York: Continuum.

Lewis, Jon. 2007. *American Film: A History*. New York: W. W. Norton.

Leys, Ruth. 2011. "The Turn to Affect: A Critique." *Critical Inquiry* 37, no. 3: 434–472.

"Li An qishilu" 李安啓示錄 (Revelations of Ang Lee). 2013. *Gongshang shibao* 工商時報 (Commercial times), March 4. Rpt. in *Zhongshi xinwenwang* 中時新聞網 (China times news net). https://www.chinatimes.com/newspapers/20130304000040-260202?chdtv.

Li, Jinhua. 2017. "National Cuisine and International Sexuality: Cultural Politics and Gender Representation in the Transnational Remake from *Eat Drink Man Woman* to *Tortilla Soup*." *Transnational Cinemas* 8, no. 2: 128–144.

Li Muci 黎慕慈. 2014. *Ai, laiqu, zhu Taiwan* 愛，來去，住台灣 (Love, let's go, live in Taiwan). Hong Kong: Joint.

Li Ya-mei 李亞梅. 2009. "Zai zheyipian yi yingxiang xingxiao chengshi de xuanxiao beihou" 在這一片以影像行銷城市的喧囂背後 (Behind the roaring scene of marketing city by film). In Tu 2009, 41–44.

Li Yilan 李邑蘭. 2011. "Cong jintian qi, wo xuanbu woshi yige 'xiaoqingxin'" 從今天起，我宣佈我是一個「小清新」 (From today, I declare I am a "little freshness"). *Nanfang zhoumo* 南方週末 (Southern weekly), April 26. http://www.infzm.com/content/58005.

Li Yumeng 李雨夢. 2015. *Daoyu, fucheng: 15 ze Xianggangren zai Taiwan de shenghuo zhaji* 島嶼·浮城：15則香港人在台灣的生活札記 (Island, floating city: 15 living journals of Hongkongers in Taiwan). New Taipei City: Nanshizixing.

"Lian Zhan 'jiuzheng' Chen Shuibian: Li An shi suoyou Zhongguoren zhi guang" 連戰「糾正」陳水扁：李安是所有中國人之光 (Lien Chan "corrected" Chen Shui-bian: Ang Lee is the glory of all Chinese people). 2006. *Shenzhen wanbao* 深圳晚報 (Shenzhen evening paper). http://news.sina.com.cn/c/2006-03-08/15348393375s.shtml.

Liang Liang 梁良. 2016. "2015 nian Taiwan Zhongwai dianying shichang ji piaofang fenxi" 2015年台灣中外電影市場及票房分析 (Analysis of Taiwan market and box office for domestic and foreign films in 2016). In Chen P-c 2016, 38–49.

Liang Liang 梁良. 2017. "2016 nian Taiwan dianying shichang ji piaofang fenxi" 2016年台灣電影市場及票房分析 (Analysis of Taiwan film market and box-office in 2016). In Chen P-c 2017, 36–49.

Liang Liang 梁良. 2018. "2017 nian Taiwan dianying shichang ji piaofang fenxi" 2017年台灣電影市場及票房分析 (Analysis of Taiwan film market and box-office in 2017). In *2018 Taiwan dianying nianjian* 2018 台灣電影年鑑 (2018 Taiwan cinema yearbook), edited by Chen Pin-chuan 陳斌全, 72–81. Taipei: Taiwan Film Institute.

Liang Liang 梁良. 2019. "2018 nian Taiwan dianying shichang ji piaofang fenxi" 2018年台灣電影市場及票房分析 (Analysis of Taiwan film market and box office in 2018). In *2019 Taiwan dianying nianjian* 2019 台灣電影年鑑 (2019 Taiwan cinema yearbook), edited by Wang Chun-chi 王君琦, 86–99. Taipei: Taiwan Film Institute.

Lim, Song Hwee. 2006. *Celluloid Comrades: Representations of Male Homosexuality in Contemporary Chinese Cinemas*. Honolulu: University of Hawai'i Press.

Lim, Song Hwee. 2007. "Positioning Auteur Theory in Chinese Cinemas Studies: Intratextuality, Intertextuality and Paratextuality in the Films of Tsai Ming-liang." *Journal of Chinese Cinemas* 1, no. 3: 223–245.

Lim, Song Hwee. 2011a. "Six Chinese Cinemas in Search of a Historiography." In Lim and Ward 2011, 35–43.

Lim, Song Hwee. 2011b. "Transnational Trajectories in Contemporary East Asian Cinemas." In *East Asian Cinemas: Regional Flows and Global Transformations*, edited by Vivian P. Y. Lee, 15–32. Basingstoke, Hampshire: Palgrave Macmillan.

Lim, Song Hwee. 2012. "Speaking in Tongues: Ang Lee, Accented Cinema, Hollywood." In *Theorizing World Cinema*, edited by Lúcia Nagib, Chris Perriam, and Rajinder Dudrah, 129–144. London: I.B. Tauris.

Lim, Song Hwee. 2013. "Taiwan New Cinema: Small Nation with Soft Power." In *The Oxford Handbook of Chinese Cinemas*, edited by Carlos Rojas and Eileen Cheng-yin Chow, 152–169. New York: Oxford University Press.

Lim, Song Hwee. 2014a. *Tsai Ming-liang and a Cinema of Slowness*. Honolulu: University of Hawai'i Press.

Lim, Song Hwee. 2014b. "The Voice of the Sinophone." In Yue and Khoo 2014, 62–76.

Lim, Song Hwee. 2016a. "Can Poetics Break Bricks?" In *The Poetics of Chinese Cinema*, edited by Gary Bettinson and James Udden, 147–165. Basingstoke, Hampshire: Palgrave Macmillan.

Lim, Song Hwee. 2016b. "Domesticating Time: Gendered Temporalities in Hou Hsiao-hsien's *Café Lumière*." *Frontiers of Literary Studies in China* 10, no. 1: 36–57.

Lim, Song Hwee. 2018. "Towards a Poor Cinema: Ubiquitous Trafficking and Poverty as Problematic in Midi Z's Films." *Transnational Cinemas* 9, no. 2: 131–146.

Lim, Song Hwee. 2019a. "Citizen-to-Citizen Connectivity and Soft Power: The Appropriation of Subcultures in 'Little Freshness' across the Taiwan Strait." *China Information* 33, no. 3: 294–310.

Lim, Song Hwee. 2019b. "Concepts of Transnational Cinema Revisited." *Transnational Screens* 10, no. 1: 1–12.

Lim Song Hwee 林松輝 and Cheung Chui-yu 張翠瑜, eds. 2018. *Pingxing wenben: Wenhua yanjiu de sixiang jiaofeng* 平行文本：文化研究的思想交鋒 (Parallel texts: Intersecting conversations in cultural studies). Hong Kong: Chinese University Press.

Lim, Song Hwee, and Julian Ward, eds. 2011. *The Chinese Cinema Book*. London: BFI Publishing, and Basingstoke, Hampshire: Palgrave Macmillan.

Lin Chun-shao 林俊劭 and Kang Yu-ping 康育萍. 2013. "Di si mu: Rongyao—Ba yisheng de bu'an bian liliang" 第四幕：榮耀——把一生的不安變力量 (Act Four: Glory—Turning anxiety of a lifetime into strength). *Shangye zhoukan* 商業週刊 (Business weekly), 1319 (March 4–10): 110–114.

Lin Mun-lee 林曼麗 and Tsai Ming-liang 蔡明亮, eds. 2016a. *Lai meishuguan jiaoyou: Cai Mingliang dazhan zhanlan tulu* 來美術館郊遊：蔡明亮大展展覽圖錄 (Catalogue of *Stray Dogs at the Museum: Tsai Ming-liang Solo Exhibition*). Taipei: Museum of National Taipei University of Education.

Lin Mun-lee 林曼麗 and Tsai Ming-liang 蔡明亮. 2016b. "Lin Manli yu Cai Mingliang duitan: Guanyu *Lai meishuguan jiaoyou: Cai Mingliang dazhan*" 林曼麗與蔡明亮對談－關於《來美術館郊遊－蔡明亮大展》 (Dialogue between Lin Mun-lee and Tsai Ming-liang: On *Stray Dogs at the Museum, Tsai Ming-liang Solo Exhibition*). In Lin and Tsai 2016a, 1–21.

Lin Shu-chuan 林淑娟, 2014. "Li Kangsheng shuile zaishang! 'Xuanzang' yan shenme? Cai Ming-liang: Wo ye buzhidao" 李康生睡了再上！《玄奘》演什麼？蔡明亮：我也不知道 (Lee Kang-sheng goes on stage after sleeping! What is *The Monk from Tang Dynasty* about? Tsai Ming-liang: I don't know too). *Xingguang yun* 星光雲 (ETtoday), April 23. https://star.ettoday.net/news/349334.

Lin Wen-chi 林文淇, ed. 2014. *2014 nian Taiwan dianying nianjian* 2014 年台灣電影年鑑 (2014 Taiwan cinema yearbook). Taipei: Taiwan Film Institute.

Lin Wen-chi 林文淇, ed. 2015. *2015 nian Taiwan dianying nianjian* 2015 年台灣電影年鑑 (2015 Taiwan cinema yearbook). Taipei: Taiwan Film Institute.

Lin, Yen-nan. 2013. "Transnational Connections in Taiwan Cinema of the 21st Century." PhD diss., University of Exeter. https://ore.exeter.ac.uk/repository/handle/10871/14386.

Lin Zonghong 林宗弘, Hong Jingshu 洪敬舒, Li Jianhong 李健鴻, Wang Zhaoqing 王兆慶, and Zhang Fengyi 張烽益. 2011. *Bengshidai: Caituanhua, pinqionghua yu shaozinühua de weiji* 崩世代：財團化、貧窮化與少子女化的危機 (The collapsed generation: The crises of tendencies toward conglomerates, impoverishment, and low birth rate). Taipei: Taiwan Labor Front.

Liu Mei-lian 劉美蓮. 2016. *Jiang Wenye zhuan: Yinyue yu zhanzheng de huixuan* 江文也傳：音樂與戰爭的迴旋 (Biography of Jiang Wenye: Whirls of music and war). Taipei: Ink.

Liu Yi-hsuen 劉懿萱. 2004. "Taizhong shizhang Hu Zhiqiang: Wenhua, dique shi men hao shengyi!" 台中市長胡志強：文化，的確是門好生意！ (Taichung mayor Jason Hu: Culture is indeed good business!). *Yuanjian zazhi* 遠見雜誌 (Good vision magazine), September 2. http://www.gvm.com.tw/Boardcontent_10074.html.

Liu, Zhen. 2018. "China's human rights record, aggressive military expansion damage its soft power rating." *South China Morning Post*, July 12. https://www.scmp.com/news/china/diplomacy-defence/article/2155051/chinas-human-rights-record-aggressive-military.

Lu Fei-i 盧非易. 1998. *Taiwan dianying: Zhengzhi, jingji, meixue 1949–1994* 台灣電影：政治、經濟、美學 1949–1994 (Taiwan cinema: Politics, economics, aesthetics, 1949–1994). Taipei: Yuanliu.

Lu Hao-ping 魯皓平. 2020. "Lian Shizhi Yuhe dou cheng le xiao fensi! He Hou Xiaoxian tongyou *Beiqing Chengshi* paishedi Jiufen: Xiang meng yiban de luxing" 連是枝裕和都成了小粉絲！和侯孝賢同遊《悲情城市》拍攝地九份：像夢一般的旅行 (Even Hirokazu Kore-eda became a little fan! Visiting Jiufen, the shooting location of *A City of Sadness*, with Hou Hsiao-hsien: A dream-like tour). *Yuanjian zazhi* 遠見雜誌 (Good vision magazine), December 1. https://www.gvm.com.tw/article/76239.

Lu, Sheldon Hsiao-peng, ed. 1997. *Transnational Chinese Cinemas: Identity, Nationhood, Gender*. Honolulu: University of Hawai'i Press.

Lu, Sheldon H., and Emilie Yueh-yu Yeh, eds. 2005. *Chinese-Language Film: Historiography, Poetics, Politics*. Honolulu: University of Hawai'i Press.

Lu, Shen, and Wilfred Chan. 2015. "Blue Sky Vanishes Immediately after Beijing's Massive Parade." CNN, September 4. http://edition.cnn.com/2015/09/04/asia/china-beijing-blue-sky-disappears-after-military-parade/.

Lu, Tonglin. 2011. "Taiwan New Cinema and Its Legacy." In Lim and Ward 2011, 122–130.

Lucia, Cynthia, Roy Grundmann, and Art Simon, eds. 2012. *The Wiley-Blackwell History of American Film*, 4 vols. Malden, MA, and Oxford: Wiley-Blackwell.

Luo Shu-nan 羅樹南, ed. 1993. *Zhonghuaminguo bashiyi nian dianying nianjian* 中華民國八十一年電影年鑑 (Cinema in the Republic of China 1992 yearbook). Taipei: Taiwan Film Archive.

Luo Shu-nan 羅樹南, eds. 2001. *Zhonghuaminguo 90 nian dianying nianjian* 中華民國90年電影年鑑 (2001 cinema yearbook in Republic of China). Taipei: Taiwan Film Archive.

Luo Shu-nan 羅樹南 and Chu Ling-yin 朱苓尹, eds. 1997. *Zhonghuaminguo bashiliu nian dianying nianjian* 中華民國八十六年電影年鑑 (Cinema in the Republic of China 1997 yearbook). Taipei: Taiwan Film Archive.

Lupke, Christopher. 2016. *The Sinophone Cinema of Hou Hsiao-hsien: Culture, Style, Voice, and Motion*. Amherst, MA: Cambria Press.

Lyons, Kate. 2019. "Taiwan loses second ally in a week as Kiribati switches to China." *The Guardian*, September 20. https://www.theguardian.com/world/2019/sep/20/taiwan-loses-second-ally-in-a-week-as-kiribati-switches-to-china.

Ma, Jean. 2015. *Sounding the Modern Woman: The Songstress in Chinese Cinema*. Durham and London: Duke University Press.

Ma, Sheng-mei. 2015. *The Last Isle: Contemporary Film, Culture and Trauma in Global Taiwan*. London and New York: Rowman & Littlefield.

Ma Yueh-lin 馬岳琳. 2011. "Cong 'Haijiao' chongshi guopian xinxin" 從「海角」重拾國片信心 (Regaining confidence in domestic films from *Cape No. 7*). *Tianxia zazhi* 天下雜誌 (Commonwealth magazine), April 13. https://www.cw.com.tw/article/5002298?aiarec=1&ercamp=article_interested_14.

Ma Yueh-lin 馬岳琳. 2016. "Ang Lee: Cinema Keeps Telling Me It Is about to Change." Translated by David Toman. *Taiwan Today*, October 7. https://taiwantoday.tw/news.php?unit=7&post=102461.

Mandelli, Elisa. 2019. *The Museum as a Cinematic Space: The Display of Moving Images in Exhibitions*. Edinburgh: Edinburgh University Press.

Mango. 2011. "Yong bu tuise de qingchun: Taiwan 'xiaoqingxin' dianying shida guanjianci" 永不褪色的青春：臺灣「小清新」電影十大關鍵詞 (Youth will never fade: Ten keywords in Taiwan "little freshness" films). *Shiguang wang* 時光網 (Mtime), November 30. Rpt. in *Mihuawang* 米花網 (imehua). http://www.imehua.com/news/2011/1130/13382.html.

Margulies, Ivone. 1996. *Nothing Happens: Chantal Akerman's Hyperrealist Everyday*. Durham and London: Duke University Press.

Marques, Sandrine. 2008. "About *Summer Hours*: Interview with Olivier Assayas." Press Kit by MK2. http://medias.unifrance.org/medias/78/144/36942/presse/dp-anglais-l-heure-d-ete.pdf.

Massumi, Brian. 1995. "The Autonomy of Affect." *Cultural Critique* 31: 83–109.

McClary, Susan. 1991. *Feminine Endings: Music, Gender, and Sexuality*. Minneapolis and London: University of Minnesota Press.

McDonough, Tom. 2009. "Introduction." In *The Situationists and the City*, edited by Tom McDonough, 1–31. London: Verso.

Mi Zou 迷走 and Liang Hsin-hua 梁新華, eds. 1991. *Xindianying zhi si: Cong* Yiqie wei Mingtian *dao* Beiqing Chengshi 新電影之死：從「一切為明天」到「悲情城市」 (Death of new cinema: From *All for Tomorrow* to *A City of Sadness*). Taipei: Tangshan.

Middleton, Jennie. 2011. "Walking in the City: The Geographies of Everyday Pedestrian Practices." *Geography Compass* 5, no. 2: 90–105.

Mills, Clifford W. 2013. *Ang Lee*. New York: Infobase Publishing.

Morris, Brian. 2004. "What We Talk about When We Talk about 'Walking in the City.'" *Cultural Studies* 18, no. 5: 675–697.

Morse, Trent. 2011. "Slow Down, You Look Too Fast." *ARTnews*, April 1. http://www.artnews.com/2011/04/01/slow-down-you-look-too-fast/.

Moskowitz, Marc L. 2010. *Cries of Joy, Songs of Sorrow: Chinese Pop Music and Its Cultural Connotations*. Honolulu: University of Hawai'i Press.

Mulvey, Laura. 1975. "Visual Pleasure and Narrative Cinema." *Screen* 16, no. 3: 6–18.

Naficy, Hamid. 2001. *An Accented Cinema: Exilic and Diasporic Filmmaking*. Princeton, NJ, and Oxford: Princeton University Press.

"National Taichung Theater Is Now Open to Public; Mayor Lin Looks to Carry Out Cultural Equality." 2016. Taichung City Government, October 14. https://english.taichung.gov.tw/731573/post.

"*Naxienian* Xianggang kaihua, 231 wan po jilu"《那些年》香港開畫231萬破紀錄 (*You Are the Apple of My Eye* opens in Hong Kong, breaking record with 2.31 million). 2011. *Pingguo ribao* 蘋果日報 (Apple daily), October 22. http://hk.apple.nextmedia.com/entertainment/first/20111022/15727876.

Needham, Gary. 2006. "Ozu and the Colonial Encounter in Hou Hsiao-hsien." In *Asian Cinemas: A Reader and Guide*, edited by Dimitris Eleftheriotis and Gary Needham, 369–383. Edinburgh: Edinburgh University Press.

Newman, Michael. 2009. "Moving Image in the Gallery Since the 1990s." In *Film and Video Art*, edited by Stuart Comer, 86–121. London: Tate.

"Niu Chengze: Hou Xiaoxian de lu wo buxiang zou" 鈕承澤：侯孝賢的路我不想走 (Niu Chen-zer: I don't want to follow in Hou Hsiao-hsien's path). 2012. *Minghui* 名匯 (Famous) 1. Rpt. in *Xinlang boke* 新浪博客 (Sina blog). http://blog.sina.com.cn/s/blog_684f8a97010147eo.html?tj=1.

"NO! Gugenhan" NO！古根漢 (NO! Guggenheim). 2004. *Pingguo ribao* 蘋果日報 (Apple daily), August 14. https://tw.appledaily.com/headline/20040814/P4RKJF2XXFALGHR2R5NCMPNVAQ/.

Norman, Neil. 2016. "Ang Lee and James Schamus." In Fuller 2016a, 36–48.

Nye, Joseph S., Jr. 1990. *Bound to Lead: The Changing Nature of American Power.* New York: Basic Books.

Nye, Joseph S., Jr. 2004. *Soft Power: The Means to Success in World Politics.* New York: Public Affairs.

Ochoa Gautier, Ana María. 2014. *Aurality: Listening & Knowledge in Nineteenth-Century Columbia.* Durham and London: Duke University Press.

Ong, Aihwa. 1999. *Flexible Citizenship: The Cultural Logics of Transnationality.* Durham and London: Duke University Press.

Ong, Walter J. (1982) 2002. *Orality and Literacy: The Technologizing of the Word.* London and New York: Routledge.

Pan Yu-chen 潘鈺楨. 2016. "Zichao mei zuanqian, chou nianzhong jiangjin. Cai Mingliang kafeidian dang goutong qiaoliang" 自嘲沒賺錢，籌年終獎金，蔡明亮咖啡店當溝通橋梁 (Tsai Ming-liang mocks himself for not making money, using café as bridge of communication to raise money for year-end bonus). *Zhongguo shibao* 中國時報 (*China Times*), December 4. https://tw.mobi.yahoo.com/news/自嘲沒賺錢-籌年終獎金-蔡明亮咖啡店當溝通橋梁-215003822.html.

"Paris Louvre tops world list with record 10m visitors." 2019. BBC News, January 3. https://www.bbc.com/news/world-europe-46748282.

Peng Hsiao-yen 彭小妍. 2010. "*Haijiao qihao*: Yiwai de chenggong? Huigu Taiwan xindianying" 海角七號：意外的成功？回顧台灣新電影 (*Cape No. 7*: A surprise hit? Looking back on Taiwan New Cinema). *Dianying xinshang xuekan* 電影欣賞學刊 (Film appreciation academic journal) 142 (January–March): 124–136.

Peterson, Anne Ring. 2010. "Attention and Distraction: On the Aesthetic Experience of Video Installation Art." *Journal of the International Association of Research Institutes in the History of Art* 9. https://journals.ub.uni-heidelberg.de/index.php/rihajournal/article/view/68537/63327.

Pocha, Jehangir. 2003. "The Rising Soft Power of India and China." *New Perspectives Quarterly* 20, no. 1: 4–13. Quoted in Nye 2004, 10.

Pollacchi, Elena. 2019. "Porous Circuits: Tsai Ming-liang, Zhao Liang, and Wang Bing at the Venice International Film Festival and the Interplay between the Festival and the Art Exhibition Circuits." *Journal of Chinese Cinemas* 13, no. 2: 130–146.

Pulver, Andrew. 2011. "Taiwan protests Venice film festival's 'China' label." *The Guardian*, August 1. http://www.guardian.co.uk/film/2011/aug/01/taiwan-protests-venice-film-festival.

Pulver, Andrew. 2013. "Ang Lee under fire from visual effects artists over Life of Pi speech." *The Guardian*, February 26. https://www.theguardian.com/film/2013/feb/26/ang-lee-visual-effects-life-of-pi.

Raju, Zakir Hossain. 2008. "Filmic Imaginations of the Malaysian Chinese: '*Mahua* cinema' as a Transnational Chinese Cinema." *Journal of Chinese Cinemas* 2, no. 1: 67–79.

Rapfogel, Jared. 2004. "Taiwan's Poet of Solitude: An Interview with Tsai Ming-liang." *Cinéaste* 4 (Fall): 26–29.

Rapold, Nicolas. 2012. "In auteur's swan song, an ode to survival." *New York Times*, February 3. http://www.nytimes.com/2012/02/05/movies/bela-tarr-says-the-turin-horse-is-his-last-movie.html?_r=0.

Rees, A. L. 2011. "Expanded Cinema and Narrative: A Troubled History." In Rees et. al. 2011, 12–21.

Rees, A. L., Duncan White, Steven Ball, and David Curtis, eds. 2011. *Expanded Cinema: Art, Performance, Film*. London: Tate.

Rehm, Jean-Pierre. 1999. "Bringing in the Rain." In *Tsai Ming-liang*, edited by Jean-Pierre Rehm, Olivier Joyard, and Danièle Rivière, 9–40. Paris: Dis Voir.

Rigger, Shelley. 2011. *Why Taiwan Matters? Small Island, Global Powerhouse*, updated ed. Lanham, MD: Rowman & Littlefield.

Robinson, Luke. 2018. "Non-State Agents, Quotidian Soft Power, and the Work of the Overseas Film Festival: Case Studies from London." In Voci and Luo 2018a, 111–127.

Roddy, Michael. 2013. "A Minute With: Director Tsai Ming-liang on Retiring, Next Film." *Reuters*, September 6. https://www.reuters.com/article/entertainment-us-venice-festival-tsai/a-minute-with-director-tsai-ming-liang-on-retiring-next-film-idINBRE9850MJ20130906.

Rodowick, D. N. 2007. *The Virtual Life of Film*. Cambridge, MA, and London: Harvard University Press.

Rosen, Philip. 2001. *Change Mummified: Cinema, Historicity, Theory*. Minneapolis and London: University of Minnesota Press.

Ross, Andrew A. G. 2014. *Mixed Emotions: Beyond Fear and Hatred in International Conflict*. Chicago and London: University of Chicago Press.

Ruberto, Laura E., and Kristi M. Wilson, eds. 2007. *Italian Neorealism and Global Cinema*. Detroit, MI: Wayne State University Press.

Samuels, David W., Louise Meintjes, Ana Maria Ochoa [Gautier], and Thomas Porcello. 2010. "Soundscapes: Towards a Sounded Anthropology." *Annual Review of Anthropology* 39 (June): 329–345.

Schoonover, Karl. 2012. "Wastrels of Time: Slow Cinema's Laboring Body, the Political Spectator, and the Queer." *Framework* 53, no. 1: 65–78.

Seigworth, Gregory J., and Melissa Gregg. 2010. "An Inventory of Shimmers." In *The Affect Theory Reader*, edited by Melissa Gregg and Gregory J. Seigworth, 1–25. Durham and London: Duke University Press.

Sharma, Devika, and Frederik Tygstrup. 2015. "Introduction." In *Structures of Feeling: Affectivity and the Study of Culture*, edited by Devika Sharma and Frederik Tygstrup, 1–19. Berlin: De Gruyter.

She Hanji 佘漢姬 and Chen Yunxuan 陳運濬. 2017. "Daoyan Zhang Dalei ai *Guhuozai*: You daluren queshao de youmogan" 導演張大磊愛《古惑仔》：有大陸人缺少的幽默感 (Director Zhang Dalei loves *Youth and Danger*: It has sense of humor that mainlanders lack). *HK01*, June 30. https://www.hk01.com/電影/101428/八月-專訪-導演張大磊愛-古惑仔-有大陸人缺少的幽默感.

"Shelun: Xiao quexing dake you honghu zhizhi" 社論：小確幸大可有鴻鵠之志 (Editorial: Little exact happiness could well have lofty ambition). 2014. *Zhongguo shibao* 中國時報 (China times), July 7. http://www.chinatimes.com/newspapers/20140707000395-260109.

Shih, Hsiu-chuan. 2007. "Mayor Hu praises transfer of Shuinan Airport to Taichung City Government." *Taipei Times*, December 23. http://www.taipeitimes.com/News/taiwan/archives/2007/12/23/2003393779.

Shih, Shu-mei. 2007. *Visuality and Identity: Sinophone Articulations across the Pacific*. Berkeley, Los Angeles, and London: University of California Press.

Shih Yuan. 2015. "'Xiao qingxin shi wuguo a!' Taiwan chuanqi yuetuan Zhuoshuixi Gongshe zhuchang Xiaoke de shehui guancha" 「小清新是誤國啊！」台灣傳奇樂團濁水溪公社主唱小柯的社會觀察 ("Little freshness is harming the nation!" Social observation by Hsiao Ke, lead singer of Taiwan's legendary band Loh Tsui Kweh Commune). *Guanjian pinglun* 關鍵評論 (The news lens), September 1. https://www.thenewslens.com/feature/soundsontheisland/23730.

Shingler, Martin. 2006. "Fasten Your Seatbelts and Prick Up Your Ears: The Dramatic Human Voice in Film." *Scope: An Online Journal of Film & TV Studies* 5 (June). http://www.nottingham.ac.uk/scope/documents/2006/june-2006/shingler.pdf.

Shouse, Eric. 2005. "Feeling, Emotion, Affect." *M/C Journal* 8, no. 6. https://journal.media-culture.org.au/mcjournal/article/view/2443.

Sims, David. 2016. "*Crouching Tiger, Hidden Dragon*: The Sad Sequel," review of *Crouching Tiger, Hidden Dragon: Sword of Destiny*. *The Atlantic*, February 27. https://www.theatlantic.com/entertainment/archive/2016/02/crouching-tiger-hidden-dragon-sword-of-destiny-review/471234/.

Sing Song-yong 孫松榮. 2010a. "'Fufang dianying' de youling xiaoying: Lun Hou Xiaoxian de *Kafei shiguang* yu *Hong qiqiu* zhi 'kua yingxiangxing'" 「複訪電影」的幽靈效應：論侯孝賢的《珈琲時光》與《紅氣球》之「跨影像性」(The phantom-effect of "cinema revisited": On the trans-imageity of Hou Hsiao-hsien's *Café Lumière* and *Le Voyage du ballon rouge*). *Zhongwai wenxue* 中外文學 (Chung-wai literary quarterly) 39, no. 4: 11–45.

Sing Song-yong 孫松榮. 2010b. "Qinglishi de xinling ganying: Lun Taiwan 'houxindianying' de liuti yingxiang" 輕歷史的心靈感應：論台灣「後－新電影」的流體影像 (The telepathy in downgrading history: On the fluid imaging of Taiwan's "post-new cinema"). *Dianying xinshang xuekan* 電影欣賞學刊 (Film appreciation academic journal) 142 (January–March): 137–156.

Sing Song-yong 孫松榮. 2014. *Rujing, chujing: Cai Ming-liang de yingxiang yishu yu kuajie shijian* 入鏡｜出境：蔡明亮的影像藝術與跨界實踐 (Projecting Tsai Ming-Liang: Towards transart cinema). Taipei: Wunan.

Sing Song-yong 孫松榮. 2016. "Chixu jiaocuo de shandongzhe: *Lai meishuguan jiaoyou—Cai Mingliang dazhan* de yingpian zhanlan" 持續交錯的閃動著：《來美術館郊遊－蔡明亮大展》的影片展覽 (The continuous crisscrossing shimmer: On *Stray Dogs at the Museum*, Tsai Ming-liang Solo Exhibition." In Lin and Tsai 2016a, 180–189.

Skoller, Jeffrey. 2005. *Shadows, Specters, Shards: Making History in Avant-Garde Film*. Minneapolis and London: University of Minnesota Press.

Smedley, Nick. 2011. *A Divided World: Hollywood Cinema and Émigré Directors in the Era of Roosevelt and Hitler, 1933–1948*. Bristol: Intellect.

Smith, Nicola. 2017. "Martin Scorsese's *Silence* Is a Win for Taiwan but Producers Are Worried about a China Backlash." *Time*, January 20. http://time.com/4640566/taiwan-silence-scorsese-movies-china/.

Sobczynski, Peter. 2015. Review of *The Assassin*. RogerEbert.com, October 16. http://www.rogerebert.com/reviews/the-assassin-2015.

Sontag, Susan. 1996. "The decay of cinema." *New York Times*, February 25. https://archive.nytimes.com/www.nytimes.com/books/00/03/12/specials/sontag-cinema.html.

"Statistics." n.d. Women and Hollywood. https://womenandhollywood.com/resources/statistics/.

Sterne, Jonathan, ed. 2012a. *The Sound Studies Reader*. Abingdon, Oxon: Routledge.

Sterne, Jonathan. 2012b. "Sonic Imaginations." In Sterne 2012a, 1–17.

Stewart, Kathleen. 2007. *Ordinary Affects*. Durham and London: Duke University Press.

Su Huei-chao 蘇惠昭. 2014. "Wo bushuo gushi: Wode dianying bushi yule—Cai Mingliang" 我不說故事：我的電影不是娛樂—蔡明亮 (I don't tell stories: My films are not entertainment —Tsai Ming-liang:). *Taiwan guanghua zazhi* 台灣光華雜誌 (Taiwan panorama), September. https://www.taiwan-panorama.com/Articles/Details?Guid=d32a0cea-b524-4776-b7bb-77884762cc56.

Sui, Daniel Z. 2000. "Visuality, Aurality, and Shifting Metaphors of Geographical Thought in the Late Twentieth Century." *Annals of the Association of American Geographers* 90, no. 2: 322–343.

Sun, Wanning. 2018. "Soft Power by Accident or by Design: *If You Are the One* and Chinese Television." In Voci and Luo 2018a, 196–211.

Tan, Shanshan 譚山山. 2012. "Xiaoqingxin suyuan" 小清新溯源 (Tracing the origin of little freshness). *Rensheng wenxuewang* 人生文學網 (Life literature net), January 8. http://www.cscecee.com.cn/qingnianwenzhai/lx/id-2236.html.

Tang Su-chen 湯素貞. 2018. "'Shaonian PI de qihuan piaoliu' dianli dianying chanzhi hepai dianfan"《少年PI的奇幻漂流》奠立電影產製合拍新典範 (*Life of Pi* sets new paradigm for co-production of films). *Taiwan dianyingwang* 台灣電影網 (Taiwan cinema web), July 6. https://taiwancinema.bamid.gov.tw/Articles/ArticlesContent/?ContentUrl=68128.

Teo, Stephen. 2009. *Chinese Martial Arts Cinema: The Wuxia Tradition*. Edinburgh: Edinburgh University Press.

Tolentino, Cynthia. 2011. "Philippine Studies and the End of the American Century." *Kritika Kultura* 16: 86–98. https://journals.ateneo.edu/ojs/index.php/kk/article/view/1435.

Truffaut, François. 2008. "A Certain Tendency of the French Cinema (1954)." In Grant 2008, 9–18.

Tsai Ming-liang 蔡明亮. 2016. "Cai Mingliang shouji" 蔡明亮手記 (Tsai Ming-liang's journal). In Lin and Tsai 2016a, 95–105.

Tseng Hsueh-chien曾雪蒨, Huang Jen-ying黃任膺, and Tsai Wei-hsin蔡維欣. 2013. "Chen Wenqian baiwan juankuan yaoshen, 'PI' 36 yi chengben zhuli, buhuiying beisuan zhanguang Li An" 陳文茜百萬捐款搖身,《PI》36億成本助力，不回應被酸沾光李安 (Sisy Chen's million-dollar donation changes into aid for *Life of Pi*'s 3.6 billion budget, she will not respond to sarcasm about benefiting from Ang Lee's limelight). *Pingguo ribao* 蘋果日報 (Apple daily), February 27. https://tw.entertainment.appledaily.com/daily/20130227/34854647/.

Tseng Jui-hua 曾瑞華. 2015. "'Xiaoquexing' zhiyu: Cong Jijieke de weiwu shenxue lun 'xiaoquexing' shangpin chongchi de wenhua xianxiang jiqi chulu" 「小確幸」之餘：從紀傑克的唯物神學論「小確幸」商品充斥的文化現象及其出路 (What remains after the enjoyment of the "small certain happiness": A study on the "small certain happiness" cultural phenomenon and its way out from the perspective of Žižek's materialist theology). *Zhongwai wenxue* 中外文學 (Chung-wai literary monthly) 44, no. 2: 107–141.

Tsu, Jing. 2010. "Sinophonics and the Nationalization of Chinese." In *Global Chinese Literature: Critical Essays*, edited by Jing Tsu and David Der-wei Wang, 93–114. Boston and Leiden: Brill Press.

Tu Hsiang-wen 塗翔文, ed. 2009. *2009 nian Taiwan dianying nianjian* 2009 年台灣電影年鑑 (2009 Taiwan cinema yearbook). Taipei: Taiwan Film Archive.

Tweedie, James. 2013. *The Age of New Waves: Art Cinema and the Staging of Globalization.* Oxford and New York: Oxford University Press.

Udden, James. 2007. "Taiwan." In Hjort and Petrie 2007a, 144–159.

Uroskie, Andrew V. 2014. *Between the Black Box and the White Cube: Expanded Cinema and Postwar Art.* Chicago and London: University of Chicago Press.

Vagenas, Maria Giovanna. 2013. "Filmmaker Tsai Ming-liang says his work should be appreciated slowly." *South China Morning Post*, August 27. http://www.scmp.com/lifestyle/arts-culture/article/1299497/filmmaker-tsai-ming-liang-says-his-work-should-be-appreciated.

Verstraete, Ginette. 2010. "Introduction: Intermedialities: A Brief Survey of Conceptual Key Issues." *Film and Media Studies* 2: 7–14.

"View from Cannes: *The Assassin* by Hou Hsiao-hsien is a visual poem." 2015. *South China Morning Post*, May 21. http://www.scmp.com/lifestyle/film-tv/article/1805063/live-cannes-assassin-hou-hsiao-hsien-visual-poem.

Vincendeau, Ginette. 2009. "Introduction: Fifty Years of the French New Wave." In Graham with Vincendeau, 1–29.

Vitali, Valentina. 2010. "Film Historiography as Theory of the Film Subject: A Case Study." *Cinema Journal* 50, no. 1: 141–146.

Voci, Paola, and Luo Hui, eds. 2018a. *Screening China's Soft Power.* Abingdon, Oxon: Routledge.

Voci, Paola, and Luo Hui. 2018b. "Screening China's Soft Power: Screen Cultures and Discourses of Power." In Voci and Luo 2018a, 1–18.

Vogel, Ezra F. 1993. *The Four Little Dragons: The Spread of Industrialization in East Asia.* Cambridge, MA, and London: Harvard University Press.

Wachman, Alan M. 1994. *Taiwan: National Identity and Democratization.* Armonk, NY, and London: M.E. Sharpe.

Wang Bo-jen 王伯仁. 2017. "Langde meiming! Ji 'Shaonian Pi' zhihou, Taizhong zaolangci zaidu bei 'Chenmo' shiyong" 浪得美名！繼《少年PI》之後，台中造浪池再度被《沉默》使用 (The wave pool deserves its good reputation! After *Life of Pi*, it has been used by *Silence*). *Minbao* 民報 (Taiwan people news), February 19. http://www.peoplenews.tw/news/62e229a4-3e97-4a0f-83e2-0b87b1c80117.

Wang Cheng-hua 王清華. 1997a. "1996 nian waipian faxing gaikuang" 1996年外片發行概況 (1996 overview of foreign film distribution). In Luo and Chu 1997, 40–44.

Wang Cheng-hua 王清華. 1997b. "1996 nian Taibeishi xipian piaofang tongji" 1996年台北市西片票房統計 (1996 statistics of foreign film box office in Taipei). In Luo and Chu 1997, 45–56.

Wang Cheng-hua 王清華. 1998. "1997 nian Taibei diqu waipian piaofang tongji" 1997年台北地區外片票房統計 (1997 statistics of foreign film box office in the Taipei region). In *Zhonghuaminguo bashiqi nian dianying nianjian* 中華民國八十七年電影年鑑 (Cinema in the Republic of China 1998 yearbook), edited by Luo Shu-nan 羅樹南 and Yang Yi-huei 楊憶暉, 101–118. Taipei: Taiwan Film Archive.

Wang Cheng-hua 王清華. 1999. "1998 nian Zhongwai dianying faxing gaikuang" 1998年中外電影發行概況 (1998 overview of Chinese and foreign film distribution). In *Zhonghuaminguo yijiujiujiu nian dianying nianjian* 中華民國一九九九年電影年鑑 (Cinema in the Republic of China 1999 yearbook), edited by Luo Shu-nan 羅樹南 and Yang Yi-hui 楊憶暉, 58–64. Taipei: Taiwan Film Archive.

Wang Cheng-hua王清華. 2001a. "2000 nian Zhongwai yingpian shichang yu faxing fenxi" 2000年中外影片市場與發行分析 (Analysis of market and distribution of domestic and foreign films in 2000). In Luo 2001, 110–120.

Wang Cheng-hua 王清華. 2001b. "2000 nian Taibei diqu waipian piaofang tongji" 2000年台北地區外片票房統計 (2000 statistics of foreign film box office in the Taipei region). In Luo 2001, 122–129.

Wang Cheng-hua 王清華. 2001c. "2000 nian Taibei diqu guopian piaofang tongji" 2000年台北地區國片票房統計 (2000 statistics of domestic film box office in the Taipei region). In Luo 2001, 130–133.

Wang Cheng-hua 王清華. 2002. "2001 nian Taibei diqu shangying yingpian piaofang tongji" 2001年台北地區上映影片票房統計 (2001 box-office statistics of films screened in the Taipei region). In *Zhonghuaminguo jiushiyi nian dianying nianjian* 中華民國九十一年電影年鑑 (Cinema in the Republic of China 2002 yearbook), edited by Luo Shu-nan 羅樹南, 58–66. Taipei: Taiwan Film Archive.

Wang Cheng-hua 王清華. 2003. "2002 nian Taibei diqu dianying shichang poxi" 2002年台北地區電影市場剖析 (2002 analysis of film market in the Taipei region). In *Zhonghuaminguo jiushi'er nian dianying nianjian* 中華民國九十二年電影年鑑 (Cinema in the Republic of China 2003 yearbook), edited by Luo Shu-nan 羅樹南, 56–65. Taipei: Taiwan Film Archive.

Wang Cheng-hua 王清華. 2004. "2003 nian dianying shichang zonglan" 2003年電影市場總覽 (Overview of film market in 2003). In *Zhonghuaminguo jiushisan nian dianying nianjian* 中華民國九十三年電影年鑑 (2004 cinema year book in Republic of China), edited by Liang Liang梁良, 76–83. Taipei: Government Information Office.

Wang Cheng-hua 王清華. 2005. "2004 nian dianying shichang zonglan" 2004年電影市場總覽 (Overview of film market in 2004). In *Zhonghuaminguo jiushisi nian dianying nianjian* 中華民國九十四年電影年鑑 (Taiwan cinema year book 2005), edited by Liang Liang梁良, 252–266. Taipei: Government Information Office.

Wang Cheng-hua 王清華. 2006. "2005 nian dianying shichang zonglan" 2005年電影市場總覽 (Overview of film market in 2005). In *Zhonghuaminguo jiushiwu nian dianying nianjian* 中華民國九十五年電影年鑑 (2006 Taiwan cinema yearbook), edited by Hsieh Jen-chang 謝仁昌, 218–242. Taipei: Government Information Office.

Wang Cheng-hua 王清華. 2007. "2006 nian dianying shichang zonglan" 2006年電影市場總覽 (Overview of film market in 2006). In *2007 nian Taiwan dianying nianjian* 2007年台灣電影年鑑 (2007 Taiwan cinema yearbook), edited by Hsieh Jen-chang 謝仁昌, 234–261. Taipei: Government Information Office.

Wang Cheng-hua 王清華. 2008. "2007 nian dianying shichang zonglan" 2007 年電影市場總覽 (Overview of film market in 2007). In *2008 nian Taiwan dianying nianjian* 2008 年台灣電影年鑑 (2008 Taiwan cinema yearbook), edited by Cheng Li-ming 鄭立明, 130–153. Taipei: Government Information Office.

Wang Cheng-hua 王清華. 2010. "2008–2009 Zhongwai yingpian piaofang jilu" 2008–2009 中外影片票房紀錄 (2008–2009 box-office record for domestic and foreign films). In Cheng L-m 2010, 90–113.

Wang Cheng-hua 王清華. 2011. "2010 nian Zhongwai dianying shichang zonglan" 2010 年中外電影市場總覽 (Overview of film market in 2010). In *2011 nian Taiwan dianying nianjian* 2011年台灣電影年鑑 (2011 Taiwan cinema yearbook), edited by Wei Pei-lei 魏蓓蕾, 40–51. Taipei: Chinese Taipei Film Archive.

Wang Cheng-hua 王清華. 2012. "2011 nian Zhongwai dianying shichang zonglan" 2011 年中外電影市場總覽 (Overview of market for domestic and foreign films in 2011). In Wei 2012, 42–63.

Wang Cheng-hua 王清華. 2014a. "2012 nian Zhongwai dianying shichang zonglan" 2012 年中外電影市場總覽 (Overview of market for domestic and foreign films in 2012). In *2013 nian Taiwan dianying nianjian* 2013年台灣電影年鑑 (2013 Taiwan cinema yearbook), edited by Wei Pei-lei 魏蓓蕾, 40–54. Taipei: Chinese Taipei Film Archive.

Wang Cheng-hua 王清華. 2014b. "2013 nian Taiwan Zhongwai dianying shichang zonglan" 2013 年台灣中外電影市場總覽 (Overview of Taiwan market for domestic and foreign films in 2013). In Lin W-c 2014, 53–79.

Wang Cheng-hua 王清華. 2015. "2014 nian Taiwan Zhongwai dianying shichang zonglan" 2014 年台灣中外電影市場總覽 (Overview of Taiwan market for domestic and foreign films in 2014). In Lin 2015, 64–114.

Wang Chi-cheng 王志成. 1991. "Zhuanfang" 專訪 (Interview). In Wang K-y 1991, 8–14.

Wang, Chih-ming. 2017. "'The Future that Belongs to Us': Affective Politics, Neoliberalism and the Sunflower Movement." *International Journal of Cultural Studies* 20, no. 2: 177–192.

Wang, David Der-wei. 2017. "Introduction: Worlding Literary China." In *A New Literary History of Modern China*, edited by David Der-wei Wang, 1–28. Cambridge, MA, and London: Harvard University Press.

Wang Keng-yu 王耿瑜, ed. 1991. *Li An* 李安 (Ang Lee). Taipei: China Times.

Wang Keng-yu 王耿瑜, ed. 2015a. *Guangyin zhi lü: Taiwan xindianying zai lushang* 光陰之旅：臺灣新電影在路上 (Film in our time: Taiwan new cinema on the road). Taipei: Department of Cultural Affairs, Taipei City Government.

Wang Keng-yu 王耿瑜. 2015b. "Taiwan xindianying lüxing biji" 台灣新電影旅行筆記 (Travel journal on Taiwan new cinema). In Wang K-y 2015a, 22–25.

"Wangmin you gaitu, shaodao Jiubadao" 網民又改圖，燒到九把刀 (Netizens alter picture again, scorching Giddens Ko). 2011. *Mingbao* 明報 (Ming pao), October 10. https://life.mingpao.com/general/article?issue=20111010&nodeid=1508111219958.

Wei Pei-lei 魏蓓蕾, ed. 2012. *2012 nian Taiwan dianying nianjian* 2012年台灣電影年鑑 (2012 Taiwan cinema yearbook). Taipei: Taiwan Film Archive.

Wei, Ti. 2005. "Generational/Cultural Contradiction and Global Incorporation: Ang Lee's *Eat Drink Man Woman*." In Berry and Lu 2005a, 101–112.

Weidman, Amanda. 2015. "Voice." In *Keywords in Sound*, edited by David Novak and Matt Sakakeeny, 232–245. Durham and London: Duke University Press.

Weinraub, Bernard. 1996. "Disney will defy China on its Dalai Lama film." *New York Times*, November 27. https://www.nytimes.com/1996/11/27/movies/disney-will-defy-china-on-its-dalai-lama-film.html.

Wen Tien-hsiang 聞天祥. 2002. *Guangying dingge: Cai Mingliang de xinling changyu* 光影定格：蔡明亮的心靈場域 (Freeze-frame of light and image: The field of Tsai Ming-liang's heart and soul). Taipei: Hengxing.

Wen Tien-hsiang 聞天祥. 2009. "2008 Taiwan dianying: Shuyu xinrui de yinian" 2008台灣電影：屬於新銳的一年 (2008 Taiwan cinema: A year that belongs to the newcomers). In Tu 2009, 16–26.

Wen Tien-hsiang 聞天祥. 2010. "Lao linghun, xin mianmu: 'Hong qiqiu' daoyan Hou Xiaoxian" 老靈魂，新面目：《紅氣球》導演侯孝賢 (Old soul, new face: *Flight of the Red Balloon* director Hou Hsiao-hsien). In *Taiwan dianying de shengyin* 台灣電影的聲音 (The voice of Taiwan cinema), edited by Lin Wen-chi 林文淇 and Wang Yu-yen 王玉燕, 71–82. Taipei: Shulin.

Wen Tien-hsiang 聞天祥. 2011. "2010: 'Mengjia' yu Taiwan dianying de sige xiti" 2010：《艋舺》與臺灣電影的四個習題 (2010: *Monga* and four questions for Taiwan cinema). In *2011 nian Taiwan dianying nianjian* 2011年台灣電影年鑑 (2011 Taiwan cinema yearbook), edited by Wei Pei-lei 魏蓓蕾, 10–29. Taipei: Chinese Taipei Film Archive.

Wen Tien-hsiang 聞天祥. 2012. "Taiwan dianying 2011: Yuhuo chongsheng jiqi huijin" 臺灣電影2011：浴火重生及其灰燼 (2011 Taiwan cinema: Rebirth in fire and its ashes). In Wei 2012, 10–31.

Wen Tien-hsiang 聞天祥. 2014. "Sheizai jiaoyou shile hun: Jianlun 2013 nian Taiwan juqing changpian" 誰在郊遊失了魂：簡論2013年台灣劇情長片 (Who lost its soul at an outing: On 2013 Taiwan's feature-length films). In Lin W-c 2014, 7–20.

Wen Tien-hsiang 聞天祥. 2015. "2014 Taiwan juqing changpian: Juejing haishi chulu?" 2014台灣劇情長片：絕境還是出路？ (2014 Taiwan feature-length films: Cul-de-sac or way out?). In Lin 2015, 12–27.

Wen Tien-hsiang 聞天祥. 2016. "2015 Taiwan juqing changpian: Laojiang xinrui jiti penfa" 2015 台灣劇情長片：老將新銳集體噴發 (2015 Taiwan feature-length films: Collective eruption by old guards and young turks). In Chen P-c 2016, 8–25.

Wen Tien-hsiang 聞天祥. 2017. "Lindong zhi zhan: 2016 Taiwan juqing changpian" 凜冬之戰：2016台灣劇情長片 (The battle in harsh winter: 2016 Taiwan feature films). In Chen P-c 2017, 8–23.

Whittaker, Tom, and Sarah Wright, eds. 2017a. *Locating the Voice in Film: Critical Approaches and Global Practices*. New York: Oxford University Press.

Whittaker, Tom, and Sarah Wright. 2017b. "Locating the Voice in Film: An Introduction." In Whittaker and Wright 2017a, 1–15.

Wicks, James. 2015. *Transnational Representations: The State of Taiwan Film in the 1960s and 1970s*. Hong Kong: Hong Kong University Press.

Willemen, Paul. 1990. "The Third Cinema Question: Notes and Reflections." In *Questions of Third Cinema*, edited by Jim Pines and Paul Willemen, 1–29. London: British Film Institute.

Williams, Raymond. 1977. *Marxism and Literature*. Oxford and New York: Oxford University Press.

Wong, Gary 王冠豪. 2017. *Dianying chaosheng—Taiwan* 電影朝聖－台灣 (Film pilgrimage: Taiwan). Hong Kong: Chaoying she.

Wong, Yvette 王樂儀. 2016. "Dangdai wenyi fengchao: Xianggang wenyiqingnian shangyehua" 當代文藝風潮：香港文藝青年商業化 (Contemporary literary trend: Commercialization of Hong Kong's literary youths). *Wenhua yanjiu@Lingnan*

文化研究@嶺南 (Cultural Studies@Lingnan) 52 (May). http://commons.ln.edu.hk/mcsln/vol52/iss1/1/.

Wu Bo-hsuen 吳柏軒. 2016. "Zeng Weiliang: Taiwan tudi you taiduo jingcai gushi" 曾威量：台灣土地有太多精彩故事 (Chiang Wei Liang: The land of Taiwan has too many fascinating stories). *Ziyou shibao* 自由時報 (Liberty times net), February 22. http://news.ltn.com.tw/news/life/paper/960584.

Wu Chao-chun 吳昭君 and Hsiao Yu-ye 蕭鈺燁. 2013. "Zhongyang difang buzhu sanyi, Li An wancheng Shaonian Pi" 中央地方補助3億，李安完成少年Pi (Central and local governments sponsor 300 million to help Ang Lee complete *Life of Pi*). *Huashi xinwen* 華視新聞 (CTS news), February 25. https://news.cts.com.tw/cts/entertain/201302/201302251199339.html.

Wu Cheng-hong 吳承紘. 2017. *Yanshidai: Dixin, pinqiong yu kanbujian de weilai* 厭世代：低薪、貧窮與看不見的未來 (Misanthropic generation: Low salary, poverty, and an inability to see the future). New Taipei City: Yuexiong chuban.

Wu, Chia-chi. 2007. "Festivals, Criticism and the International Reputation of Taiwan New Cinema." In *Cinema Taiwan: Politics, Popularity and State of the Arts*, edited by Darrell William Davis and Robert Ru-shou Chen, 75–91. London and New York: Routledge.

Wu Shang-hsuen 吳尚軒. 2020. "Zhang Ji'an 'Nanwu' pai huaren lisanshi duo zuijia xindaoyan, ganxie Hou Xiaoxian jiyu yangfen" 張吉安《南巫》拍華人離散史奪最佳新導演，感謝侯孝賢給予養分 (Chong Keat Aun's *The Story of Southern Islet* films history of Chinese diaspora and wins Best New Director award, thanks Hou Hsiao-hsien for providing nutrition). *Feng chuanmei* 風傳媒 (The storm media), November 21. https://www.storm.mg/article/3227493.

Wunderlich, Filipa Matos. 2008. "Walking and Rhythmicity: Sensing Urban Space." *Journal of Urban Design* 13, no. 1: 125–139.

Xiao, Ying. 2017. *China in the Mix: Cinema, Sound, and Popular Culture in the Age of Globalization*. Jackson: University Press of Mississippi.

Xiong Liao 熊寥, Zhang Yingying 張瑩瑩, Jiang Wenjuan 蔣文娟, and Chang Xiaohu 常小琥. 2012. "Taiwan dianying: Bie jiao wo xiaoqingxin 台灣電影：別叫我小清新 (Taiwan cinema: Don't call me little freshness). *Minghui* 名匯 (Famous), January 20. Rpt. in *Xinjingbao wang* 新京報網 (New Beijing news net). http://www.bjnews.com.cn/ent/2012/01/20/179036.html.

Yeh, Emilie Yueh-yu, and Darrell William Davis. 2005. *Taiwan Film Directors: A Treasure Island*. New York: Columbia University Press.

Yeh Huang-chi 葉湟淇. 2010. "'Ruanshili': Woguo tuizhan 'huolu waijiao' de zhuzhou." 「軟實力」——我國推展「活路外交」的主軸 ("Soft power": The main axis of our country's flexible diplomacy). *Waijiaobu tongxun* 外交部通訊 (MOFA news and report), 28, no. 5 (June). http://multilingual.mofa.gov.tw/web/web_UTF-8/out/2805/2-3_page.html.

Yu Chang-min 于昌民. 2012. "Kafei shiguang: Cai Mingliang chuangzuo mantan" 咖啡時光：蔡明亮創作漫談 (Café lumiere: On Tsai Ming-liang's creative work), *Fangying zhoubao* 放映週報 (Fun screen) 348 (March 9). http://www.funscreen.com.tw/headline.asp?H_No=397.

Yu, Hsiang, and Ko Lin. 2020. "Hong Kongers granted residency in Taiwan jump 116%." *Focus Taiwan*, August 15. https://focustaiwan.tw/cross-strait/202008150010.

Yue, Audrey, and Olivia Khoo, eds. 2014. *Sinophone Cinemas*. Basingstoke, Hampshire: Palgrave Macmillan.

Yulezu 娛樂組. 2019. "Dayingle que buchuxi, Zhao Deyin fangniao Jinma zao pi wang'enfuyi" 答應了卻不出席，趙德胤放鳥金馬遭批忘恩負義 (Agreed to but did not attend, Midi Z's absence from Golden Horse criticized for ungratefulness). *Jing zhoukan* 鏡週刊 (Mirror media), December 1. https://www.mirrormedia.mg/story/20191201ent009/.

Zhan Hongzhi 詹宏志. 1988. "Minguo qishiliu nian Taiwan dianying xuanyan" 民國七十六年台灣電影宣言 (1987 Taiwan cinema manifesto). In *Taiwan xindianying* 台灣新電影 (Taiwan new cinema), edited by Chiao Hsiung-ping 焦雄屏, 111–118. Taipei: Shibao wenhua.

Zhang Jingbei 張靓蓓. 2002. *Shinian yijiao dianying meng* 十年一覺電影夢 (Ten years of cinematic dreams). Taipei: Shibao.

Zhang Kerong 張克榮. 2005. *Li An* 李安 (Ang Lee). Beijing: Xiandai chubanshe.

Zhang, Yingjin. 2000. "A Typography of Chinese Film Historiography." *Asian Cinema* 11, no. 1: 16–32.

Zhang, Yingjin. 2018. "Afterword: Shifting Perspectives on Soft Power and Chinese Screens." In Voci and Luo 2018a, 252–260.

Zhao, Deyin 趙德胤 [Midi Z]. 2015. *Ju, li, Bingdu: Zhao Deyin de dianying rensheng jishi* 聚。離。冰毒：趙德胤的電影人生紀事 (Gathering, separating, *Ice Poison*: Chronicle of Midi Z's film life). Taipei: Commonwealth Magazine.

"Zhonghuaminguo yingpian, kanglu yingpian ji qita waipian piaofang tongji" 中華民國影片、港陸影片暨其他外片票房統計 (Box-office statistics for films from the Republic of China, Hong Kong, the Mainland, and other foreign regions). n.d. *Wenhuabu yingshi ji liuxing yinyue chanyeju* 文化部影視及流行音樂產業局 (Bureau of Audiovisual and Music Industry Development, Ministry of Culture). Accessed on January 10, 2021. https://www.bamid.gov.tw/downloadfilelist_248_2.html.

"Zhongshi Wufeng 'zhong Taiwan yingshi jidi' zhengshi kaigong, mingdao Li An, Wei Desheng tonghe" 中市霧峰「中台灣影視基地」正式開工，名導李安、魏德聖同賀 (Central Taiwan film and TV base in Taichung Wufeng's formally launched, famous directors Ang Lee and Wei Te-sheng sent congratulations). 2016. Taichung City Government Tourism and Travel Bureau, October 20. https://travel.taichung.gov.tw/zh-tw/Event/NewsDetail/1715/中市霧峰-中台灣影視基地-正式開工-名導李安-魏德聖同賀.

Zhu Yuan 祝媛. 2014. "Xiaoqingxin: Yizhong xinxing de wenhua chaoliu" 小清新：一種新興的文化潮流 (Little freshness: A newly emerged cultural trend). MA diss., Shanghai Normal University. http://gb.oversea.cnki.net/KCMS/detail/detail.aspx?filename=1014337883.nh&dbcode=CMFD&dbname=CMFDREF.

"Zijin mei daowei, Haijiao Qihao yinyueju tingyan" 資金沒到位，海角七號音樂劇停演 (*Cape No. 7* musical halted owing to lack of funding). 2017. *Zhongyangshe* 中央社 (Central News Agency), February 21. Rpt. in *Zhongshi xinwenwang* 中時新聞網 (*China Times*). https://www.chinatimes.com/realtimenews/20170221004954-260404?chdtv.

Index

For the benefit of digital users, indexed terms that span two pages (e.g., 52–53) may, on occasion, appear on only one of those pages.

Tables and figures are indicated by *t* and *f* following the page number

3D. *See* digital technology

Academy Awards, 15, 94, 95–96, 97–98, 145–46
    See also Oscars
affect, 18–19, 20–23, 33, 41–43, 44, 56–57, 85, 86, 110, 116, 122–26, 134–35, 136, 139–40
    affective cinema, 41–44, 136–40
    affective turn, 116, 122–24
art galleries, 68–69, 75–78, 80–81, 88, 91, 92
    See also intermediality
Assassin, The (Hou Hsiao-hsien), 10*t*, 15–16, 45–46
Assayas, Olivier, 10*t*, 24–26, 27–29, 40, 41–43, 46–47, 142–44
    See also HHH: Portrait de Hou Hsiao-hsien
aurality, 45–46, 48–50, 54–56, 57–59, 61–62, 66–67
    acousmêtre, 61–62
    aural turn, 48–50, 58–59, 66–67
    displacing visuality, 50, 55–59
    gendered, 45–46, 50–52, 54–55, 57–59, 63–64, 66–67
    materiality of voice, 55–57, 62–67
auteur, 14–15, 17, 25–26, 35, 44, 46–47, 54–55, 63–64, 68–69, 70, 90, 97–98, 112–14, 116–17, 123, 138, 147–50
    See also authorship
authorship, 2–3, 6, 25–26, 27, 32, 46–47, 63–64, 69, 97–98, 99, 112–14, 117, 123, 146–48
    authorship as soft power, 7, 14–15, 21–22, 146–48, 153–54
    See also auteur

Bao, Weihong, 21
    See also affect
Berlant, Lauren
    on cruel optimism, 139–40
    on intimate publics, 122, 124, 139
    See also affect
Bi Gan, 141, 145, 147, 153–54
    See also Kaili Blues

Billy Lynn's Long Halftime Walk (Ang Lee), 96–97, 100, 101*t*, 112, 189n.8
Binoche, Juliet, 47, 54–55, 60–61, 62*f*, 63–64, 66
Blue Gate Crossing (Yee Chih-yen), 127–29
Braester, Yomi, 107
    on cultural brokers (*see* Lee, Ang: as cultural broker)
Buddhism, 70–71, 86–87, 90, 92–93
    butoh, 86–87

Café Lumière (Hou Hsiao-hsien), 41–44, 45–46, 47, 52, 53–54, 55–59, 61–62, 63
Cape No. 7 (Wei Te-sheng), 8–9, 16–17, 105–6, 115–24, 119*t*, 136, 137–39, 147–48, 152–53
    as box office miracle, 116–22
Central Motion Picture Corporation (CMPC), 16, 24–25, 30–31, 71–72, 98–99
Chen Kuo-fu, 24–26, 136–37, 190n.21, 194n.12
Chiao, Peggy Hsiung Ping, 128–29, 186n.9
Chion, Michel, 51–52, 55–56, 58–59, 61–62, 63, 64–65, 183n.27
Chow, Rey, 49–50, 51–52
Chu Tien-wen, 63–64, 183n.20
cinephilia, 26, 33, 35–40
    as soft power, 7, 25–26, 33–40, 146–47
city branding, 100, 103–6, 108–14
City of Sadness, A (Hou Hsiao-hsien), 10*t*, 25, 28–29, 38, 45, 48, 64, 110–11, 123, 146–47
corporeality, 58–59, 60–63, 70–71, 85, 90–91
cross-cultural influence. *See* cinephilia
cultural policy, 4–5, 104–5, 138

Deleuze, Gilles and Guattari, Felix, 151
digital technology, 70–71, 80–81, 90–91, 92–93, 111–14
    3D, 100, 111–14
    virtual reality (VR) film, 71, 73–75
Dinnie, Keith, 103–4, 108–14
documentary, 24–26, 27–28, 41
    as a form of historiography, 25, 27, 29–31, 40–44